Musician's Resource

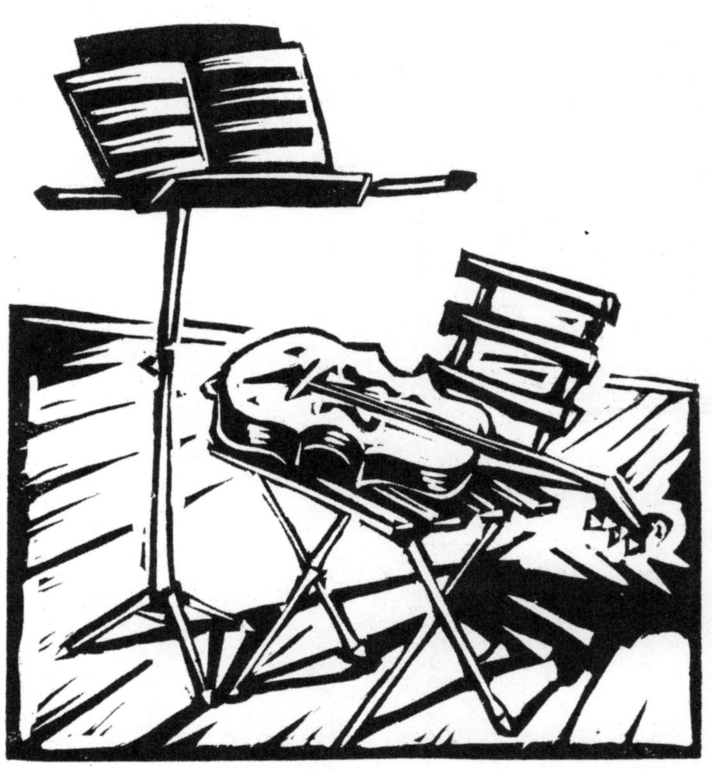

Musician's Resource

The Watson-Guptill Guide to

- Workshops
- Conferences
- Residential Programs
- Academic Programs
- Festivals
- Masterclasses

Gwendolyn Freed

Getting Your Act Together™

Produced for Watson-Guptill Publications by
David Emblidge — Book Producer

Watson-Guptill Publications
New York

Getting Your Act Together™

Series Concept: David Emblidge

Series Editor: David Emblidge

Researcher: Emily Rabin

Database design: Chris Blair, David Emblidge

Copy Editor: Rodelinde Albrecht

Book design: Bill Cooke

Icons: Bill Cooke, Robin O'Herin

Page makeup: Robin O'Herin

Interior Illustrations: Roy Germon

Photographs: See credits with each image.

Indexer: Letitia Mutter

The text of this book was created in Microsoft Word and Q&A for Windows, and pages were subsequently designed in Quark XPress. Program descriptions were imported from the database using the X-Data extension. Display typefaces used include Frutiger and Officina Sans. Veljovic is used for the main text.

Library of Congress Cataloguing-in-Publication Data
Freed, Gwendolyn.
Musician's resource : the Watson-Guptill guide to workshops, conferences, artists' colonies, and academic programs / by Gwendolyn Freed.
p. cm. — (Getting your act together series)
Includes bibliographical references and index.
ISBN 0-8230-7652-0
1. Music trade—Vocational guidance.
2. Music—Economic aspects.
I. Title. II. Series.
ML3790.F72 1997
780'.71'073—dc21 97-11997
CIP
MN

10 9 8 7 6 5 4 3 2 1
Printed in the United States

Contents

7 **Foreword**

9 **Introduction**

- How to Use This Book
- Definitions
- How You Can Participate
- Acknowledgments

PART ONE
Living to Make Music, Making Music to Live

17 **On Becoming a Musician**

- A Career in Music
- The Decision to Become a Professional
- The Decision to Remain an Amateur
- Getting Your Act Together

PART TWO
Music Programs in North America Today

27 **Only Connect**

- Associations and Organizations
- Unions and Other Labor Organizations

32 **Selecting a Program**

- Special Advice on Academic Programs
- Special Advice on Festivals

37 **Music Programs**

- State by State: Workshops, Conferences, Residential Programs, Academic Programs, Festivals, Masterclasses

PART THREE
The Business of Music

137 **Financial Aid—The Inside Scoop**

- Grants, Fellowships and Awards for Musicians

139 **Setting Up Shop**

- Marketing Your Skills

141 **The How-To Bit**

142 **Tools of the Trade**

- Your Instrument
- Shipping and Postage

143 **Cutting the Deal**

- Copyright
- Contracts

143 **The Price Tag on Your Work**

144 **Starting a Music Business**

- Incorporation
- Taxes
- Investing for Your Future

PART FOUR
Bibliography & Index

149 **Bibliography**

151 **Index**

176 **About the Author**

176 **About Getting Your Act Together™**

Foreword

MUSIC HAS BEEN A CONSTANT and joyous presence in my life. My mother played the viola in orchestras in St. Louis and Cleveland and was a member of a string quartet in both cities. Some of my earliest memories involve being put to bed and hearing my mom and her colleagues rehearsing Beethoven, Schubert or Ravel down the hall.

For the past quarter century I've been involved with music from the broadcasting end. My current perspective as host of a national radio program allows me to see just how much musical activity there is in late-1990s America; quite literally, there are concerts, recitals and operas going on in cities and towns 365 days a year. And when you factor in the dozens of festivals that take place on islands and mountainsides and in meadows and forests across the country each summer—not to mention rock 'n' rollers, country musicians, folk, jazz and gospel artists, and session players—it becomes increasingly clear that there are lots of opportunities for a lover of music to actually make a buck by serving his muse.

But where does a lover go to serenade his love? "Only connect," says Gwen Freed, quoting E.M. Forster, in this invaluable resource book. In witty and sympathetic prose she reveals just how many Howard's Ends there are in America today, where a musician can study, obtain a degree, latch on to a mentor, sign a contract or simply make music with other smitten men and women. She also has some frank and sobering words to say about the tremendous odds facing anyone contemplating a life in music. Only a tiny fraction of people have the luxury of earning a living exclusively through their music. But Freed reminds the reader of the many opportunities for amateur musicians in this country: church choirs, community orchestras and chamber music among friends. And she takes pains to remind us that the root meaning of the word "amateur" is "lover."

Music is one of the greatest gifts the human animal has given to itself. "Music can name the unnameable and communicate the unknowable," as Leonard Bernstein said. *Musician's Resource* is a gift of that gift.

Martin Goldsmith
Host, NPR's *Performance Today*

Introduction

WELCOME TO *Musician's Resource*, a compendium of information and ideas for the musician—professional or amateur or anywhere in between. Whether you want to develop new skills, schmooze with managers, club owners and concert presenters, or network with fellow musicians, in this book you will find scores of opportunities. Before you get down to particulars, cruise the aisles as though this were a department store, and have fun dreaming about the programs you might someday attend and what the musical results might be. I wish you all the best.

How to Use This Book

USE THIS BOOK AS YOU WOULD the counsel of a wise friend. Absorb the information that seems noteworthy to you; take heed of opinionated statements; consider the logic behind suggested strategies for getting into, and through, the kind of music program you want. But remember that your own personal preferences for type of program, location, cost and schedule will be just as important or even more so than any information you may find in these pages. Music, like all the arts, is intensely personal; so, too, are education and training in the craft of making it. What works well for Musician A will be a disaster for Musician B. Wallace Stevens gave us a poem called "Sixteen Ways of Looking at a Blackbird." This book should indicate that there are at least that many ways to further your development as a musician.

In Part One, "Living to Make Music, Making Music to Live," I talk about the need to think of music as a *vocation* before plunging into the struggle of making music your *business*. There's a certain chemistry, perhaps alchemy, that needs to be achieved to make a go of it as a musician, whether you are financially self-sustaining or not. A mix of determination, confidence, vulnerability, openness and practical savvy must come into focus in you, the musician, whether you're fiddling at a barn dance or singing opera at the Met.

Part Two, "Music Programs in North America Today," forms the bulk of the book. After listing associations and organizations you may want to join, the book switches to a gazetteer format and moves state by state through descriptions of Workshops, Conferences, Residential Programs, Academic Programs, Festivals and Masterclasses.

Part Three, "The Business of Music," covers the numbers game from soup to nuts: financial aid, marketing your skills, negotiating deals, and setting yourself up in the music business.

Definitions

Six icons make it easy for you to navigate through the book and locate what you are seeking.

 Workshop

You say potayto, I say potahto. What's a masterclass to you may be a workshop to someone else, or a conference to me. The terms are used casually in the music field, and I've done my best to balance two goals here. One, to honor the terminology used by the programs themselves; two, to distinguish workshops and masterclasses from conferences by a simple rule when conditions permit. To wit: A workshop is generally a small group of musicians, meeting once or regularly over a period of days or weeks, for the clear purpose of learning from one or more teachers. Music performance is often the shared activity, though some workshops in this book focus on other areas of concern to musicians, such as performance anxiety and body alignment.

 Conference

A conference is generally a large gathering of musicians (larger than a workshop) and can frequently include folks from other aspects of the music industry as well. It meets for a day, a weekend, or a week, perhaps annually or, for special topics, one time only. Within a conference there may be smaller group sessions that operate like workshops (hence the confusion of terminology). More typical, however, are plenary sessions in which experts hold forth on topics of practical usefulness (musical skill development, making a buck) or give readings from their own work. Some conferences offer interaction between the experts and the attendees; many do not.

 Residential Program

The term "residential" is used in this book to describe programs devoted to housing musicians and/or other artists for periods of a week, several months or even a year; and providing anything from total seclusion to scheduled daily confabs and critiques of residents' work, or at least a high degree of musical camaraderie. "Colony" and "retreat" are synonymous here.

 Academic Program

If the program leads to a degree (BM, MM, DMA) or a genuine academic certificate, it's listed as an academic program in this book.

Yet even this simple definition fails to cover all cases. Many universities have extension programs (or continuing education programs) providing classes and special events that are sometimes called simply "courses" or, more confusingly, "workshops" or even "conferences." Most of these programs are listed as workshops or conferences per se. Some of them are genuinely excellent programs, and some are the best bargains in this book. Often such programs grant continuing education units (CEUs) or another kind of academic credit.

It casts no aspersions on any academic music program to say that many of them are nearly clones of many others, hard to distinguish without a level of detail (particularly a description of faculty) that is beyond the scope of this book. Of course there are vast differences in quality. Podunk Junior College for the Musically Challenged is not the same as the Eastman School of Music. For this reason, this book is rather selective. If an academic program is included here it's because I recommend it, either because it is clearly the best program available for miles around or because it is of superior musical and academic quality compared to its competition nationwide.

Part Two provides some advice about choosing and following the academic track as a musician.

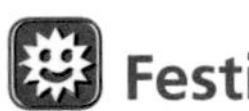

Festival

Music festivals come in all types and can take place at any time during the year (though most happen in the summer). Despite the variations, two elements seem to unite them. One is public events. Every festival in this book presents concerts and/or other events to its surrounding community. Second, all the festivals here have great locations. From woods to seascapes to deserts to glittering urban skylines, all the festivals here feature exceptional things to do, see and enjoy.

Part Two gives you some hints about choosing a festival to suit your needs.

Masterclass

Masterclasses stand apart because performance is always the focus, and masterclasses are always led by a single experienced, well-known master teacher. Good masterclasses give participants a chance to perform under a fair dose of pressure, get feedback from peers, and come away with nuts-and-bolts advice from a serious pro. Masterclasses are almost always rather small gatherings, to allow for plenty of interaction and as much intense, productive work as possible.

How the Information Is Displayed

Think "Upstairs" and "Downstairs." Upstairs is the information block that looks like the example on page 12.

Downstairs you'll find one or more paragraphs of description.

In the Upstairs section, most items are self-explanatory, but a few categories bear explanation.

Icons:

= Workshop

= Conference

= Residential

= Academic

= Festival

= Masterclass

JazzTimes Convention

For vocalists, composers *New York metropolitan area — Sheraton Meadowlands Hotel, East Rutherford, NJ 0707; 38737 Colesville Rd., 5th Fl., Silver Spring, MD 20910* **Voice:** 301-588-4119 ext. 23 **Fax:** 301-588-5531 **E-mail:** JTimes@aol.com **Contact:** Cheryl T. Goodman, Asst. Dir. **Founded:** 1984 **Open:** Early–mid-Nov. **Admission:** Registration **Deadlines:** May 31 (early registration) **Cost:** $219–$299 **Size-Attendees:** 1,000 **Handicapped Access**

Addresses: The on-site mailing address where, usually, the program takes place. If a second address is given, typically it's for the off-season or for the application only. When mailing an application, make sure you put the program name first, because many are small projects under the umbrellas of large universities.

Country: Always the U.S. or its territories unless otherwise stated.

Contact person: The one to ask for if you want well-informed, up-to-date information. The bigger the program, the harder it is for would-be applicants to get through to the director, but go ahead and ask. Many programs have coordinators, secretaries or administrative assistants who are helpful and informative.

Open: Program dates shift annually. Likely times are given here.

Admission: Almost all programs require an application form, but after that the road divides into many paths, with some asking for everything just short of an FBI clearance. Rule of thumb: programs requiring tapes, auditions, resumes and/or references are by far the most selective and most rigorous of the lot. The converse is generally true, too.

Concerning application fees: Sometimes they're broken out, sometimes they're folded into general tuition. If the fee seems egregious relative to overall quality, then caveat emptor. Most programs require a modest fee with the application, to be applied to the tuition if you attend.

Deadlines: Can't live with 'em, can't live without 'em. Some programs are sticklers for deadlines; others are open until the room fills (presumably to permit good last-minute applicants to sneak through the door). The best advice is to apply early, increasing your chances of connecting with specific teachers you may want. Financial aid applicants often must apply earlier than others. Read the fine print. Concerning deadlines, what you see is what the programs said. In the absence of information here, be sure to inquire.

Cost: I've done my best to untangle a confusing web. Program fee (or tuition) is followed by room and board. Programs may have fees for materials or extras. Sometimes there are discounts for early registration. Often there are discounts for members of relevant professional organizations. Where attendees arrange their own housing, cost is not given (check for advice in the program description). For programs with complicated cost schedules, a range is displayed here. Call for the details.

Financial Aid: Potayto and potahto again. A "scholarship" in one program is a "fellowship" in another. Often a "work/study" grant is linked to a "scholarship." The bigger and older programs may have various endowed scholarships, not necessarily mentioned in the program's general brochure. Be sure to request a financial application at the outset if you're in need (as noted above, watch out for early deadlines, different from those for general applications). Often a financial aid application requires additional supporting documents (letters of recommendation, audition tape). Because of the welter of confusing data, the amount of financial aid available in the specific programs is not listed.

Size—Attendees and **Size—Class:** Some programs give the total number of attendees; some give typical class size; some give both. What seems most representative is reported here.

Handicapped Access: Programs at institutions receiving federal tax dollars are likely to have handicapped-accessible facilities, but still the specific rooms used for the music program may be difficult to reach. Handicapped access is reported only when the program itself makes this claim. Many programs that do not claim to be handicapped accessible actually are because the meetings take place in convenient hotels or on campuses with appropriate facilities. It's best to ask the contact person, being sure to review access to classrooms, dining facilities, sleeping quarters, and so forth, especially if the program takes place in a rustic setting.

How the Information Was Gathered

It would have been fun to visit every program, but that would have taken a lifetime, and then you would not have this book in your hand. I called program directors and chatted with them about the history and direction of their programs; I read brochures, catalogues and application forms; I spoke to participants in some programs; I contacted arts administrators in some state agencies and private foundations. And I kept my ear to the ground. In the world of music festivals, masterclasses, conferences and academic programs, rumor is rampant, and while sometimes a hint worth following emerges, more often it's about as reliable as the weather in New England (where Mark Twain said, if you don't like it, wait five minutes).

The upshot is that this book makes a serious effort to be objective and accurate about facts and information while also indulging itself, and you, in opinionated descriptions of the programs.

Bear in mind the research time frame: I started research in 1996, wrote and edited in 1996–1997, and published in fall 1997. The world of nonprofit arts programs is always in flux, and costs (almost) never go down. Make your own inquiry for current information. The plan is to update this book every two years.

How You Can Participate

READERS ARE INVITED TO RESPOND. Please correct my mistakes, offer your perspectives, and let me know what else you'd like to see in the next edition. Please indicate where you bought or borrowed this book.

Use the postcard that was bound into this book or write to: Editors, Getting Your Act Together™, ℅ Watson-Guptill Publications, 1515 Broadway, New York, NY 10036.

Acknowledgments

FOR A LONG TIME, I'VE HEARD MUSICIANS talk about the need for such a guidebook as this. It turns out that we owe its existence not to a professional musician or music educator, but to series editor David Emblidge, who recognized that artists of all kinds need help sifting through today's myriad educational options. David tells me that Candace Raney and Glenn Heffernan at Watson-Guptill saw the series' potential from the beginning, as did Liz Harvey and Bob Nirkind, my editors there. (Bob, who is particularly interested in popular music, gave me some excellent advice.) In putting together this music volume, I depended on program directors and admissions personnel from around the continent for detailed information, and every one of them came through for me. Thanks to my research assistant, Emily Rabin, who put her compulsive side to good use in this project, last summer somehow seemed like more fun than work. I owe much to Rodelinde Albrecht for her patience and fortitude in copy editing the manuscript. Thanks to Chris Blair for imaginative yet practical database design. Bill Cooke, who designed the book, gave me his time and kindness, helping me through several computer nightmares. Kudos go to Robin O'Herin for her work on page makeup. Artist Roy Germon provided really lovely drawings. Our fearless indexer was Letitia Mutter. Finally, my husband, Ken, also fearless, deserves credit here for getting me through this project with plenty of strong coffee and lots of funny jokes.

PART ONE

Living to Make Music, Making Music to Live

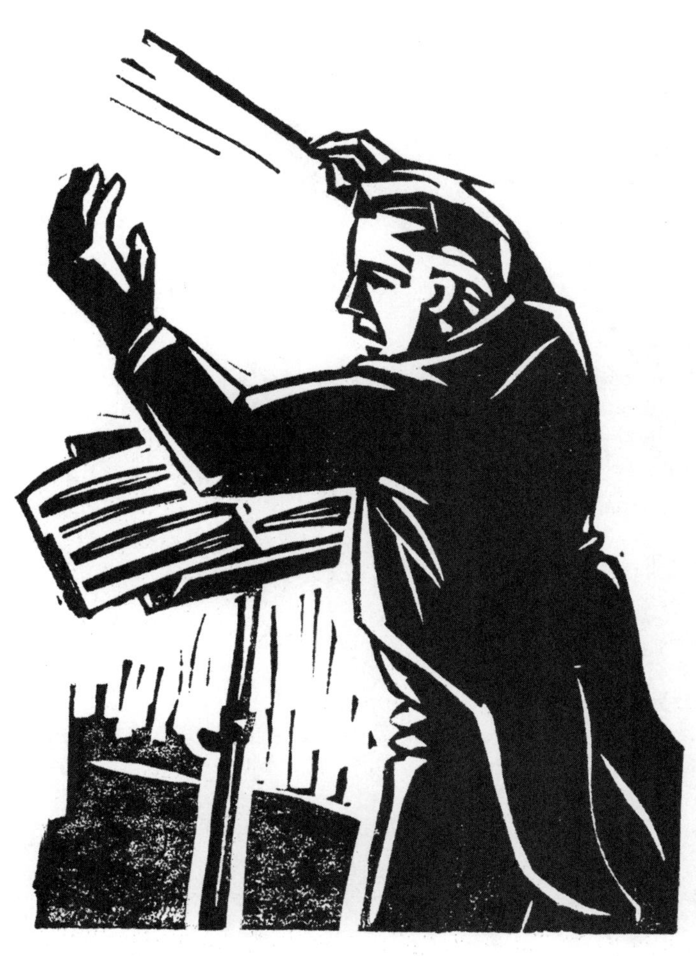

On Becoming a Musician

For many musicians, there was a moment in early life when they recognized for the first time that theirs was a world of sound, that they loved great music, that they wanted to express themselves through playing, singing or writing music.

For some it begins with a listening experience, perhaps in a club or at a concert hall, hearing music and feeling profoundly moved in a way they never have felt before. For others, it's the first act of making music, starting lessons on an instrument, singing in the shower, even banging on pots and pans. One way or another, for every musician, there is a period of time when it seems that the universe of music is gradually opening and that the creative possibilities are without limit.

A budding musician's ears are open to musical detail, shades of sound, nuance of meaning. And bringing one's own music making closer and closer to the sounds one hears deep within becomes an all-consuming passion.

Once the floodgates of self-expression are opened, there's usually no shutting them. From that time on, a musician-to-be seeks opportunities and outlets, or at least keeps practicing in pursuit of perfection.

This book is meant for the musician who takes himself or herself seriously, who wants to grow, to make contact with others practicing the same craft, to build a network of professional contacts who can provide help along the often meandering road toward the concert stage or the recording studio. And it's meant for those who take delight in music played well for its own sake.

In this age one might naturally ask whether certain types of music are dying—classical music and jazz especially. While it's true that those genres together represent less than 10 percent of the current music market, music taken as a whole is a healthy industry. By most standard measures—industry volume, purchasing trends and the collections of performing rights organizations—there is indeed money to be made in music, lots of it.

Rock, pop and country music dominate the music market, but if you aspire to break into other, less popular genres, your courage and confidence in the vitality and viability of all forms of music will revive as you thumb through this book.

What brings people to the craft and business of music? Some are attracted to what they perceive to be the musician's life. Having arrived at this fork in the road, you will need to ask some serious questions.

If you have the skills of a competent musician, what do want to do with them? How big a part of your life do you want music to be? What do you want to accomplish with your music, and for whose benefit? Perhaps you want to have your own solo act, perhaps you'd like to play chamber music or be a member of a big band.

The key question is: What will satisfy you? Will you be content just practicing your scales in the event that someone calls you on a rainy day, or do you want to make a living from your craft, as an orchestral player, a songwriter or a church organist?

If the professional track is for you, you will need a lot more than just the hunger to make music. You need to know how musicians work and what it is like to be a professional, facing auditions, adapting to styles you may not fully endorse, negotiating for (and chasing after) money. It's not all just a matter of sipping sherry with musical friends and discussing your favorite tenor's latest CDs. Indeed, it's more a matter of brewing that extra cup of coffee and staying up late to push yourself to improve, improve, improve. A decision of this importance—turning professional—requires the very best information you can get and a sensitive ear to the murmurings of your heart.

The best way to find out what musicians do and how they live is to talk to experienced pros about all aspects of their work. Talk to people at different levels in their careers and in different specialties to get the most complete view. Ask all the questions you can think of. At the very least, you should know what options you face in stepping up to the ranks of the professional and be able to imagine yourself living and working that way.

A Career in Music

Choosing a career in music is a bold step. As a profession, music is alluring but also fraught with peril. It can yield great personal and professional rewards, but the demands are high. For every glamorous, packed-house gig, there are a dozen failed auditions, unreturned phone calls and days spent questioning the fundamental premises of your life. Along with every glass-shattering high C you hit exactly on pitch come 10 or 100 that are not quite right or are just plain awful.

What follows here is a partial list of the avenues a musician might choose, and a brief description of what each type of music entails.

To locate music industry publishers, writers, record companies, producers, artists, managers, publicists and agents, consult the following standard reference books or ask a reference librarian for other similar tools. Full details are in the Bibliography.

Musical America International Directory of the Performing Arts, a comprehensive sourcebook of the classical music industry.

Songwriter's Market, an especially helpful resource for writers and performers in various forms of popular music.

This Business of Music, a compendium of business information for all types of musical artists.

Commercial Music

You might hate it in the dentist's office, but you can learn to love arrangements of "Let It Be" for 101 strings. It may seem silly to sit in a booth for three hours recording thirty seconds of music for a Puppy Chow commercial, but there's nothing silly about getting a check for your portion of the proceeds once every few months for as long as it airs. If you sightread very well, perform cleanly and consistently and behave like a professional, you don't have to be Vladimir Horowitz or Garth Brooks to make a very good living in studio music. The best opportunities for commercial work exist in places like New York and Los Angeles, where there is the highest volume of advertising, film and television business.

Orchestral Music

According to the American Federation of Musicians, the national labor organization that publishes *The International Musician,* there are usually fewer than 100 full-time orchestral job openings each year in the U.S. With more than 13,000 musicians graduating from college with music degrees each spring, you can do the math yourself.

It's not uncommon for more than 300 people to show up for an audition for a single spot in a good orchestra. This disastrous state of affairs signifies two things. One, as long as music schools continue to profit from bringing in aspiring musicians, they are not going to make a point of warning them about how hard it is to get an orchestra job. Two, short of joining the very highest echelon of obscenely overpaid musicians working as soloists, membership in a major orchestra is one of the best financial bets in the classical music industry. In the top ten orchestras (Chicago, New York, Cleveland, and so on) section salaries start at around $70,000. Certain titled chairs can far exceed $100,000. The trade-off, of course, is artistic. Some instrumentalists work for years to get into a great orchestra, only to win the audition and spend the next thirty years resenting conductors and their own less-than-autonomous musical role. Some players do love it, however, particularly section leaders and wind players. Take note though: There are fewer than fifty American orchestras currently paying players base salaries above $20,000. (No, that's not a misprint.)

Chamber Music

Chamber music is usually what orchestral players say they wish they were doing. The artistic grass may be greener in chamber music land, but as the service organization Chamber Music America reports, the average full-time chamber musician makes only about $11,000 annually from playing music. (That's not a misprint either.)

An important factor to consider on both the pro and con sides of chamber music is that in chamber music you work intensely for long periods in a small, sometimes tiny, group of people. That's great, if the others play like angels and speak in full sentences. It's less great if their high notes are always out of tune or they don't use deodorant.

Jazz

As a market category, jazz is apparently an even smaller and more obscure world than that of classical music, and is considered every bit as "endangered." In spite of this, hundreds of colleges and universities offer variations on the jazz studies major. As in the classical field, jazz musicians frequently round out their incomes playing studio or show music, and many of them teach.

Opera

Opera seems to be enjoying a good period in America. According to the National Endowment for the Arts, the U.S. opera audience grew by nearly 25 percent between 1982 and 1992. Total attendance at all North American opera productions exceeded the 7-million mark in the 1994–1995 concert season, more than a 10 percent increase over 1993–1994.

If you like opera, though, you'd better like Italian opera. A lot. Of the ten most frequently performed operas last season, all were in Italian, except *Die Zauberflöte,* which ranked ninth.

Choral Music

Some of the best religious and concert music of all time has been composed and/or arranged for chorus. Unfortunately, though, it's close to impossible to make a full-time living in choral music, says Karen Richter, member services director of the service association Chorus America. "Most choral musicians attempting to make a living are probably involved in five or ten or more different musical endeavors. In other words, come tax time, they are buried in W-2 forms." There are two particularly lucrative exceptions to this rule, however: the San Francisco–based ensemble Chanticleer and the U.S. Armed Forces choruses. Despite the generally low pay, gratification in chorus life must be high: Chorus America boasts some 540 member choral groups not affiliated with any church or school.

Rock Music

Rock music includes hard rock, soft rock, alternative modern rock, new wave, punk, heavy metal, rock 'n' roll, pop rock and other forms of rock. The vision many of us have when we think of rock is of the fans: throngs of them packing the bleachers of a sports arena, teeming masses of them rubbing shoulders at an outdoor event, their numbers sprawled out as far as the eye can see.

The possibility of being loved this much by this many people—or even by some of them—is doubtless what draws so many into the rock profession. Rock has dominated the music market for decades and will probably continue to do so for many decades to come. Through the 1990s to date, it has held more than a third of the music recordings market. Timothy White, editor-in-chief of *Billboard* magazine, says "Rock and Roll has advanced in the last 50 years from a maverick pursuit to a blue-collar profession to the white-collar status it enjoys today. There are lots more opportunities now to draw rock audiences than anyone thought possible in the late fifties. Today, rock is one of America's biggest businesses; it's a leading exporter, right up there with the aeronautics and film industries."

But for emerging artists, the stakes are higher than in other genres. In the classical music record industry, for example, a new group selling 5,000 to 10,000 copies of a first release is considered worthwhile. A new artist in rock, says Sony Music's Linda Ury Greenberg, is expected to sell 200,000 to 500,000 copies of a first album just to keep going.

Country Music

Country music is currently the fastest-growing American musical genre, more than doubling its overall sales in the past five years. And according to John Knowles, executive director of the Country Music Foundation, the country music world orbits around Nashville.

"As a community, Nashville trains country music's future talent," he says. In addition to two major country music college programs in the area, Nashville is home to innumerable informal training venues. The Nashville Songwriters Association holds weekly get-togethers, for example. Cafes, restaurants, hotels, motels and bookstores hold songwriters' nights. "It's a whole way of life around here. People like Garth Brooks came of age here," says Knowles. It's not by accident that more than 20 major country record labels are based in Nashville headquarters.

Gospel Music

Once relegated to the fringe, gospel music has enjoyed a kind of transformation and renewal in recent years. Owing in part to their new emphasis on the mainstream, gospel record labels and gospel retailers are gaining clout. A related musical format, sometimes called "positive country," or "Christian country," is also gathering momentum. It's a format to watch.

The Decision to Become a Professional

Many musicians never make a formal decision to specialize in one kind of music versus another. The process just happens. They start playing or singing or composing because they enjoy it or feel they have something to say, and their personal styles evolve. In time, they find themselves gravitating toward one type of music or another. This form of self-selection is a healthy way to discover one's own best path. Each person ends up doing the kind of music to which he or she is best suited by dint of skill, preference and personality.

In choosing to become a professional musician, you evaluate your commitment to the medium. It is no longer an infatuation but more like a marriage, complete with responsibilities and sacrifices. It begins to shape the way your life unfolds. In exchange for that heightened commitment, you expect to reap rewards in terms of financial gain, social benefits and personal satisfaction. All these are possible. But in music, as in many professions and in all marriages, the good stuff does not always come easily.

Music is competitive. For many of the same reasons you might want to make a career out of being a musician, plenty of other people do, too. It's a fact of life that there will always be more people who want to make a living at music than there will be paying markets to support them. In time, the less talented, less passionate, less highly motivated musicians will drop away and take up other work. The desire of every new professional is to be one of those who can weather the competition and build a successful career.

The demands on professional musicians are quite different from those on even the most gifted amateurs. Professionals need to be able to produce music that fulfills the demands of audiences. In the best of situations, that means musicians finding listeners who love the way they sound.

Professionals must produce top-quality work at every gig, no matter how they feel or what logistical limitations they may face. It doesn't matter if the conductor breathes fire, or if the notes are too high to sing or the amp is broken. Professionals produce professional-grade work. No presenter, club owner or contractor, upon hearing music that exceeds expectations, will ever ask you how you did it. A fine restaurant's reputation is based not on a few fabulous meals but on a consistent string of excellent ones. The same holds true for professional musicians.

Music is one of those fields that calls so strongly to some people that they never actually work through the process of making the decision to become professionals. They know right from the beginning that they are and always will be musicians. They have a love affair with music that leaves them no other choice. Establishing a career is a manifestation of the inevitable.

For most of us, though, the decision to become a professional needs to be carefully considered.

Do not become a musician by accident or default. Do not take up professional musicianship just because you find diddling around enjoyable and cannot think of anything else to do. It is too challenging a career. If the well-documented minimal income of most would-be musicians isn't enough to scare you off, then the likelihood of a long string of rejections may be. Before composer Philip Glass hit the big time with *Einstein on the*

Beach, he had received and suffered through enough bad reviews and rejection letters to wallpaper the taxicab he had to drive to make ends meet. You simply have to want it with everything you've got, and then you have to build your career in music carefully, and strategically, as you would in any other field. The decisions you make deliberately and carefully, rather than just fall into, will ultimately yield greater satisfaction.

The Decision to Remain an Amateur

The root meaning of the word "amateur" is "lover." The amateur gets to do what he or she loves, without the need to answer to anyone else. Many of the most passionate musicians prefer to remain amateurs all their lives rather than sacrifice their deep personal relationship with the medium of music to the exigencies of earning a living.

They have a career, an occupation elsewhere, and spend their evenings, weekends and vacations pursuing their truest love, making music. Amateur musicians have many opportunities, including the chance to perform in minor or even major ways on a freelance basis.

Serious amateur musicians may be as skilled as professionals. They may have the technical expertise and personal vision for which Carnegie Hall or Madison Square Garden would gladly pay. Instead, they remain amateurs to preserve their harmonious relationship with their own work. They simply don't want to objectify their own talent, or turn it into a commodity and put in on the auction block. Anyone who loves music should think carefully about what will be lost by becoming a professional, as well as what will be gained. It would be a shame to have one's love affair with music ground down by the need to turn notes into cash.

Getting Your Act Together

Whether music is a career or an avocation for you, your desire to use this book shows that you take it seriously. You recognize the need to hone your skills and learn new ways to grow as a musician. You see how shifting market forces, technological advances and the never-before-so-important game of networking have changed the way music is made and sold.

In picking up this book, you seek to expand your knowledge about music, to acquire specific skills or to advance your vision.

This book has been created to help you. It catalogues hundreds of different ways in which to advance your musical life, whether you choose to make music your profession or to pursue it as an amateur. You will find descriptions of workshops and training facilities for all types of music, plus organizations of and for musicians, artists' colonies, specialized music schools and academic institutions that have strong music programs.

All musicians thrive on the satisfaction of crafting the unforgettable musical performance. It is my wish that the information offered here will help you become the musician you want to be.

PART TWO

Music Programs in North America Today

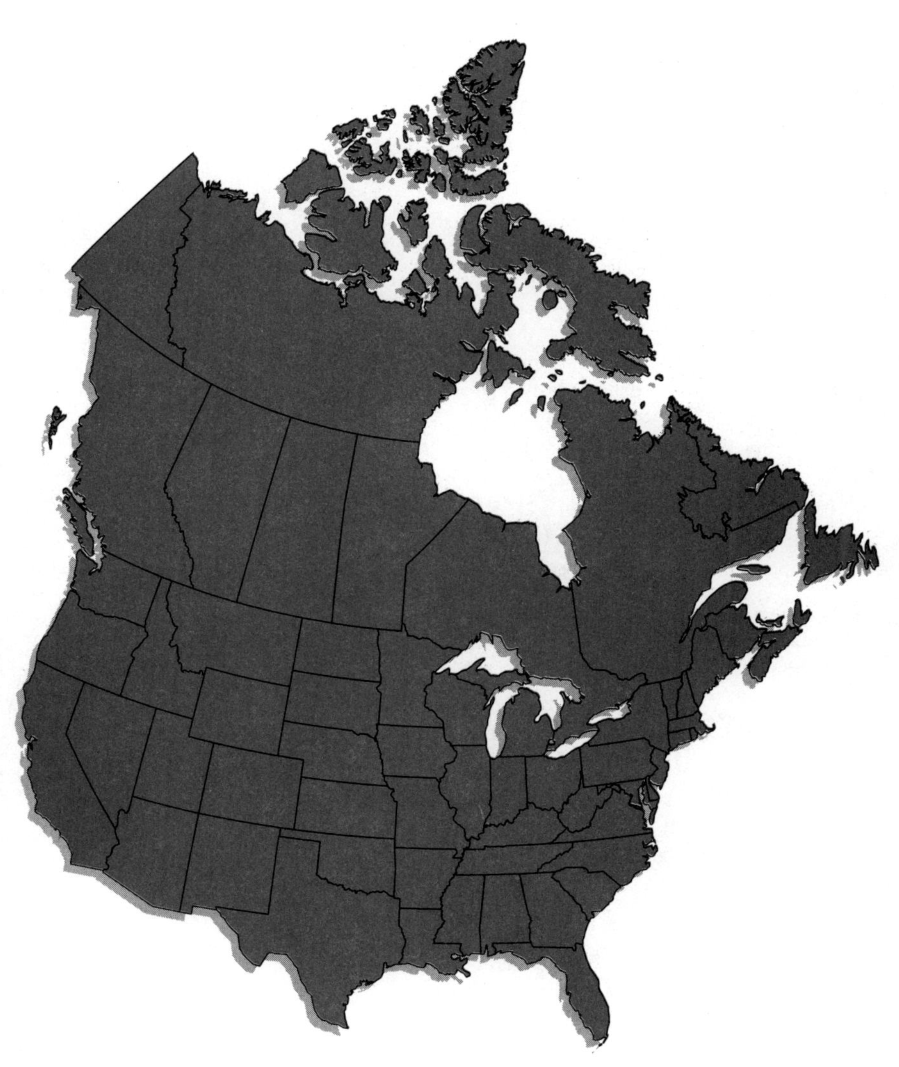

Only Connect

IMMEDIATELY BELOW YOU'LL FIND A LISTING of national associations, organizations and unions (or other labor organizations) that you may want to join. For similar state, regional and local organizations, ask your reference librarian or call your state arts council. In the gazetteer of program descriptions that follows, you will see certain programs (workshops, conferences ...) sponsored by regional associations for musicians and other artists. If noteworthy, some information is given about the association at that point.

Music is hardly a solitary act. The yin and yang of it mean that the relative solitude of practicing and rehearsing needs to be balanced by association, fraternity and sorority, and sometimes by going to the barricades together. Hence this section's title, "Only Connect," borrowed shamelessly from novelist E. M. Forster.

There is much to be said for joining appropriate professional or amateur musicians' organizations. We all learn from one another, both on the music side and on the business side. Especially for people who live and work in far-flung places, away from the hub of musical activity in major cities like New York, Boston, Chicago and San Francisco, an organization's newsletter and annual meeting may be the best (and sometimes the only) places to hear what peers and colleagues are doing about the same opportunities and problems you may be facing. The better organizations emphasize service: insurance plans, job networking, how-to skills workshops, and so forth. I advise spending your membership dollars only for these real benefits.

Too many resumes list memberships in shell organizations that provide no real services and offer no warmth, camaraderie or collegial networking to their members. Musicians are no more immune than other workers to that American penchant for "joining up," what Garrison Keillor pokes fun at when he says his *Prairie Home Companion* radio show is brought to us by the "American Federation of Associations."

You'll do better if you choose the one or two associations that actually serve your purposes as a specific kind of musician. Certainly if you are an opera singer, then the opera associations are for you. If you are a dulcimer player, find your specialty group of folk musicians. And so on.

The one overarching organization all musicians may want to consider is the American Federation of Musicians (AFM), the national umbrella association for all America's local musicians' unions. It's a must for all performers who seek protection against exploitation and who want to support the cause of raising the economic status of musicians in our country.

The AFM, an affiliate of the AFL-CIO, works hard to provide its 185,000 members with the services associated with traditional labor organizations: contract and payment advice, legal counsel, and a clearinghouse of work-related business information. One AFM bonus is access to a health insurance plan.

Because most musicians have to negotiate on their own behalf, rather than collectively, negotiations can be dicey if the fellow on the opposite side of the table is the "hit man" for a corporation. Enter the AFM with model contracts, precedents you can review and moral support (which was part of the winning formula when David negotiated with Goliath).

For the past several years, the AFM has been in the forefront of many key struggles, one of them against the IRS, seeking to overturn decades of tax-law precedent in the case of Richard and Fiona Simon. The Simons, violinists in the New York Philharmonic, believe they have the right to depreciate their rare, 200-year-old violin bows as tools of their trade. The government has said no because it regards the bows as antiques and collectibles. The AFM has been raising money in support of the Simons, who may take their case to the highest courts in the land before all is said and done.

Associations and Organizations

Academy of Country Music

Who: Artists, songwriters, producers, agents and others in the country music business. **What:** Promotes country music through its talent contests, artist showcases, seminars and assistance to members who seek to place songs. **Contact:** Academy of Country Music, 6255 Sunset Blvd., #93, Hollywood, CA 90028; 213-462-2351 **Membership:** Open to all. $60 annual fee.

American Composers Forum

Who: About 1,000 composers, performers and lovers of new music. **What:** Founded 1973. Links communities with composers and performers, encourages the making, playing and enjoyment of new music. **Contact:** American Composers Forum, 332 Minnesota St., Ste. East 145, St. Paul, MN 55101; 612-228-1407; e-mail: compfrm@maroon.tc.umn.edu; http://www.umn.edu/nlhome/m111/compfrm **Membership:** Open to all. $45 annual fee.

American Music Center

Who: 2,300 members, including performers, composers, presenters, directors, conductors and others who concentrate in the area of contemporary American concert music, jazz or opera. **What:** Promotes performances of contemporary music through advocacy, grants and a library of more than 60,000 perusal scores. Founded in 1939 by Aaron Copland, Quincy Porter and other leading American composers of that era. **Contact:** David Matthews, American Music Center, 30 West 26th St., Ste. 1001, New York, NY, 10010; 212-366-5260 ext. 23; e-mail: Dwcm@ix.netcom.com; http://www.amc.net/amc **Membership:** Open to all. $55 annual fee.

Broadway on Sunset

Who: Musical theater librettists, lyricists and composers of all levels. **What:** lectures, consultation and evaluation services, production opportunities, workshops and instruction offered in the Los Angeles area. **Contact:** Kevin

Kaufman, Broadway on Sunset, 10800 Hesby, Ste. 9, North Hollywood, CA 91601; 818-508-9270; e-mail: bosmt@aol.com; http://www.members.aol.com/bosmt **Membership:** Open to all. No fee.

Canadian Country Music Association

Who: Canadian songwriters, musicians, producers, managers and others involved in country music. **What:** Founded in 1976 to provide its constituency with workshops, performance opportunities, awards and a newsletter. **Contact:** Canadian Country Music Association, 3800 Steeles Ave. W., Ste. 127, Woodbridge, ON, L4L 4G9, Canada; 905-850-1144 **Membership:** Open to all. No fee.

Chamber Music America

Who: 5,000 members, mostly professionals in the chamber music field. **What:** Promotes chamber music and works to improve the working lives of American chamber groups through grant programs, residencies, advocacy efforts, publications including *Chamber Music* magazine and an annual directory, technical assistance and a yearly conference. **Contact:** Jim Dauer, Chamber Music America, 305 7th Ave., New York, NY 10001; 212-242-2022 ext. 107 **Membership:** Open to all. $35 annual fee.

Chorus America

Who: 540 ensembles, administrators, instructors and conductors in the choral field. **What:** Offers publications, an annual conference, a summer management institute for choral managers, a conducting workshop and internships. **Contact:** Karen Richter, Chorus America, 1811 Chestnut St., Ste. 401, Philadelphia, PA 19103; 215-563-2430; e-mail: chorusam@libertynet.org; http://www.libertynet.org/~chorusam **Membership:** Open to all. $100–$500 annual fee for organizations; $50 for conductors; $25 for all others.

Early Music America

Who: 2,400 professionals, amateurs and early music enthusiasts. **What:** Founded in 1985 to foster and promote the performance, enjoyment and understanding of music before our time and to encourage the use of historically appropriate instruments and performance styles. Publishes *Early Music America* magazine, an annual membership directory, discounts on concert tickets, festivals, recordings, health and instrument insurance and technical assistance. Participates in annual early music festivals that take place in Boston and Berkeley in alternate years. **Contact:** Early Music America, 11421½ Bellflower Rd., Cleveland, OH 44106; 216-229-1685; e-mail: emaoffice@aol.com; http://www.cru.edu/orgs/ema **Membership:** Open to all. $40 for full membership; discounts for students.

Folk Alliance

Who: 1,800 people, mostly musicians and dancers, involved in the performing folk arts in America and Europe. **What:** Founded in 1989. Seeks to bind together the community of folk music and dance throughout North America. Provides networking opportunities, educational programs, advocacy and professional development assistance as well as a large-scale national conference. **Contact:** Folk Alliance, 1001 Connecticut Ave. NW, Ste. 500, Washington, DC 20036; 202-835-3655; http: // www. hidwater.com/folkalliance/ **Membership:** Open to all. Fees vary according to type of membership.

Gospel Music Association

Who: Performers, songwriters and others in the gospel music industry. **What:** Founded in 1964 to further the cause of Jesus Christ through all forms of gospel music. Maximizes opportunities for Christian music in the marketplace, has a major resource center and offers educational programs and publications such as the *Christian Music Networking Guide*. **Contact:** Member Services, Gospel Music Association, 1205 Division St., Nashville, TN 37203; 615-242-0303 **Membership:** Open to all. $75 for professionals; $50 for associate members.

International Bluegrass Association

Who: More than 2,500 bluegrass professionals and fans. **What:** A trade association that helps promote the business of bluegrass and encourages unity within it. Publishes bimonthly magazine, holds an annual trade show/convention, represents the field in other contexts and keeps members informed and connected. **Contact:** Member Services, International Bluegrass Association, 207 Second St., Owensboro, KY 42303; 502-684-9025 **Membership:** Open to all. $125 for organizations; $50 for professionals; $25 for fans.

Nashville Songwriters Association International

Who: 4,600 professional and aspiring songwriters in the U.S. and several foreign countries. **What:** A nonprofit service organization for songwriters working in all musical genres. Members get music industry information and advice, song evaluations, publications, networking opportunities, workshops and other educational programs. **Contact:** Nashville Songwriters Association International, 15 Music Sq. W., Nashville, TN 37293; 615-256-3354; http://www.songs.org/nsai **Membership:** $35–$100 annual fee depending on professional status.

National Academy of Recording Arts and Sciences

Who: 10,000 people in the recording industry including artists, students, teachers, lawyers, industry managers and other business people. **What:** Recognizes excellence through the Grammy Awards, educates people in the professional community and in the general public about music and the music business through the Grammy in the Schools program, puts out publications and provides general assistance. **Contact:** Membership Services, National Academy of Recording Arts and Sciences, 3402 Pico Blvd., Santa Monica, CA 90405; 310-392-3777; http://www. grammy.com **Membership:** Open to all. Fees vary.

OPERA America

Who: Professional opera and music theater companies, composers, musicians and other individuals. **What:** Established in 1970 to promote opera and musical theater. Maintains America's largest opera archive, offers conferences, publishes directory of opera and musical theater worldwide. **Contact:** OPERA America, 1156 15th St. NW, Ste. 810, Washington, DC 20005; 202-293-4466; e-mail Liz@operam.org **Membership:** Open to professionals in the field. Fees vary.

Songwriters Guild

Who: More than 5,000 songwriter members around the world including professional songwriters, heirs of deceased writers and amateurs. **What:** Founded in 1931. Run by and for songwriters to help promote its members and assist them in the creative, administrative and financial aspects of their work through seminars, workshops, a newsletter and more. **Contact:** Songwriters Guild, 1222 16th Ave. S., Ste. 25, Nashville, TN 37212; 615-329-1782 **Membership:** $70 for professionals; $55 for associate members.

Unions and Other Labor Organizations

American Federation of Musicians

Who: An international umbrella organization of more than 500 local affiliates in the U.S. and Canada. **What:** World's largest performing artists' union. Directs musicians to their local unions, serves members with publications such as the *International Musician* newspaper, provides emergency union protection to traveling musicians. **Contact:** American Federation of Musicians, 1501 Broadway, Ste. 600, New York, NY 10036; 800-762-3444 **Membership:** Available through local affiliates.

American Society of Composers, Authors and Publishers (ASCAP)

Who: More than 76,000 U.S. music writer and music publisher members. **What:** World's largest performing rights society, both in constituency size and in license fee collections ($435 million in 1995). Also, the only U.S. society created and controlled by music writers and publishers. Collects licensing fees on behalf of its members. Represents more than 200,000 foreign society members. Offers a credit union and medical, dental, life and instrument insurance. **Contact:** ASCAP, One Lincoln Plaza, New York, NY 10023; 212-621-6000; http://www.ascap.com **Membership:** For associate membership, a copy of copyright form for Library of Congress is required; for full membership, evidence of performance of composed music in an ASCAP-licensed venue or a commercially available product is required.

Broadcast Music, Inc. (BMI)

Who: American music publishers and composers. **What:** Collects performance royalties on behalf of affiliates when their music is played on radio or television. **Contact:** BMA Writer/Publisher Relations Department, 320 W. 57th St., New York, NY 10019; 212-586-2000; http://www.bmi/com **Membership:** Open door policy (no proof of performance required). No annual dues for composers; publishers pay $100 one-time fee.

Dramatists Guild

Who: 6,300 playwrights, composers and lyricists. **What:** Founded in 1920. Fights for fair royalties, protection of subsidiary rights, artistic control and copyright ownership. Maintains contracts for all levels of theatrical production; provides advice on all theater-related business matters. Gives information on agents, producers, contests, theaters and conferences. Publishes a literary quarterly, a newsletter and an annual resource guide. Sponsors symposia nationwide. Provides access to health insurance. **Contact:** Dramatists Guild, 234 W. 44th St., 11th Fl., New York, NY 10036; 212-398-9366 **Membership:** Eligibility requirements for active members; associate membership open to all theater writers and composers without precondition.

SESAC

Who: More than 5,000 songwriter and publisher affiliates. **What:** The smallest of America's three performing rights organizations and the only such organization operating on a for-profit basis. Has a more selective process for affiliation. The only U.S. organization to use Broadcast Data Systems, a large computer database that collects signals from radio and television stations around the country and records exactly when and where music is being played. **Contact:** SESAC Writer/Publisher Relations Department, 55 Music Sq. E., Nashville, TN 37203; 800-826-9996 **Membership:** No fee. Upon songwriter inquiry, the SESAC selection committee reviews musical material to deem whether or not affiliation will be mutually beneficial.

Selecting a Program

YOU'RE SHOPPING FOR SHOES. Your feet tell you they need new ones in order to do well what they were born to do. In the shoe store there is an overwhelming array of possibilities. Loafers and sandals, wing tips and high heels, Wellingtons and Aqua-mocs, Reeboks and Nikes and Converse. What you need is a shoe-shopping consultant!

In the music programs department, the array of possibilities can be dizzying. Until, that is, you take inventory of what you really want or need. I suggest a process that goes, loosely, like this:

Imagine the best place to do your musical work. Is it urban or rural? Busy with artistic compatriots or far away from everybody? Does working in the presence of famous or highly successful musicians inspire or intimidate you?

Do you work best with structured time (structured for you by a teacher) or in a free-floating atmosphere where work, meals, sleep, indeed night and day, blend into one another while you're in the working mode?

Do you want to perform while in a workshop, or do you want to listen to others talk about performing, or do you want a mix of both?

Are you hungry for skill development instruction, or is it hard-nosed business management advice you need?

How do you feel about exposing your work to peers, or to a mentor? Are you looking for private one-on-one critiques of your work, or are you ready to bring your performing or composing out into the (sometimes harsh) light of day?

Do you like events with hundreds of people scurrying about to this seminar or that, or are you looking rather for six good folks with whom you can meet for quiet, sustained dialogue about your music?

Is it your current performing or composing project you want to push forward, or are you looking for a workshop teacher who will coach you through a series of musical aerobics classes with exercises and guided discussion, perhaps in a genre that's new to you?

Do you want to travel to the workshop (can you afford to?), or do you need something near home with little or no added expense beyond the program itself?

Do you want to meet managers and concert presenters and press the flesh as a networker? Are you willing to pay to schmooze with those who may pay for your musical services, or does the mere thought of such activity make you vaguely seasick?

The list will expand a bit as you pose your own useful questions. If you sort out these entirely personal issues first, then the process of sorting through the array of musicians' workshops and conferences will be easier and more fun.

If this is the first time you've considered a workshop or conference experience, read randomly through the entries for half an hour; then go back to the self-inventory suggested above; then read again, using the index to find programs suited to your needs. It won't be long before you have a substantial list, then a winnowed list, of programs to contact for brochures and application forms.

Start a few months in advance if possible. In your local community, read the bulletin boards at the coffee shop or the YMCA or the college or university. Sometimes a great one-time-only workshop opportunity shows up on your doorstep—no need to fly to Montana! If you want to enter an ongoing program, ask the program director for names of a few recent participants whom you might query. Be sure you understand all the costs and whether the application fee is refundable. I believe this book is the most extensive guide of its kind, but I know I haven't captured the entire universe of music programs in these pages: keep a sharp lookout yourself.

And don't let the potentially endless job of searching for the ideal music workshop become a substitute for music making itself. Your most important workshop will always be your own voice or instrument and whatever time you can devote to your own creative work.

Special Advice on Academic Programs

It seems there are statistics that show that a college degree raises your likely lifetime earnings by a substantial amount over what you could expect if you bailed out after high school. But the difference between the lifetime earnings of those with undergraduate degrees compared to those with graduate degrees presents a cloudier picture. Sure, an astrophysicist with a PhD will do better than someone in rocks for jocks at Podunk Junior College. The question here is: What if you're a musician? Is a graduate degree worth the trouble and the expense?

For musicians, the statistics are generally useless. In fact, don't even approach the question of getting an academic degree in music from the angle of its likely impact on your earnings. Why? Because for most musicians, income from music is a crap shoot. At your first gig, you could earn nothing or a fat check. You could earn a measly $50 and yet a recording executive could be seated in the front row who signs you on the basis of what she heard. Composing and performing music, like philosophy, bake no bread, and to be heard at all, many musicians spend their own money rather than earn anything for their labors. And so forth. Economically speaking, music is an irrational adventure.

If you want to teach music, that's a different story. In most schools (secondary and college level), a graduate degree is necessary, if not to get the job then certainly to advance. But this isn't a book about how to become a teacher of music. If that's your goal, talk to the music chairperson at the largest university near you. Many music professionals are far less enthusiastic about music education departments, where the emphasis is more on process and quantification than on quality, content and imagination. Ask the music department not only about the content of the program but also about job placement of recent graduates, and try to query some of those graduates about the actual usefulness of the degree program. If you go for it, and if you become a good teacher of music—no matter how humble, and trust us, a few years of teaching freshman music appreciation will humble anyone—you will garner applause for sure.

The concern here is the graduate degree in music per se, for those who want to be musicians, full or part time. Often these are the master of music (MM) and doctor of musical arts (DMA) programs, though there are variations, such as music education artist diploma programs. Musicians headed for the groves of academe should read the catalogue fine print carefully. If you want music only, don't sign up for a degree requiring that you spend half your time and money on the abstractions of music scholarship (which these days ranges from highly politicized multiculturalism studies to in-depth musical analysis).

On the other hand, there is much to be gained from the extramusical offerings of schools like Eastman that are now adding a great many business of music courses to their offerings. It's high time music schools made a serious effort to equip graduates with useful entrepreneurial skills.

The good and bad news is that there are scores of academic music programs all across the country. Good news because you can probably find an appropriate program close to home if that's necessary; bad news because deciding which one will serve you best isn't easy. Advice follows.

The best music programs tend to be the smaller ones, where a close, dynamic relationship between teacher and student is possible or even required. So the first suggestion is: Think small. Next, it's generally true that the best music teachers—with some exceptions, of course—tend to be musicians themselves, people who teach as a form of service to younger musicians coming along (and no doubt to pay the bills). Look for a program staffed by musicians with active performing or composing careers (whether with famous groups or in the limelight isn't always the point). The best student-teacher relationships in music are essentially protégé-mentor relationships, which means that new students ought to know or have reason to believe that the faculty in their chosen programs have good candidates for this invaluable and highly sensitive role.

Then there is the content of the program. There are numerous curricular approaches to the teaching of music (including the one that says it can't be taught at all). My preference (you might not share this view) would be for programs that require (yes, I said require) the student to work extensively in several genres while concentrating on one. Alexander Glazunov's Concerto for Alto Saxophone might be your specialty, but your playing arguably will improve if you learn improvisation on the jazz charts. A grounding in theory and ear training is a must for *all* musicians, and virtually every academic program in this book offers coursework in these areas. And again, music schools with good career offices and serious course requirements in the business of music area do their students a real service in today's competitive marketplace.

Last, inquire about the final project required for graduation. Go for a program that will push you to do something better and bigger than ever before. Won't you feel better about yourself as a serious musician after having done a full recital of your own rather than just having played one piece in a departmental concert?

If you turn up evidence that a music program has a lot of hangers-on who have spent years "finding themselves" on campus while eking out a living as clerks in the local record store—well, as your mama told you long ago, "You'd better shop around."

Quite a number of academic programs are listed in this book because in music they are vitally important, particularly in the classical music and jazz fields where, for every successful artist who did not attend college or conservatory, there are hundreds more who did. I believe the programs listed are among the noteworthy ones. If there is another one near you that seems convenient to your plans, apply the criteria discussed above, and if the answers are good, open the door and walk through.

Special Advice on Festivals

It's a dream most musicians entertain at one point or another: a week, a month, a whole season or even a year away from other mundane responsibilities and frivolous distractions. Nothing but blue skies and beautiful mountains to inspire you to play your best and make great music. The music festival is a venerable tradition in America, and for serious musicians who can disconnect temporarily from the everyday world, such programs can be paradise regained.

Most, but not all, festivals are situated in idyllic rural settings. Many serve a variety of artists in addition to musicians. Most require attendees to audition and demonstrate some kind of track record of formal study, often in the form of recommendation letters.

Some festivals are Cadillacs, some are Chevrolets, and some, frankly, are donkey carts. Some will cost you a fortune; others will pay you a stipend just to be there whether you get anything done there or not. Some make a virtue out of the Spartan life (be alert to the brochure that says "rustic yet comfortable"), while others, like the Sarasota Music Festival, put their residents up in nice hotels. Some have prestige that will advance your career, and others are a distraction from career and work as well.

Remember, we live in an age of advertising hype. Anyone with a desktop publishing program can whip up a handsome brochure. If you are contemplating the expense (in dollars or time, or both) of a residential music program at a festival, look below the surface before you quit your day job or write any checks.

Daily rhythm differs widely between festivals. The scuttlebutt on a few festivals is that not much work gets done but the schmooze factor is high and, for the adventurous, the likelihood of a romantic or sexual romp is equally high. (Don't bother checking the index; it's not sorted in the latter category.)

Most festivals expect musicians to be serious on some level. Festivals known for intensive work schedules can be physically exhausting and emotionally draining. Be sure before you go to such places that high gear is indeed what you want.

And if you apply and are accepted, be wary of other extremes. You may think you'll love to get away from it all, but make a plan to check in periodically with the family at home. You may think you'll make great musical strides, but you won't if you are overwhelmed with loneliness. Be realistic about expectations.

Most of all, if you go, be sure to leave some time to be grateful. A stint at a music festival should be decidedly hard work, but it is also a rare privilege. You may never see much remuneration for your craft, but at the festival you are free to indulge your imagination. That's a freedom you simply cannot buy back home in a kitchen full of caterwauling kids or at your school or business or day job.

Music Programs

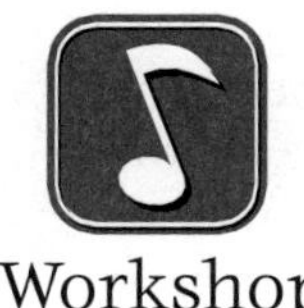

Workshop

Conference

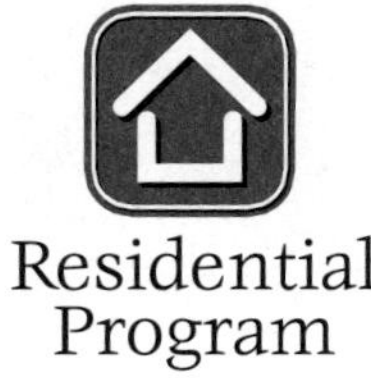

Residential Program

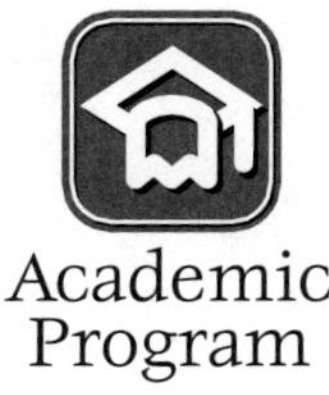

Academic Program

Festival

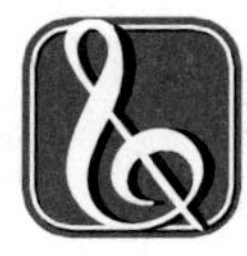

Masterclass

Alabama

Samford University School of Music

For instrumentalists, vocalists, composers, conductors, church musicians *800 South Lakeshore Drive, Birmingham, AL 35229* **Voice:** 205-870-2851 **Contact:** Milburn Price, Dean **Founded:** 1841 **Open:** Sept.–May **Admission:** Application ($25), audition, transcripts, letters of recommendation, test scores **Cost:** $12,492 (all-inclusive) **Financial Aid:** Scholarship **Size-Attendees:** 125 **Degree or Certification:** MM **Handicapped Access**

LOCATED IN SUBURBAN Birmingham, Samford University is a small, independent religious school run by the Alabama Baptist State Convention. There are 7 colleges and 20 different degree programs at the university. At the School of Music, all areas of traditional study are offered. In the graduate realm, there is particular emphasis on voice, piano, music education and church music. In addition to traditional instruments, the school also provides instruction in carillon playing, a must for many church musicians that is rarely taught in music schools. Facilities include 30 practice rooms and no fewer than 5 high-quality organs (Aeolian-Skinner, Holtkamp, Schlicker, and 2 von Bekerath). Again for the religious musician, the school library houses a number of special hymnal and tunebook collections. Samford has an exchange program with its companion school in England, the London Study Centre.

University of Alabama School of Music

For instrumentalists, vocalists, composers, arrangers *Box 870366, Tuscaloosa, AL 35487* **Voice:** 205-348-1463 **Fax:** 205-348-1473 **Contact:** Dr. Dennis Monk, Dir. Grad. Admissions **Founded:** 1831 **Open:** Sept.–May **Admission:** Application ($25), audition, transcripts **Cost:** $2,374 (resident), $5,924 (nonresident); $3,658 room and board **Financial Aid:** Scholarship **Size-Attendees:** 265 **Degree or Certification:** MM, MA, DMA **Handicapped Access**

TO THE SOUND OF bugles, no doubt, the University of Alabama was all but burned to the ground during the Civil War. It's come back strong, and today you'd never hear a few bugles over all the music that's playing on campus. Southwest of Birmingham, the university has some 14,000 students, many of whom choose to get involved in performance groups at the School of Music, like its Million Dollar Marching Band. For music majors, the course of study is serious and professional. Areas of focus include jazz and classical music. Many of the 21 music faculty members hail from the Birmingham and Montgomery symphony orchestras. This accredited program offers degrees in all performance areas, music therapy, music education and music administration. There are literally scores of ensembles in which to participate, and scholarships are often made available to those people lucky enough to play instruments that are especially needed in a given year.

Alaska

Fairbanks Summer Arts Festival

For instrumentalists, vocalists, composers *University of Alaska, P.O. Box 80845, Fairbanks, AK 99708* **Voice:** 907-474-8869 **Fax:** 907-479-4329 **Contact:** Jo Ryman Scott, Producing Dir. **Founded:** 1980 **Admission:** Must be 18 or high school graduate **Deadlines:** None; but reduced fee for early registration **Cost:** $300 **Size-Attendees:** 600 **Size-Class:** 10–12 **Handicapped Access**

THIS LIGHTHEARTED festival stands out for the breadth of artistic disciplines featured and for the variety of participants it draws, from novices to serious pros. Jo Ryman Scott of Fairbanks and Edward J. Madden from Boston founded the festival in 1980 as a 1-week jazz festival which has since expanded to 2 weeks. By 1982, the program—situated on the campus of the University of Alaska—grew to include not only jazz but also classical and popular music, dance, musical theater, opera, storytelling, ice skating, visual arts and more. The faculty roster is strong, with many members from Alaska, the Pacific Northwest and Los Angeles. Classes cover topics from performance to theory, improvisation to arranging. The festival boasts some 600 participants and total audience counts of more than 12,500. Many residents of the Fairbanks area participate as volunteers, and the directors consider the festival very much a community effort.

JO SCOTT'S CENTER

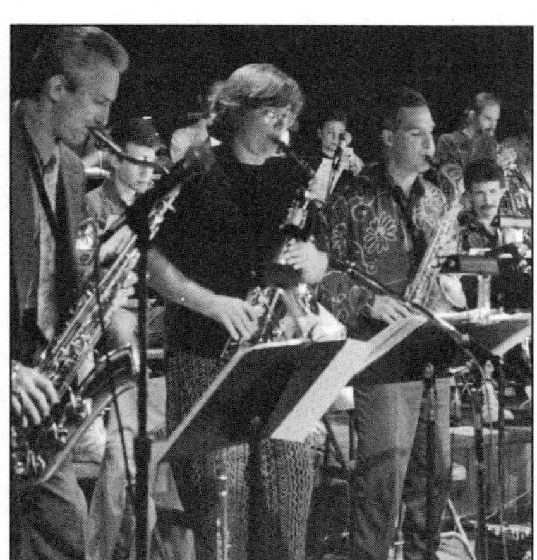

Jazz Band at Fairbanks Summer Arts Festival.

University of Alaska Fairbanks Music Department

For instrumentalists, vocalists, composers *100 mi. S of Arctic Circle — Signers' Hall, Ste. 102, Fairbanks, AK 99775* **Voice:** 907-474-7555 **Contact:** Madeleine Schatz, Dept. Head **Founded:** 1922 **Open:** Sept.–May **Admission:** Application ($35) **Deadlines:** Aug. 1 **Cost:** $2,070 (resident), $6,210 (nonresident); $3,690 room and board **Financial Aid:** Scholarship **Size-Attendees:** 500 **Degree or Certification:** BM, BA, MA, MA in education

THE MUSIC DEPARTMENT of the University of Alaska at Fairbanks has more than 500 music majors and a music faculty of 12 full-time and 7 part-time teachers. The program is aimed at those musicians who would like to get a full liberal arts education and then go on to a career of teaching or performing classical or jazz repertoire. One of the special focuses is preparing performers to do outreach work in rural areas. There is a full calendar of performances each semester. The music department is accredited by the Northwest Association of Schools of Music and by the National Association of Schools of Music. The university as a whole offers degree programs in 65 areas of study. It is situated on 2,250 gorgeous acres and is part of a statewide university system.

Arizona

Northern Arizona State University School of Performing Arts

For instrumentalists, vocalists, composers, conductors *North-central Arizona — P.O. Box 6040, Flagstaff, AZ 86011* **Voice:** 520-523-3731 **Web Site:** http://www.nau.edu/~spa **Contact:** Mary Huston-Somerville, PhD Asst. **Founded:** 1899 **Open:** 3 semesters: fall, spring, summer **Admission:** Application, audition **Deadlines:** Dec. 1 (Jan.–May); Mar. 1 (Aug.–Dec.); May 15 (June–Aug.) **Cost:** Per credit hour: $99 (resident), $296 (nonresident), $102 (summer) **Financial Aid:** Loans; Scholarship; Work/Study **Size-Attendees:** 90 **Size-Class:** 24 **Degree or Certification:** MM **Job Placement:** Yes **Handicapped Access**

Northern Arizona State University, approaching its centennial celebration in 1999, is a comprehensive state university with more than 19,000 students. The music program at NASU's School of Performing Arts stands out particularly in the area of jazz. The school has 3 fine jazz ensembles, the most advanced one of which has appeared at the Playboy Jazz Festival and the Hollywood Bowl, and has made recordings that have received favorable reviews in such magazines as *Downbeat.* The director of jazz studies is Dr. Peter M. Vivona, a graduate of the Eastman School of Music. NASU offers extensive study in conducting and in vocal music, with majors encouraged to participate in the University Chorale and Chamber Singers and in opera productions. Half a dozen other musical ensembles are open to all university students. The NASU Marching Band is one of the largest of these, the most active and well-respected of all the organizations on campus. No doubt marching around the campus, at 7,000 feet above sea level, is good for the cardiovascular system.

Arkansas

Arkansas State University Department of Music

For vocalists, instrumentalists, composers *75 mi. NW of Memphis, TN — P.O. Box 779, Jonesboro, AR 72469* **Voice:** 501-972-2094 **Fax:** 501-972-3932 **E-mail:** wholmes@aztec.astate.edu **Web Site:** http://www.astate.edu **Contact:** Dr. William D. Holmes **Founded:** 1925 **Open:** Year-round **Admission:** Application, audition **Deadlines:** Aug. 15; Jan. 2 **Cost:** Per semester: $975 (undergraduate resident), $1,800 (undergraduate nonresident), $1,170 (graduate resident), $1,990 (graduate nonresident) **Financial Aid:** Loans; Scholarship; Fellowship; Work/Study **Size-Attendees:** 150 **Size-Class:** 15 **Degree or Certification:** BA, BM, BME, MM, MME **Job Placement:** Yes **Handicapped Access**

Established as one of 4 state agricultural schools in 1909, Arkansas State University has become a typical large state school. The department of music offers the BA and MM degrees, as well as degrees in music education. Somewhat intriguing, only 2 courses are required for MM candidates, namely one in advanced conducting and one on research techniques. Another unusual requirement at ASU is that all keyboard majors must study languages.

Otherwise, ASU's Department of Music seems to be a fairly boilerplate institution. In addition to performance and music education, program areas include sacred music, composition and music theory. Performing groups include marching band, laboratory band, concert band, jazz ensemble, wind ensemble, ASU concert choir, madrigal singers and an opera production class. The school has approximately 150 music majors at the undergraduate and graduate levels, 21 faculty members and 30 practice rooms. ASU does not require auditions for admittance. Rather, applicants are accepted on a rolling basis.

Hot Springs Music Festival

For instrumentalists, conductors *Historic downtown district — 634 Prospect Ave., Hot Springs National Park, AR 71901* **Voice:** 501-623-4743 **Fax:** 501-624-6440 **E-mail:** hsmf@asms3.k12.ar.us **Contact:** Laura Rosenberg, Exec. Dir. **Founded:** 1996 **Open:** First 2 wks. June **Admission:** Application ($10), tape **Deadlines:** From Jan. till positions filled **Cost:** Full scholarship for all participants; $150 optional meal plan **Financial Aid:** Scholarship **Size-Attendees:** 80–90 **Handicapped Access**

THE STILL RELATIVELY new Hot Springs Music Festival focuses on musicians making the transition from student to professional. Under the guidance of experienced mentors talking with them and playing alongside them, apprentices—as participants are called—rehearse and perform orchestral and chamber music. The schedule is demanding, on purpose. It offers business of music courses in order to prepare young players for the real world to come. The festival made its debut in June 1996 in Hot Springs National Park, which is a spa town 60 miles southwest of Little Rock. The calendar of festival events featured some 20 concerts in just 2 weeks. The Bergonzi Quartet and the Rose Trio were among the teaching and performing ensembles. Laura and Richard Rosenberg, the founding directors, are out-of-towners who arrived in Arkansas with a mission to bring high-level music to the area. So far they are succeeding.

University of Arkansas Department of Music

For instrumentalists, vocalists, composers, conductors *201 Music Bldg., Fayetteville, AR 72701* **Voice:** 501-575-4701 **Fax:** 501-575-5409 **Contact:** Dr. Stephen Gates, Asst. Chair, Dept. of Music **Founded:** 1871 **Open:** Sept.–May **Admission:** Application ($15), audition, transcripts **Deadlines:** Apr. 1 **Cost:** $2,200 (resident), $5,392 (nonresident); $3,468 room and board **Financial Aid:** Scholarship **Size-Attendees:** 200 **Degree or Certification:** BM, MM **Handicapped Access**

THERE ARE MORE than 36,000 students at the University of Arkansas, some 200 of them majoring in music. The department of music offers undergraduate and advanced degree study in applied music, ensemble, and music education, history, literature and theory. It has a special Departmental Honors Program in music for university juniors and seniors who want to participate formally in scholarly music activities in the areas of performance, music history and literature, theory or composition. Candidates in the program work in independent study, do research under the guidance of music faculty and take part in special honors classes and seminars. As music departments do in most large universities, the UA Department of Music welcomes nonmajors in its activities.

California

Broadway on Sunset

For composers, songwriters, lyricists

Downtown — L.A. Theatre Center, 514 Spring St., Los Angeles, CA 91601; 10800 Hesby St., North Hollywood, CA 91601 **Voice:** 818-508-9270 **Fax:** 818-508-1806 **Web Site:** http://www.members.aol.com/bosmt **Contact:** Kevin Kaufman, Exec. Dir. **Founded:** 1991 **Open:** Year-round **Admission:** All courses have fees attached except musicals selected for development **Cost:** $165–$495; course in craft and business (most popular) is $225 plus $10 materials fee **Financial Aid:** Scholarship; Work/Study **Size-Attendees:** 200 **Size-Class:** 12–20 **Handicapped Access**

BROADWAY ON SUNSET is a musical theater development organization founded by writers for writers. It's a nonprofit, nonmembership program with different programs intended to help various participants, from those who want to write a musical, to those who have written an outline including a few songs, to those who are the proud creators of completed shows. All the BOS programs emphasize the need for a well-structured libretto before writing lyrics or composing music, thus minimizing book problems before a show is up and running.

BOS programs educate writers on lyric writing, musical dramatization and the expectations of the profession at every stage of the writing process. In addition, courses cover finding a collaborator, securing rights to a property, economic factors that influence a show's produceability and how to present a work to producers in a professional manner. It offers a step-by-step 6-week general course, a guide to libretto writing, a writers' reading program, an interview series and symposia, a musical scene workshop, a lyric-writing class, staged readings, consultations and what's called a "musical theatre referral service." BOS workshop instructors include the playwright, lyricist and librettist Libbe S. HaLevy, lyricist Marshall Barer and musical dramatist Kevin Kaufman. BOS has been active in education and development since 1991. In 1997 it mounts its first commercial production, of BOS executive director Kevin Kaufman's musical, *Little Witch*.

Djerassi Resident Artists Program

For classical and jazz composers and composer/performers *45 mi. S of San Francisco — 2325 Bear Gulch Rd., Woodside, CA 94062* **Voice:** 415-747-1250 **Fax:** 415-747-0105 **E-mail:** Drap@djerassi.org **Founded:** 1979 **Open:** Apr.–Oct. **Admission:** Application ($25), 2 recordings of full pieces, score if available, project proposal **Deadlines:** Mid.–Feb. **Cost:** None **Size-Attendees:** 8–12

JUST AN HOUR'S drive from San Francisco and only 10 minutes from Palo Alto, Djerassi nonetheless seems remote amid 600 wooded acres high in the Santa Cruz mountains. Though the program is best known to writers, it invites artists of many stripes, including dancers, painters, sculptors, photographers and composers. Participants are housed

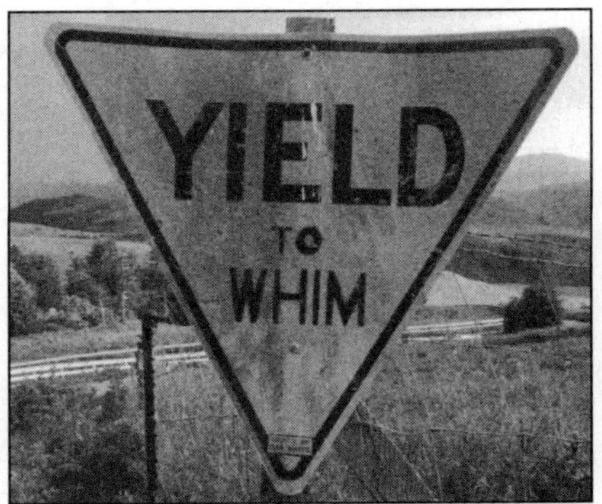

ROBIN CLARK

Welcome to the Djerassi Resident Artists Program.

in an old farmhouse and in an old circular barn, partitioned into many odd-shaped studios, one of which is specially equipped with a piano and soundproofed for a composer's use. The colony was established in 1979 and named for Dr. Carl Djerassi, a professor at Stanford University and an inventor of the birth control pill. Djerassi is now administered as a public charity, and artists receive their residencies fully free of charge. A panel of San Francisco area artists chooses participants from among applicants from around the world.

Headlands Center for the Arts

For performers, composers, audio artists *Northern edge of SF Bay — 944 Fort Barry, Sausalito, CA 94965* **Voice:** 415-331-2787 **Fax:** 415-331-3857 **Founded:** 1987 **Open:** Feb.–Dec. **Admission:** Application, example of recent work (on CD, audio- or videotape) **Deadlines:** Early June **Size-Attendees:** Varies

ABOUT 15 MINUTES from San Francisco, the Headlands Center for the Arts is one of America's more offbeat artist residency sites. It's situated on 13,000 acres of coastal wilderness once used by the U.S. Army for a number of military installations. The center's main buildings are former army barracks, built early in this century. The Army left the Headlands in the 1970s, turning the land over to the National Park Service. Eventually the land was divided up among nonprofit organizations willing to help renovate its historic buildings. At HCA, such major artists as Ann Hamilton, John Randolph and Mark Mack have helped transform the former barracks and their grounds into works of art. According to HCA, there is still much work for interested residents to do on site.

Besides its one-of-a-kind setting, what sets Headlands apart is its mission as an artists' residence. The center invites participants to come explore and investigate rather than focus on the completion of a project per se. Although it's fine to write a symphony at Headlands, it's also fine to spend time there making notes on the idea of a symphony or one's approach to working with sound. The emphasis is not so much on projects and results as on the artistic process itself.

Thirty-five affiliate artists from the Bay Area live at the center for periods of up to 3 years, in 3 fully furnished buildings. The residents do their own housekeeping and, 5 nights a week, the center's chef prepares dinner in the Mess Hall. In addition to the live-in artists, 10 artists in residence from other parts of the U.S. and abroad come and spend shorter periods (usually 4 to 12 weeks). The center takes visual artists, choreographers, writers, musicians and film and video artists.

Residents are selected on the merit of their work, but the center is especially looking for artists who stretch conventional boundaries and/or demonstrate that they consider the social, cultural or political issues of today. The center currently offers residencies for artists living in California, North Carolina and Ohio and for artists from Sweden, Denmark, Taiwan, the Czech Republic and Slovakia. Artists from anywhere else are responsible for securing funding for their residency from their home region.

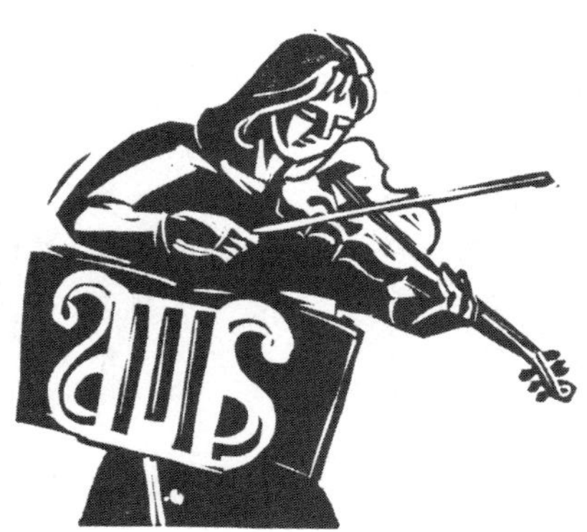

Mills College Music Department

For instrumentalists, vocalists, composers *5000 MacArthur Blvd., Oakland, CA 94613* **Voice:** 510-430-2171 **Contact:** Chris Brown, Dept. Head **Founded:** 1852 **Open:** Sept.–May **Admission:** Application, audition, test scores **Deadlines:** Apr. 1 **Cost:** $8,400; $4,100 room and board **Financial Aid:** Loans; Scholarship; Work/Study **Size-Attendees:** 75 **Degree or Certification:** BA, MA, MFA **Handicapped Access**

An all-female school established in 1852 as a seminary for women, Mills has become a prominent college and graduate school. Still a women's school, Mills has made a serious dent in music history. Going back to the 1940s, when Darius Milhaud was briefly on the faculty, Mills has been turning out some of the 20th century's most famous women composers, Pauline Oliveros for one.

The school tries to get beyond thinking in a box, aiming to turn out individual artists rather than people with diplomas in rigidly structured areas of study. Basic offerings include baroque music, composition, electronic music, ethnomusicology, music education, music history, music literature, performance and recording media, but specific study programs can be tailored to the individual. The MFA, for example, can be obtained in composition and performing within special areas of concentration, such as in interdisciplinary work based on music but involving a variety of media forms, such as video and film production, staging, lighting and scriptwriting. Among the instruments taught are clavichord and gamelon.

Mills College's Center for Contemporary Music is very strong and up to date, housing electronic instruments, studios and laboratories.

In addition, the music department brings in well-known guest artists to lecture and work with students in its Formal Methods program.

Music Academy of the West Summer School and Festival

For instrumentalists, vocalists *1070 Fairway Rd., Santa Barbara, CA 93108* **Voice:** 805-969-4726 **Fax:** 805-969-0686 **E-mail:** 102770.131@compuserve.com **Contact:** Dr. David L. Kuehn, Pres. **Founded:** 1947 **Open:** 4th wk. June–3rd wk. Aug. **Admission:** Application ($40), audition (vocal, accompanying), tape (instrumental) **Deadlines:** Mid-Jan. (vocal, accompanying); Feb. 28 (instrumental); Mar. 15 (piano) **Cost:** $3,200 (room and board incl.); $100 (registration fee) **Financial Aid:** Scholarship; Fellowship **Size-Attendees:** 135 **Size-Class:** 4–40 **Handicapped Access**

For half a century, the Music Academy of the West Summer School and Festival has been one of the West Coast's most distinguished summer music programs. About 135 voice, piano and instrumental students are provided experiences there that directly relate to expectations of the current musical marketplace.

The academy was founded in 1947 by a group of Southern California musicians and arts patrons. Its early history is star-studded. Metropolitan Opera soprano Lotte Lehmann was one of the first organizers, and her faculty members included the likes of Ernest Bloch, Darius Milhaud and Arnold Schoenberg.

Just 4 years after the academy opened, it was bequeathed the John Percival Jefferson estate in Santa Barbara. The main building, Miraflores, is a large and gracious structure in the Spanish Renaissance style overlooking the Pacific, surrounded by 10 acres of gardens.

Voice students participate in a balanced curriculum of opera scene presentations and art song interpretation; pianists choose to emphasize either solo performance, instrumental accompanying or vocal accompanying; and instrumental students participate in the 90-piece Festival Orchestra and in an extensive chamber music program.

There is an active music theater program as well.

The festival has one of the best student to faculty ratios available, at 5 to 1. This is significant, considering that the faculty roster is of the highest order. Such globally famous performers as Marilyn Horne, Catherine Comet and Jerome Lowenthal teach alongside powerhouse pedagogues like violist Donald McInnes. It would be hard to find a better all-round faculty list anywhere on the West Coast.

Musicians Institute

For instrumentalists, vocalists, composers *1655 McCadden Pl., Hollywood, CA 90028* **Voice:** 213-462-1384; 800-255-PLAY **Fax:** 213-462-6978 **E-mail:** Musicinst@earthlink.net **Web Site:** http://www.mi.edu **Contact:** Admissions Dept. **Founded:** 1976 **Open:** Year-round **Admission:** Application ($100); audition/tape (vocational program); audition/videotape, exam, essay (degree program) **Deadlines:** Aug. 1 (degree program); first day of each class (vocational program) **Cost:** $300 per wk. (noncertificate program); $200 per credit unit (certificate program). **Financial Aid:** Loans; Scholarship; Work/Study **Size-Attendees:** Varies **Size-Class:** 15–20 **Degree or Certification:** BM, Voc. Cert., Assoc. Deg. **Handicapped Access**

For more than 20 years bass players, singers, guitarists, bassists, drummers and keyboard players, as well as recording artists, have benefited from the offerings at the Musicians Institute, where the emphasis is on comprehensive preparation for the work world. The school offers vocational and degree programs. It has business of music courses and offers an active referral service and job placement program.

Its learning facilities are state-of-the-art, including an audio/video library, audio and video recording facilities, 24-track digital and analog studios, as well as multimedia and midi training facilities. Concerts and clinics are ongoing. The school also offers 3- and 6-month courses of study.

San Francisco Conservatory of Music

For instrumentalists, vocalists, composers *1201 Ortega St., San Francisco, CA 94122* **Voice:** 415-564-8086 **Fax:** 415-759-3499 **Web Site:** http://www.sfcm.edu **Contact:** Colleen Katzowitz, Dir. of Student Services **Founded:** 1917 **Open:** Sept.–May **Admission:** Application ($60), transcripts, test scores, recommendations, audition **Deadlines:** Mar. 1 **Cost:** $14,800 **Financial Aid:** Loans; Scholarship; Stipend; Work/Study **Size-Attendees:** 270 **Size-Class:** 10 **Degree or Certification:** BM, MM, Art. Cert. **Handicapped Access**

The San Francisco Conservatory of Music is the only major independent conservatory of music on the West Coast, and one of the top music schools in the country. It's also one of the smallest, with a total student body of about 270.

Founded as a piano school in 1917 by Ada Clement and Lillian Hodgehead, the conservatory incorporated in 1923. Composer Ernest Bloch was its first director. Among the conservatory's early students were Isaac Stern and Yehudi Menuhin.

The conservatory's programs and reputation grew steadily. A summer chamber music program started by the Griller String Quartet in 1948 attracted students from around the country and established a tradition of chamber music at the school.

In fact, the SFCM is well known as the first U.S. music school to offer an MA in chamber music. Chamber music continues to be an extremely important element in the conservatory's programs, with an exceptional faculty and a program that encourages students and faculty to perform together alongside guest artists. Alumni of the chamber music program include members of the Peabody Trio, and the Arditti, Ridge and New Zealand string quartets.

The SFCM was also the first conservatory to offer degrees in classical guitar. This remains a distinguished program at the school. The guitar department, chaired by David Tanenbaum, is one of the most progressive in the country, with a particular emphasis on new music for the instrument.

Students have many opportunities to perform. The school's long list of regular ensembles includes an orchestra, an opera theater, a new music ensemble, a baroque ensemble, a brass choir, chamber ensembles of all configurations, a cantata singers group, a guitar ensemble and a percussion ensemble.

As is becoming common in music schools around the country, community service concerts are integral to the performance curriculum at SFCM. Every year, the conservatory sends students out into the community to perform concerts at convalescent homes, hospitals, schools and other institutions. In addition, the job placement office offers paid performance opportunities.

Many SFCM faculty members come from the San Francisco Symphony and the San Francisco Opera. Others of note include the cellist Bonnie Hampton, the violinist Stuart Canin (former concertmaster of the San Francisco Symphony) and conductor Denis de Coteau of the San Francisco Ballet. The faculty-student ratio at SFCM is 6 to 1.

Graduate course offerings range from the basics, like one called Dramatic Structures in Opera, to the highly intriguing, as in Music in James Joyce's *Ulysses.*

Student life has its attractions. The conservatory is located in a comparatively affordable, residential area near Golden Gate Park about 2 miles from the Pacific Ocean.

KINGMOND YOUNG

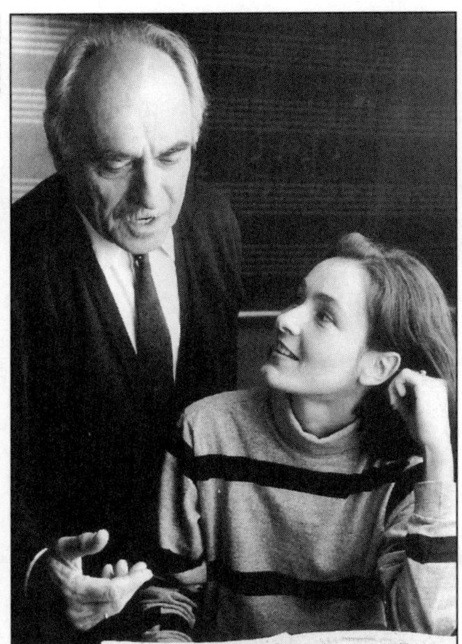

San Francisco Conservatory of Music faculty chair Zaven Melikian and graduate student Angeline Branson.

San Francisco State University Department of Music

For instrumentalists, vocalists, composers *1600 Holloway Ave., San Francisco, CA 94123* **Voice:** 415-338-1344 **Fax:** 415-338-3294 **E-mail:** ptlee@sfsu.edu **Web Site:** http://www.sfsu.edu/~music **Contact:** Dr. Patricia Taylor Lee, Dept. Chair **Founded:** 1898 **Open:** Year-round **Admission:** Written application ($55), tape audition, recommendations, placement tests in theory, musicianship **Deadlines:** Rolling **Cost:** Per semester: $246 (resident), $1,000 (nonresident) **Financial Aid:** Loans; Scholarship; Fellowship; Work/Study **Size-Attendees:** 250 **Size-Class:** 15 **Degree or Certification:** BA, BM, MA, MM **Job Placement:** Yes **Handicapped Access**

THE DEPARTMENT of music at San Francisco State University offers both professional and liberal arts degree programs in music and courses that enrich the general education and cultural life of the university. The faculty of the department of music includes the members of the Alexander String Quartet and such San Francisco Symphony members as bassoonist Rufus Olivier and French hornist William Klinghoffer. A variety of individual and ensemble performance opportunities in classical music, jazz and pop are available to students in the department. Facilities include McKenna and Knuth theaters, seating 750 and 320 respectively; an up-to-date electronic music laboratory; 2 piano labs; choral and instrumental rehearsal space; classroom and practice facilities; and a major music library.

Songwriters Guild of America Workshops

For composers, lyricists, performers *Los Angeles, New York and Nashville — 6430 Sunset Blvd., Hollywood, CA 90028* **Voice:** 213-462-1108, 212-768-7902, 615-329-1782 **E-mail:** SGANews@aol.com **Founded:** 1931 **Open:** Year-round **Admission:** Application ($55), list of published works **Deadlines:** Rolling **Cost:** Various fees, some free **Size-Attendees:** 15–50 **Handicapped Access**

THE SONGWRITERS GUILD of America is probably the nation's largest and oldest songwriters' association. Since its founding in 1931, SGA has provided songwriters with services and activities they need to succeed in the business of music. SGA's membership includes authors and composers in all phases of music: pop, R&B, rock, folk, country, jazz, theater, classical, motion picture and television. The Songwriters Guild Foundation is SGA's nonprofit foundation created to assist artists through various programs at SGA offices in Los Angeles, New York and Nashville. Recent workshop topics have included Supershop Pitch, in which participants pitched their songs to record artists and repertory reps and/or producers; the Creativity Workshop, designed to help songwriters channel their creativity; and the Phil Swan Country Workshop, in which students got behind-the-scenes information about the country music marketplace.

Stanford Jazz Workshop

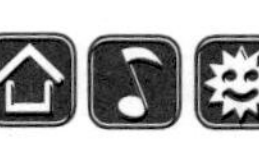

For instrumentalists, vocalists *Stanford University — P.O. Box 11291, Stanford, CA 94309* **Voice:** 415-386-8535 **Fax:** 415-386-8535 **E-mail:** sjazzw@netcom.com **Web Site:** http://www.leland.stanford.edu **Contact:** Jim Nadel, Dir. **Founded:** 1972 **Open:** Late July–mid-Aug. **Admission:** Application **Deadlines:** June 1 **Cost:** $500; $300 room and board **Financial Aid:** Scholarship; Work/Study **Size-Attendees:** 500 **Handicapped Access**

THE STANFORD JAZZ Workshop, now more than a quarter of a century old, is one of America's best summer jazz programs. The faculty includes internationally celebrated jazz artists as well as many fine San Francisco Bay Area players. Some 500 participants turn out to study music performance, music theory, the business of music and more each summer.

SJW's Jazz Residency is of special appeal to graduate-level students and professionals. It's a self-paced program of jazz playing and study with instrumentalists and vocalists, including daily classes, lectures, masterclasses, concerts and special events. Adult amateurs and high school students may participate, but only if approved by audition tape. Faculty members include John McKenna, Ndugu Chancler and Albert "Tootie" Heath.

Stanford also offers the Summer Evening Combo, Theory and Arranging Program. These evening classes meet for six weeks and focus on jazz theory, arranging, small combo, piano trio and guitar trio playing.

There are special workshops from year to year, held in San Francisco's Cafe du Nord. These have included an African-Cuban workshop led by Chucho Valdes, with the Cuban ensemble Irakere. Another series of workshops has included The Web and You, and Performance Anxiety: Use It or Lose It.

For a number of years, SJW has included a special workshop called Improvisation for Strings. David Balakrishnan and Mark Summer of the Turtle Island String Quartet have led it in the past. It's a week-long program of challenging, supportive study of jazz improvisation on bowed string instruments. Rhythmic techniques available to string players, jazz chamber music and solo work are among the areas of study.

In part because of the sheer volume of activity going on at SJW, the San Francisco Chronicle has called the Stanford Jazz Workshop jazz heaven. In addition to string improvisation, and its jazz residency program, the 1996 SJW offered a jazz camp for young musicians aged 12 to 17.

There was also the Steve Coleman Community Residency Project, a community outreach effort that brought Coleman and his 10-piece ensemble, Metrics, out for free performances, lecture-demonstrations and clinics incorporating jazz, hip hop, dance, percussion, spoken word and other art forms, held at various locations throughout the Bay Area.

All this takes place against the backdrop of the Stanford Jazz Festival, in which faculty and guests present more than 35 concerts in intimate settings on the Stanford campus.

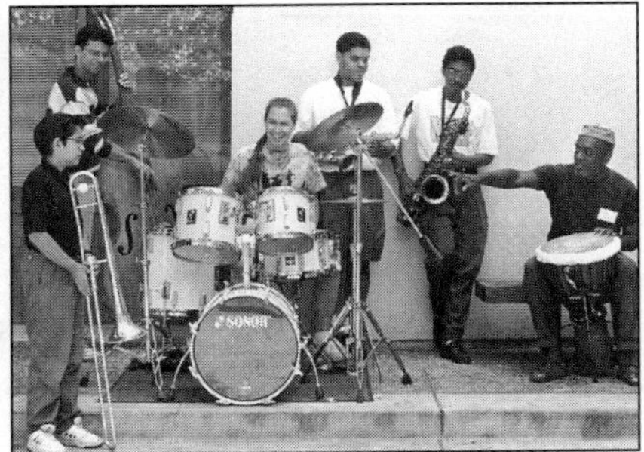

K. GYPSY ZABOROSKIE

Albert "Tootie" Heath teaching the Stanford Jazz Workshop.

Symphony at Sea

For amateur and professional instrumentalists *Seminar/cruise of the Caribbean Islands — P.O. Box 718, ℅ Eugenio Gaddini, Nevada City, CA 95959* **Voice:** 916-478-1551; 800-386-8646 **Fax:** 916-273-2853 **Contact:** Jerry Preseler **Founded:** 1996 **Open:** Late Mar.–early Apr. **Admission:** Application **Deadlines:** 2 mos. before departure **Cost:** $1,150 plus tax, excl. airfare **Size-Attendees:** 25–80 **Size-Class:** 55 **Handicapped Access**

PROVING THE ADAGE that there is something for everyone in this world, the Symphony at Sea is a one-of-a-kind program designed to appeal to orchestral musicians who want to get away from it all. For $1,150 per person plus a $129 port tax, you can embark at Ft. Lauderdale and cruise the Caribbean on Holland America's *Westerdam* and make (mostly light-encore) music to your heart's content. Music director Eugenio Gaddini leads 2 on-board orchestras. One, the Symphony at Sea, is geared for proficient amateurs and professionals. The other, the Sea Gull Symphonette, is for those who play well but are a little rusty. The program includes full orchestra rehearsals daily, alternating sectionals, optional chamber ensemble playing and a performance. The orchestra manager is actually a travel agent named Jan. To reach her, just call 1-800-Fun-To-Go.

UCLA Department of Music

For instrumentalists, vocalists, composers *Westwood — 405 Hilgard Ave., Los Angeles, CA 90024* **Voice:** 213-825-4321 **Contact:** Robert H. Gray, Dean, College of Fine Arts **Founded:** 1881 **Admission:** Application ($35), test scores, music aptitude and achievement tests **Deadlines:** July, Oct., Nov. **Cost:** Free (resident), $4,086 (nonresident) **Financial Aid:** Loans; Scholarship; Work/Study **Size-Attendees:** 455 **Degree or Certification:** BM, MA, MFA, PhD **Handicapped Access**

ARNOLD SCHOENBERG put UCLA on the musical map when he taught composition there from 1936 to 1944. The school named its music department site after him; it's called the Schoenberg Hall and Annex. Today, of the 8 music departments within the University of California system, UCLA's is the largest and almost certainly the best known. The basic foundation of study is traditional, emphasizing theory, history, analysis and performance. At the same time, the school has a strong profile in the areas of nonwestern, historically informed and experimental music. The department offers not only performance degrees but also the MA and PhD degrees in the fields of historical musicology, ethnomusicology, systemic musicology, composition and music education. Of interest to enterprising musicians, UCLA's Graduate School of Management offers an MBA in arts management and entertainment.

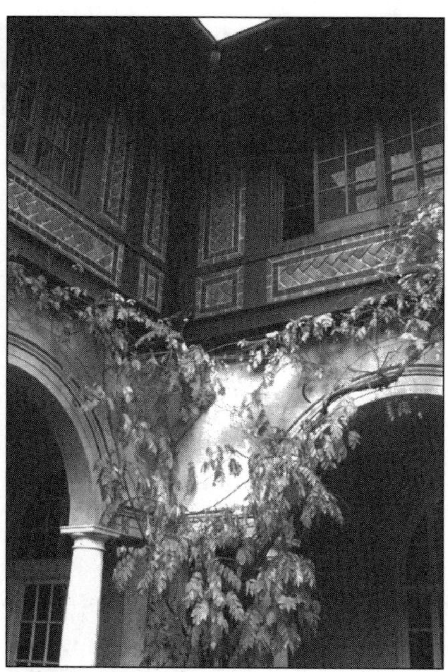
MICHAEL COLLOPY

Villa Montalvo, Saratoga.

Villa Montalvo Artist Residency Program

For performers, composers *1 hr. S of San Francisco — P.O. Box 158, 15400 Montalvo Rd., Saratoga, CA 95071* **Voice:** 408-741-3421 **Fax:** 408-741-5592 **Founded:** 1942 **Open:** Year-round **Admission:** Application ($20), 3 copies of cassette recording of a recent work **Deadlines:** Mar. 1 (for Oct.–Mar.); Sept. 1 (for Apr.–Sept.) **Cost:** $100 security deposit **Financial Aid:** Loans; Fellowship **Size-Attendees:** 5

LOCATED IN THE FOOTHILLS of the Santa Cruz Mountains, Villa Montalvo is a 1930s estate built by U.S. Senator James D. Phelan in the style of a Mediterranean villa. Since the 1940s it has been open to visual artists, musicians and writers as a year-round residential program.

The program encourages performers and composers to apply for participation in what it calls its "quiet" season, which takes place in fall and winter. (Montalvo's "active" spring/summer season features dozens of somewhat intrusive public events.) All artists are given private apartments; composers receive quarters equipped with a grand piano and extra rehearsal space. Meals are the artists' responsibility. The atmosphere is highly suitable for long hours of uninterrupted work. Montalvo accepts artists at all stages of their careers and seeks a diverse international community of residents.

Colorado

Aspen Music Festival and School

 *For instrumentalists, vocalists, composers* *2 Music School Rd., Aspen, CO 81611* **Voice:** 970-925-3254 **Fax:** 970-920-1643 **E-mail:** amf-publicity@aspenmusic.org **Web Site:** http://www.aspenonline.com/musicfestival **Contact:** Debbie Ayers, Publicity Dir. **Founded:** 1949 **Open:** Mid-June–Aug. **Admission:** Application (fee), tape **Deadlines:** Apr. 15 **Cost:** $2,100; $2,250 room and board **Financial Aid:** Scholarship; Fellowship; Stipend; Work/Study **Size-Attendees:** 900 **Size-Class:** 1–20 **Job Placement:** Yes **Handicapped Access**

DUBBED BY SOME the Juilliard of the West, Aspen Music Festival and School has traditionally drawn heavily from among students at Juilliard and other major music schools.

Aspen's is a competitive atmosphere. For instrumentalists, for example, there are 5 orchestras, and assignments can vary from week to week. Orchestra assignments and seating are determined by audition and overall performance. In the Festival Orchestra and the Chamber Symphony, players have the chance to perform alongside well-known faculty members, so the stakes are high.

There is no doubt that for very serious musicians the ability to play among talented peers has significant musical and professional benefits. For the savvy and talented, Aspen presents significant networking possibilities. Many now-famous individuals and ensembles can trace their success back to associations formed there.

The faculty lineup at Aspen is extremely impressive. Dorothy Delay, a Juilliard fixture, has a violin studio at Aspen, as do many other world-renowned teachers and performers. The Emerson String Quartet has been working with young groups for years in the festival's special program for string quartets.

The typical student's schedule is packed. Private lessons are given in all major fields. Students may also select courses from a curriculum that includes theoretical studies, seminars, ensemble classes, movement classes, and orchestral, choral, opera and jazz training. Masterclasses conducted in each department are open to all. These classes offer students the opportunity to observe studies outside their major field.

The Aspen Music School campus is situated outside the town of Castle Creek and rests among groves of aspen trees and a series of trout ponds. Built on the location of a former silver mine, the campus boasts 2 rehearsal rooms, a library and 2 buildings that house a student lounge, a dining hall and additional practice rooms. The festival also uses school and community facilities within Aspen, including the renovated Wheeler Opera House. Free bus transportation between town and campus is provided by the city of Aspen.

Concurrent with the Aspen Music School summer session is the Aspen Music Festival. Members of the school's artist faculty perform alongside students and guest artists in the festival concerts and events. The Aspen Music Festival draws audiences from all over the world.

The chief downside of Aspen is often the expense. Tuition is relatively high, but its real estate is the killer. Even for students on full scholarships, finding af-

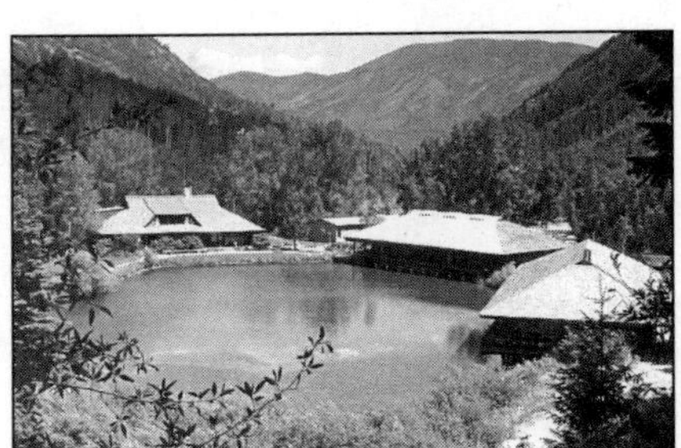

ALEX IRVIN

Aspen Music Festival and School.

fordable living arrangements can be frustrating. Modest accommodations in the world-famous resort town can reach $800 per month per person.

Central City Opera

For vocalists *30 mi. W of Denver — Box 218, Central City, CO 80218; 621 17th St., Ste. 1601, Denver, CO 80293* **Voice:** 303-292-6500 **Web Site:** http://www.ossinc.net/opera **Contact:** Curt Hancock, Artistic Admin. **Founded:** 1978 **Open:** June–mid-Aug. **Admission:** Application (no fee), audition **Deadlines:** Nov. 1 (audition) **Size-Attendees:** 26–28 **Handicapped Access**

FOR 8 WEEKS EACH summer, Central City Opera engages qualified young singers for its Apprentice Artist Program and its Studio Artist Program. The Apprentice Artist Program is a career-entry vehicle intended for singers aged 24 to 30. The Studio Artist Program is for younger singers, between 21 and 25.

Both programs provide extensive training classes in stage movement, acting, stage combat and diction, as well as masterclasses in makeup, audition techniques and career planning. Operas are sung in English.

Central City Opera provides housing in Central City, a weekly stipend and a transportation allowance. Apprentices understudy CCO cast members and perform operas at youth concerts. Some will play supporting and understudy roles in the opera company during the regular season. Studio artists will appear in major productions featuring chorus and perform on the CCO's Salon Recitals series.

MARK KIRYLUK

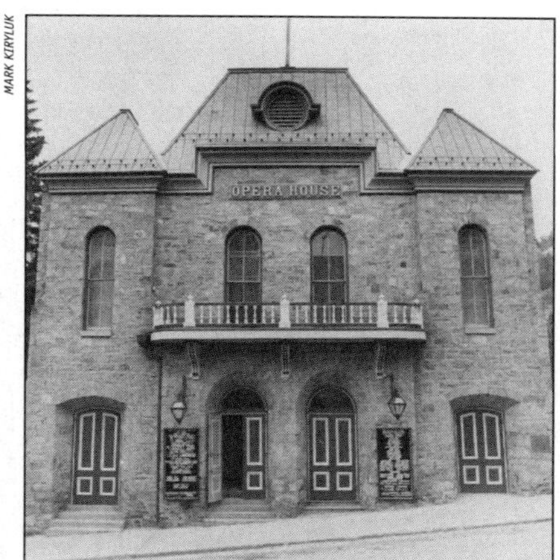

Central City Opera.

Christian Artists' Seminar in the Rockies

For instrumentalists, vocalists, composers, songwriters *YMCA of the Rockies, 2515 Tunnel Rd., Estes Park, CO 80511; Christian Artists' Corp., 7100 Broadway, Ste. 3K, Denver, CO 80221* **Voice:** 303-428-5995; 800-755-7464 **Fax:** 303-428-9308 **Contact:** Joelle Krankota **Founded:** 1974 **Open:** Last wk. July **Admission:** Registration fee (conference); additional fee (competitions) **Deadlines:** Up to the event **Cost:** $425 (programs); $60 (special conference tracks); $200/wk. and up (housing) **Size-Attendees:** 1,100–1,200 **Handicapped Access**

THE THEME IS MUSIC and ministry, but the nuts-and-bolts instruction offered is standard for the music industry. Into just 1 week, the Christian Artists' Seminar the Rockies squeezes in a prestigious competition offering more than $100,000 in prizes; more than 150 classes, with topics ranging from performance techniques to concert booking, recording and MIDI technology; and 6 nightly concerts.

Featured artists have included Twila Paris, Larnelle Harris, Steve Camp and Joe Gautier. Daily general sessions feature acclaimed speakers and music industry panelists. New artists are showcased by major record labels. There are dance training sessions, a songwriters' gathering and conferences in drama training and how to combine music and worship. Running in tandem with the seminar is a kids' bible camp, designed to make the conference a must for the whole family.

Colorado College Summer Conservatory and Music Festival

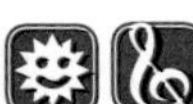

For instrumentalists
South-central Colorado — 14 E. Cashe Lapoudre, Colorado Springs, CO 80903 **Voice:** 719-389-6653 **Fax:** 719-389-6955 **E-mail:** Conservatory@cc.colorado.edu **Contact:** Susan Grace **Founded:** 1985 **Open:** Late June **Admission:** Application ($40), tape, letter of recommendation **Deadlines:** Apr. 1 **Cost:** $575; $375 room and board **Financial Aid:** Scholarship **Size-Attendees:** 40 **Size-Class:** 1–40 **Handicapped Access**

UNDER THE DIRECTION of distinguished composer and teacher Rubin Goldmark, Colorado College established its first summer music program in the late 1880s. Since then, a succession of gifted performers and students have been summer guests of the college. In its present form, run by Susan Grace, artist-in-residence at Colorado College, the program allows outstanding young musicians to spend 3 weeks working closely with faculty coaches in chamber groups, orchestra rehearsals, masterclasses, private lessons and independent practice. They perform 3 evening orchestra concerts and a series of lunchtime programs, all free and open to the community.

The conservatory's Festival Artists Concerts, an integral component of the Summer Conservatory and Music Festival, give listeners an opportunity to hear performances of great chamber music played by virtuoso faculty members, including pianist William Wolfram, violinist Glenn Dicterow and violist Karen Dreyfus.

University of Colorado at Boulder College of Music

For instrumentalists, vocalists, composers, conductors, church musicians
Campus Box 301, Boulder, CO 80309 **Voice:** 303-492-2207 **Fax:** 303-492-5619 **Contact:** Deborah Hayes, Dean for Grad. Studies **Founded:** 1861 **Open:** Sept.–May **Admission:** Application ($40), audition, letters of recommendation **Deadlines:** Apr. 30 **Cost:** To $2,672 (resident), $13,374 (nonresident); $4,162 room and board **Financial Aid:** Scholarship **Size-Attendees:** 500 **Degree or Certification:** BM, MM, BME, MME, DMA **Handicapped Access**

THE UNIVERSITY OF Colorado at Boulder is located at the foot of the Rocky Mountains, at an altitude of 5,000 feet. With more than 500 students and 50-plus faculty members, UC Boulder's College of Music is one of the 2 largest music schools in the state, the other being UC Denver. A typical professional training curriculum is offered to graduate students, with concentration possible in performance, church music, music literature, composition, conducting and pedagogy. The DMA is a professional degree for composers and performers with appropriate skill, experience, vision and academic strength. The PhD in music is also offered, with an emphasis in music education, musicology and other fields.

A point of interest on campus is the music library which contains, in addition to tens of thousands of scores, books and recordings, a special collection of folk music including hillbilly and western music recorded between 1923 and 1932.

University of Colorado at Denver Department of Music

For instrumentalists, vocalists, composers, arrangers *Downtown — P.O. Box 173364, Campus Box 162, Denver, CO 80127* **Voice:** 303-556-2727 **Fax:** 303-556-2325 **Web Site:** http://www.cudenver.edu/public/SOA **Contact:** Dick Weissman, Asst. Prof. of Music **Open:** Year-round **Admission:** Application ($40), audition (for some programs), transcripts **Deadlines:** July (for fall); Dec. (for spring) **Cost:** Per semester: $1,115 (resident), $5,190 (nonresident); room and board not available **Financial Aid:** Loans; Scholarship; Fellowship; Work/Study **Size-Attendees:** 100 **Size-Class:** 15–25 **Degree or Certification:** BS **Job Placement:** Yes

The University of Colorado at Denver Music Department offers 4 music programs: in music performance, in composition and arranging, in engineering and in management. The school has world-class recording studios and boasts that many graduates are now working for top record companies, in personal management concerns and in many aspects of engineering and production. Playing to these strengths, the school recently instituted a new degree program in what it calls music industry studies. Whereas the other 4 majors at the department feature a basic 2-year package of music history, theory and performance coursework, this new music industry program features minimal music class requirements because it's intended for nonmusicians who are interested in working in the production and business sides of the industry.

Connecticut

Hartt School of Music

For instrumentalists, vocalists, composers *200 Bloomfield Ave., West Hartford, CT 06117* **Voice:** 203-768-4465 **Fax:** 203-768-4441 **Contact:** James Jacobs, Dir. of Admissions **Founded:** 1920 **Open:** Sept.–May **Admission:** Application, audition, transcripts, 3 letters of recommendation **Cost:** $21,875 (all-inclusive) **Financial Aid:** Scholarship **Size-Attendees:** 485 **Degree or Certification:** BM, MM, DMA **Handicapped Access**

The Hartt School of Music was one of the founding institutions of the University of Hartford in 1920. It draws hundreds of music students each year, and some of them get the opportunity to study with a few of the better-known teachers and ensembles on the faculty. It so happens, for example, that Hartt is the teaching home of the Emerson String Quartet.

The MM degree is offered in instrumental performance and teaching, liturgical music, choral conducting, voice, opera, composition, theory and music history. The school is a strong presenter of concerts; its faculty series draws audience members from around the state. The school is accredited by the New England Association of Schools of Music, the National Council for Accreditation of Teacher Education and the National Association of Schools of Music.

KentMusic

For string players only: experienced adult amateurs, professionals, and semiprofessionals *Litchfield Hills — c/o Marvelwood School, 476 Skiff Mountain Rd., P.O. Box 3001, Kent, CT 06757; 26 Old Rt. 7, West Cornwall, CT 06796* **Voice:** 860-927-0047 **Contact:** Rae Eastman, Dir. **Founded:** 1989 **Open:** Last wk. June **Admission:** Application; nonrefundable deposit ($150) **Deadlines:** May 1 **Cost:** $500 (double room, meals incl.); single room $50; nonresidential tuition and meals $375; room and board for nonparticipating spouse $250 **Financial Aid:** Fellowship **Size-Attendees:** 60 **Size-Class:** 4

BEGUN IN 1989 AT Kent School, KentMusic is a continuation of the program instituted by the Manhattan String Quartet at Music Mountain in Falls Village in 1981. This is a strings-only chamber music conference focused on quartet playing. Enrollment is limited to 60 players to insure close contact with the Manhattan coaches. The faculty welcomes preformed quartets as well as individual musicians. The program has enjoyed a loyal following, with participants coming from as far away as California, Guatemala and Israel.

Members of the Manhattan String Quartet make up the faculty at this weeklong summer conference for professional, semiprofessional and experienced amateur players.The music is challenging; assigned pieces in recent years have included Beethoven's String Quartet, op. 132, and Bartok's String Quartet no. 2. The atmosphere is informal, supportive, and fun. It's not unusual for friends to stay up all night sightreading just for the joy of it.

New Haven Festival Masterclasses

For vocalists, organists *Yale campus, downtown New Haven — Association of Yale Alumni, Box 209010, New Haven, CT 06520* **Voice:** 203-498-1212 **Contact:** Joan Kneeland **Founded:** 1996 **Open:** Late June **Admission:** Application **Cost:** $250 **Size-Attendees:** 50 **Size-Class:** 10–20 **Handicapped Access**

OFFERED TO ALUMNI and friends of Yale by the Association of Yale Alumni, the New Haven Festival masterclasses take place in conjunction with New Haven's burgeoning, citywide International Festival of Arts and Ideas. The classes, not only in music but also in drama, art, architecture and writing, are taught by teachers from the Yale community and run for 4 mornings during the late-June festival. Two music classes are offered: one in choral performance and the other in organ playing. The choral class, taught by Yale professor emeritus of choral music and retired Yale Glee Club director Fenno Heath, focuses on the study and rehearsal of choral music from many periods and in a variety of styles. Charles Krigbaum, professor emeritus of music, teachers the organ masterclass, which affords participants a chance to prepare and perform music on any of 3 different Yale organs.

Norfolk Chamber Music Festival

For preformed chamber ensembles; special workshops for vocalists, composers, etc. *Litchfield Hills — Ellen Battell Stoeckel Estate, Rtes. 44 & 272, P.O. Box 545, Norfolk, CT 06058; 96 Wall Street, P.O. Box 208246, New Haven, CT 06520 (Oct.–May)* **Voice:** 860-542-3000 **Fax:** 860-542-3004 **E-mail:** norfolk@yale.edu **Web Site:** http://www.yale.edu/norfolk/ **Contact:** Michael Geller, Admin. Dir. **Founded:** 1941 **Open:** Mid-June–mid-Aug. **Admission:** Application ($35–$50), audition (first round taped, second round live), 2 letters of recommendation **Deadlines:** Feb. 15 (early application); Mar. 15 (final) **Cost:** All participants on full fellowship covering tuition; housing $675, meals $672 **Financial Aid:** Scholarship; Fellowship; Work/Study **Size-Attendees:** 60 **Size-Class:** 2–40 **Handicapped Access**

The Norfolk Chamber Music Festival is Connecticut's best-known and best-loved summer music festival. Situated on the Ellen Battell Stoeckel Estate in the rural town of Norfolk in Litchfield County, it focuses on chamber music, with concerts by faculty, guest artists and students.

The strong tradition of music in Litchfield County dates back more than a century to when Ellen Battell Stoeckel, an accomplished pianist and singer, first began informal musical gatherings in Whitehouse, the estate's 35-room family mansion. Mrs. Stoeckel and her husband, Carl, son of Gustav Stoeckel, the first professor of music at Yale, founded the Litchfield County Choral Union in 1899 and built a music festival around its concerts. The Norfolk Chamber Music Festival quickly became one of the most prestigious musical events of its time.

The Stoeckels brought instrumentalists from the New York Philharmonic and the Metropolitan Opera to Norfolk. Luminaries from the early years included Fritz Kreisler, Sergei Rachmaninoff, Enrico Caruso and Jan Ignace Paderewski.

Mrs. Stoeckel died in 1939 and left her estate to the Yale School of Music. Since that time, both the festival and the school have remained true to her original vision, offering musicians the opportunity for relaxation, growth and the pursuit of chamber music study and performance at the highest level.

All those accepted to the school receive full fellowships covering the cost of tuition for their period of study. With no more than 70 fellows and nearly 50 artist-faculty, chamber music study is both intimate and varied.

Each year, Norfolk offers several sessions focusing on different areas of the chamber music repertoire. The festival also conducts a biennial Composer Residency Program.

Fellows are given the opportunity for regular performances as part of Norfolk's Young Artists Recital Series. Concerts take place twice weekly and are professionally recorded. Norfolk's Outreach Program enables fellows to perform at events in and around the Nor-

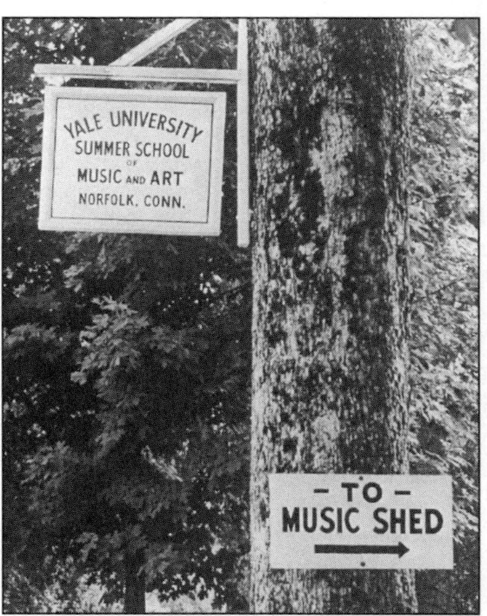

NORFOLK CHAMBER MUSIC FESTIVAL

Norfolk Chamber Music Festival at Yale's summer music and art campus.

folk area as well. Students perform for local schools, camps, senior centers, and other community organizations.

Sessions are intensive without being frenetic. A typical day includes a morning rehearsal, afternoon coaching, and an evening recital, leaving ample time for individual practice and study. Festival activities take place Monday through Saturday; Sundays are generally left open for individual pursuits.

Yale School of Music pianist and composer Joan Panetti has guided Norfolk since 1982. The Tokyo String Quartet, the New York Woodwind Quintet and the Guarneri Quartet are among the ensembles that have coached at Norfolk in recent years. Visiting composers have included Joan Tower and Jacob Druckman.

The serene, intimate atmosphere at Norfolk encourages inspired music-making, and fosters the development of long-lasting musical bonds and friendships. It is very highly respected among musicians.

Yale Institute of Sacred Music

For organists, choral conductors *Downtown — 409 Prospect St., New Haven, CT 06511* **Voice:** 203-432-5180 **Fax:** 203-432-5296 **Contact:** Ruth Lackstrom, Dean **Founded:** 1973 **Open:** Sept.–May **Admission:** Application ($50), tape, transcripts **Deadlines:** Jan. 15 **Cost:** $13,350; $10,515 room and board **Financial Aid:** Fellowship; Work/Study **Size-Attendees:** 300 **Size-Class:** 2–30 **Degree or Certification:** MM, MMA, DMA, MA in Religion, Master of Divinity, Master of Sacred Theology **Job Placement:** Yes **Handicapped Access**

At a time when changes are affecting churches and synagogues around the country, Yale music students heading for careers in religious music have the opportunity to prepare for challenges. In 1973, the Yale Institute of Sacred Music was established as a continuation of New York's Union Theological Seminary. It is the belief of the institute that its students must have the finest musical training, but should also be able to argue persuasively for music, knowing enough of liturgical and church history, and of modern theology, to do so.

Institute students choose to enroll either in the Yale School of Music or in the Yale Divinity School. They focus primarily on choral conducting and organ playing, and participate in weekly seminars, lectures, workshops and performances in these areas.

Yale School of Music

For instrumentalists, vocalists, composers, conductors *Downtown — 458 College St., P.O. Box 208246, New Haven, CT 06520* **Voice:** 203-432-1960 **Fax:** 203-432-7542 **Contact:** Robert Blocker, Dean **Founded:** 1890 **Open:** Sept.–May **Admission:** Application ($60), tape/audition **Deadlines:** Jan. 31 **Cost:** $16,740; $8,810 room and board **Financial Aid:** Loans; Scholarship; Work/Study **Size-Attendees:** 200 **Degree or Certification:** MM Perf., MMA, DMA, Cert., Art. Dipl. **Handicapped Access**

By virtue of the Yale name and the campus's proximity to both New York and Boston, the Yale School of Music has always attracted a fine and rather well-known faculty. For the same reasons, the school has been something of a draw for talented students from around the world. But with total expenses at the school estimated at $25,500, and few available scholarships, the school seems to have trouble competing for the very best students in some departments.

The school places emphasis on the availability of Yale University's rich intellectual life, and the fact that Yale

School of Music students can extend their studies to take advantage of the intellectual opportunities all around. This broadening of horizons is not required, however, and—music students being music students—not as many choose to broaden themselves in this way as one might assume. Without a doubt, however, this environment makes all the difference for the curious, and it accounts indeed for the high number of respected scholars and music critics who have graduated from the School of Music.

Most of the Yale music campus is organized around a single city block in the heart of the Yale campus in downtown New Haven. And like all of Yale, it is a tour guide's dream come true. Stoeckel Hall houses Norfolk Summer School headquarters and faculty studios and the Oral History American Music Project, with its extensive collection of tape-recorded and videotaped interviews with and about such major figures as Copland, Ives, Hindemith and Ellington. Down the street is the Yale University Collection of Musical Instruments, which contains over 1,000 instruments of which the majority document Western European art music tradition, especially the period between 1550 and 1850. Concert halls on campus include the 700-seat Arnold Sprague Memorial Hall, the Louis Sudler Recital Hall and Woolsey Hall, which houses the Newberry Memorial Organ and the Center for Studies in Music Technology.

A big emphasis at Yale is chamber music, which gets close supervision by faculty coaches. There are opportunities to perform in other genres as well. Opera and conducting at Yale enjoy strong reputations. Interestingly, Yale is the only music school in the country geared exclusively toward graduate study. The School of Music has just 200 students and 60 faculty members, about a 3-to-1 ratio.

New Haven abounds in good graduate housing. Life in the city, if you remember to lock your car, can be close to ideal. With the ease of travel to New York and Boston, many are able to get one foot into professional life while finishing up graduate study, always a wise approach.

YALE UNIVERSITY

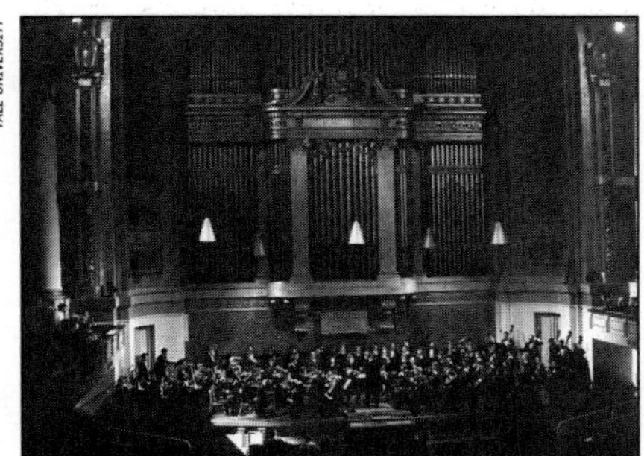

Yale Philharmonia and Newberry Organ, in Woolsey Hall, Yale University, New Haven.

Delaware

University of Delaware Department of Music

For instrumentalists, vocalists, composers *Willard Hall—Educational Building, Newark, DE 19716* **Voice:** 302-831-2129 **Contact:** Lloyd Shorter, Admin. for Music Programs **Founded:** 1743 **Open:** Sept.– May **Admission:** Application, audition, transcripts **Deadlines:** Mar. 1 **Cost:** $3,860 (resident), $10,730 (nonresident); $4,420 room and board **Financial Aid:** Scholarship **Size-Attendees:** 115 **Degree or Certification:** BM, MM **Handicapped Access**

PART OF A LARGE STATE school nestled in the relatively small town of Newark and surrounded by the cultural hubs of New York, Philadelphia, Baltimore and Washington, the University of Delaware Department of Music makes a nice spot for aspiring professional musicians. Probably the most distinctive feature about the music department is the quality of its music technology instruction. There are opportunities here to fuse music of electronic keyboards, computers and synthesizers. The music department's *Videodisc Music Series* is an educational tool that helps familiarize computer users with musical masterworks. And its new computer-based instruction project, Jazz Theory Lessons, recently funded by the U.S. Department of Education, will allow the development of innovative teaching methods at the university level. Special events at the department include a student concerto competition, the University of Delaware Winter Institute for String Quartets and an annual new music festival.

District of Columbia

Folk Alliance Annual Conference

For artists and business people in the folk music industry *Held in a different North American city each year — 1001 Connecticut Ave. NW, Ste. 501, Washington, DC 20036* **Voice:** 202-835-3655 **Fax:** 202-835-3656 **E-mail:** fa@folk.org **Web Site:** http://www.hidwater.com/folkalliance/ **Contact:** Margaret Loomis, Admin. Dir. **Founded:** 1989 **Open:** Mid-Feb. **Admission:** Conference registration (cheaper with membership in Folk Alliance); graduated rate structure dependent on membership status and time of registration **Deadlines:** Registration is possible up to start of conference. **Cost:** Changes annually **Financial Aid:** Scholarship **Size-Attendees:** 1,500

THIS 4-DAY CONFERENCE is probably the only one of its type. It attracts people from all sides of the folk-music industry, offering workshops, formal and private showcases, an all-folk exhibit hall, lifetime achievement awards, peer group and regional sessions and lots of networking. The conference is dedicated to folk music, storytelling and related performing arts. It is a critical gathering for artists, presenters, record companies, media, agents and educators. It's a great opportunity to mix fun with education and business. Founded in 1989, the Folk Alliance is the realization of a vision that one organization could bind together the folk music and dance community in North America. The alliance seeks to raise public awareness of the artistic and cultural importance of folk performing arts forms and to create new opportunities for all those who make the performances possible.

Rome School of Music

For instrumentalists, vocalists, conductors *Harewood Rd. (Brookland metro stop) — The Catholic University of America, Washington, DC 20064* **Voice:** 202-319-5414 **Fax:** 202-319-6280 **E-mail:** roberts@cua.edu **Web Site:** http://www.cua.edu/www.musu/ **Contact:** Dr. Paul Taylor, Asst. Dean, Grad. Adm. **Founded:** 1950 **Open:** Aug.– Dec.; Jan.–May **Admission:** Application (fee), transcripts, letters of recommendation **Deadlines:** Rolling admission until 1 mo. before semester begins **Financial Aid:** Loans; Scholarship; Stipend **Size-Attendees:** $180 **Size-Class:** 10–15 **Degree or Certification:** BM, MLM, MM, MA, DMA, PhD **Job Placement:** Yes **Handicapped Access**

AT THE CATHOLIC University of America's Benjamin T. Rome School of Music, the focus is on performance. Students, faculty and guest artists present more than 300 concerts annually on and off campus. The symphony and chorus appear each year at the John F. Kennedy Center for the Performing Arts. Some students have played with the National Symphony when additional players were needed.

Many current and former members of the NSO teach at the school.

In addition to instrumental majors, CUA offers study in subjects including chamber music, conducting, liturgical music, musical theater, opera, voice and music education. Catholic University's student population is 96 percent lay and 4 percent religious, and the school welcomes members of all faiths. The campus is located on 154 quiet acres, close to a metro rail station, giving students easy access to all corners of the city.

Florida

Atlantic Center for the Arts

For composers *East coast, between Daytona Beach and Kennedy Space Center — 1414 Art Center Ave., New Smyrna Beach, FL 32168* **Voice:** 904-427-6975; 800-393-6975 **Fax:** 904-427-5669 **Contact:** Nick Conroy, Dir. **Founded:** 1977 **Open:** Year-round **Admission:** Each resident master artist defines criteria for his or her associates **Deadlines:** Revolving; usually 2 mo. before residency **Cost:** $100 per wk.; housing $500 for 3-wk. residency **Size-Attendees:** 30 **Handicapped Access**

FOUNDED IN 1977, the Atlantic Center for the Arts was the brainchild of Doris Leeper, sculptor, painter and environmentalist. It was her dream to create a community in which artists of different disciplines could live and work together. Since then it has become a high-profile residency site, drawing well-known artists from all walks.

ACA offers 3-week residencies, providing midcareer artists ("associates") the opportunity to work with "master artists" in their art. A typical residency features 3 big-name master artists from different disciplines, each choosing up to 10 associates with whom to work. Though the associates are apprenticing in this way, they also have time set aside at ACA for their own artistic pursuits.

ACA is not a colony for artists seeking solitary confinement. Quite the opposite, in fact: it's open to the public for a number of events including readings, exhibitions and performances.

Since its inception, ACA has been acquiring new acreage and building new work and living spaces. The Leeper Studio Complex, a series of buildings that comprise 5 discipline-specific studio

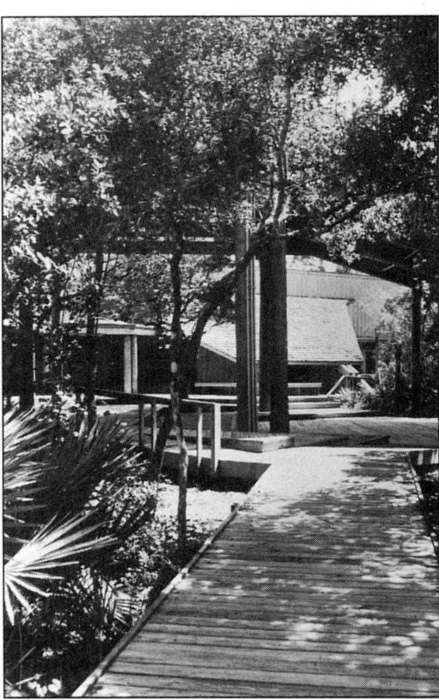

Atlantic Center for the Arts, New Smyrna Beach.

spaces, was opened in 1996. One of the studios, the Ruth Scorgie Hubbard Music Studio, is specially equipped for composers.

Lukas Foss and David Baker are the 2 composers on the 16-member National Council for the Atlantic Center for the Arts, a group that guides the center's artistic direction.

Close Encounters with Music

For all levels of chamber musicians *South Florida — Biltmore Hotel, 1200 Anastasia Ave., Coral Gables, FL 33134; P.O. Box 34, Great Barrington, MA 01230* **Voice:** 305-445-1926; 800-843-0778 **Contact:** Wendy Best, Administrator **Founded:** 1985 **Open:** Oct.–May **Admission:** Application **Deadlines:** Rolling **Cost:** $229 double room per night **Size-Attendees:** 50 **Handicapped Access**

Close Encounters with Music, a popular concert series run by cellist Yehuda Hanani in Williams Island, has branched out to include 2 annual luxurious amateur music workshop weekends. They take place amid the grandeur of the Biltmore Hotel. Guests check in for these Biltmore Complete Classics Weekends on Friday, and spend until Sunday working with acclaimed artists on repertoire organized by theme. For example, one weekend was called "Bach, Beethoven and Brahms—What Makes Them Timeless?" Another was called a French Festival; with performer-teachers from the Pablo Casals Prades Festival, it included enjoyment of fine regional wines. The festival's series of 4 concerts are worthy of note: my personal favorite was called "Musical Whodunit—Reeds vs. Strings," and featured the fabulous bassoon talent Kim Walker in recital with string player friends.

New Arts Festival

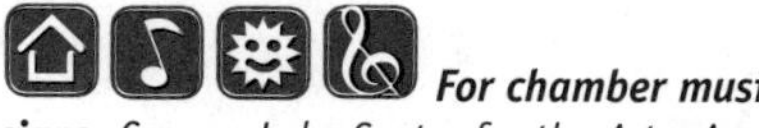

For chamber musicians *Cypress Lake Center for the Arts, Arcade Theatre — 3788 Harold Ave., Fort Myers, FL 33916* **Voice:** 941-332-4643; 800-335-ARTS **Fax:** 941-939-4756 **Contact:** James Griffith, Artistic Dir. **Founded:** 1989 **Open:** Mid-July–mid-Aug. **Admission:** Application ($25), audition/tape, letters of recommendation **Deadlines:** June 1 **Cost:** $550; $375 hotel accommodations, $275 meal plan **Financial Aid:** Scholarship; Work/Study **Size-Attendees:** 30 **Handicapped Access**

The 3-week-long New Arts Festival is one of Florida's better summer programs for artists in theater, dance, and chamber music. It is geared for professionals and students, offering more than 40 performances and masterclass events, and a comprehensive study program in a beautiful Florida coastal environment.

Chamber musicians find the festival attractive for its faculty, which includes Eric Pritchard of the Ciompi String Quartet, Maria Kitsopoulos of CELLO, and Andres Diaz of the Diaz Trio.

New Arts Festival classes take place at the newly renovated Arcade Theatre and at the Cypress Lake Center for the Arts. Participants are housed at the Sheraton Harbor Place Hotel, a 24-story luxury hotel. The surrounding southwestern Florida area offers recreational opportunities such as excursions to beaches, islands, historic sites, nature habitats, and local entertainment spots.

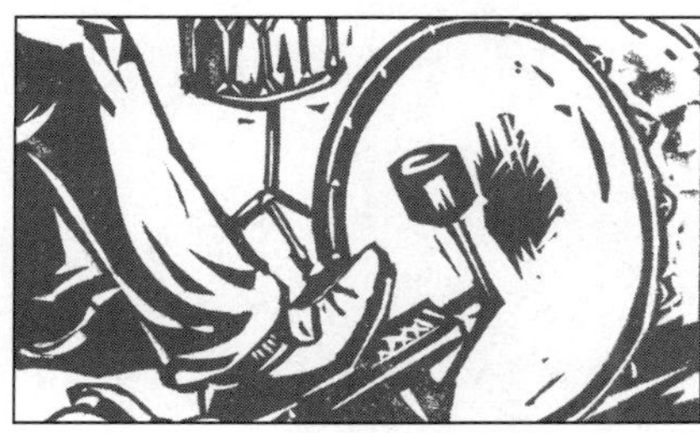

New World Symphony

For instrumentalists *South Beach, minutes from downtown Miami — 541 Lincoln Rd., Miami Beach, FL 33139* **Voice:** 305-673-3330 **Fax:** 305-673-6749 **Web Site:** http://www.nws.org **Contact:** Heather Hills **Founded:** 1987 **Open:** Sept.–May **Admission:** Application ($40), audition **Deadlines:** Rolling; audition tour Feb.–May **Cost:** Fellowship musicians receive $330 weekly stipend **Financial Aid:** Fellowship **Size-Attendees:** 150 **Job Placement:** Yes **Handicapped Access**

Michael Tilson Thomas is the artistic director of the New World Symphony, a dynamic training orchestra founded in 1987. Its mission is to provide an educational environment for the gifted graduates of America's leading music schools. As a place to learn from the great master teachers and work with peers, the NWS is a perfect gateway to a successful career in music. That's a polite way of saying they want their graduates to actually get jobs.

So far the track record is impressive. To date, alumni have landed jobs around the world. Many of them go on to steppingstone orchestras, like the Indianapolis Symphony and the Fort Worth Symphony, and a surprisingly high number make it directly into groups like the Cleveland Orchestra and the Boston Symphony. This level of achievement is highly unusual for such young players.

FRANCIS GILES

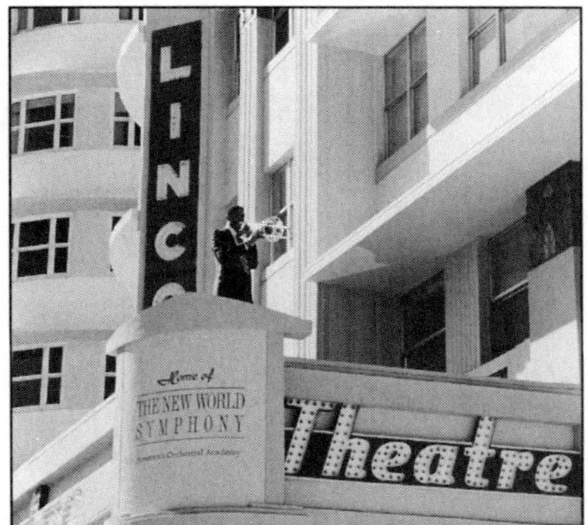

Lincoln Theatre, home of the New World Symphony, Miami Beach.

The beauty of NWS is its simplicity and practicality. It's free (all participants have fellowships), it's preprofessional (the demands mimic that of a real orchestra) and its primary educational goal is to prepare participants to snag great jobs.

The NWS's season runs from September to May and includes full symphony and chamber orchestra series. In addition, several weeks each season are devoted to masterclasses and private lessons with distinguished artists and teachers. These special sessions focus on advanced orchestral techniques and audition preparation.

Recording projects, tours and community outreach are all part of the NWS program.

A look at the list of guest teachers artists and teachers from any given season reveals a major key to the program's success. By virtue of the NWS's special mission, and probably also because of Tilson Thomas's strong commitment to the program, famous names from every major orchestra show up. In just one month in 1996, for example, participants got to work with none other than the concertmaster of the Buffalo Philharmonic, the principal violist and the principal cellist of the Cleveland Orchestra, the principal oboist and the principal trombonist of the New York Philharmonic and Donald McInnes, regarded as one of the world's all-time great gurus of the viola.

Participants pay nothing. Rather, the symphony awards 3-year fellowships and kicks in an additional weekly stipend, free housing, and affordable health insurance.

NWS musicians are selected through an intensely competitive national audition. To be a member of the NWS, musicians must have at minimum an undergraduate degree or diploma.

The NWS is an exciting development in American musical training. One could argue it does more good, quicker and cheaper than most conventional music schools. The focus is on preparedness for the working world. And that makes good sense.

Sarasota Music Festival

For instrumentalists *Gulf Coast, SW Florida — 709 N. Tamiami Tr., Sarasota, FL 34236* **Voice:** 941-952-9634; 800-287-9634 **Fax:** 941-953-3059 **Web Site:** http://www.sarasota-online.com/symphony/ festival **Contact:** Trevor Cramer, Admin. Dir. **Founded:** 1965 **Open:** First 3 wks. June **Admission:** Application ($35), tape **Deadlines:** Feb. 1 **Cost:** $65; housing $250 (double), $200 (triple); food $115 (36 meals/3 wks.) **Financial Aid:** Scholarship **Size-Attendees:** 100 **Handicapped Access**

FOR 3 WEEKS EVERY June, 100 students from around the world come to Sarasota for the study of chamber and orchestral repertoire.

The Sarasota Music Festival was founded in 1965 as the New College Summer Chamber Music Festival. It consolidated with the Florida West Coast Symphony 20 years later in order to become one of the largest cultural institutions in Florida and one of the best summer chamber music programs in the country.

Paul Wolfe, conductor of the Florida West Coast Symphony and violinist with the Florida String Quartet, has led the festival from its inception. His faculty is high gear. Among the internationally known soloists and major orchestra players on the teaching roster are cellist Timothy Eddy of the Orion String Quartet, English Chamber Orchestra principal oboist Neil Black and flute soloist Carol Wincenc.

University of Miami School of Music

For instrumentalists, vocalists, composers, conductors *Metropolitan Miami — P.O. Box 248165, Coral Gables, FL 33124* **Voice:** 305-284-2446 **Fax:** 305-284-6375 **Contact:** Dr. David J. Boyle, Asst. Dean, School of Music **Founded:** 1925 **Open:** Sept.–May **Admission:** Application ($35), audition, essay, transcripts, letter of recommendation **Deadlines:** Mar. 1 **Cost:** $24,552 (all-inclusive) **Financial Aid:** Scholarship; Work/Study **Size-Attendees:** 640 **Degree or Certification:** BM, MM, DMA **Handicapped Access**

THE UNIVERSITY OF MIAMI has an eclectic profile. Nonclassical genres are popular, and competition is stiff to play in the Funk, Bebop and Monk/Mingus ensembles. The music library's diversity mirrors the prevalent musical diversity of musical tastes here, and includes special collections of jazz, Latin American and Yiddish music.

The University of Miami was the first American university to offer a degree in music engineering technology. The program is designed for students who would like a career in audio engineering, music recording, audio equipment design, sound reinforcement, broadcasting, audio sales or studio maintenance. It has pioneered as well in the areas of music industry studies, studio music and jazz. The faculty-student ratio is particularly low, allowing for intense and serious work. There are many opportunities for students to take in world-class music, with the Florida Philharmonic Orchestra, the New World Symphony and the Greater Miami Opera Company all right nearby. The School itself presents more than 300 events annually.

University of South Florida Department of Music

For instrumentalists, vocalists, composers *Suburban Tampa — University of South Florida, 4204 E. Fowler Ave., Tampa, FL 33620* **Voice:** 813-974-3976 **Fax:** 813-974-2091 **Contact:** Don Owen, Grad. Advisor **Founded:** 1956 **Open:** Sept.–May **Admission:** Application ($20), audition, portfolio **Deadlines:** Rolling **Cost:** $1,877 (resident), $6,764 (nonresident) **Financial Aid:** Loans; Scholarship; Work/ Study **Size-Attendees:** 250 **Degree or Certification:** BM, MM **Handicapped Access**

THE UNIVERSITY OF SOUTH Florida Department of Music offers regular music classes, but probably the most outstanding feature of the department is something it calls the Systems Complex for the Studio and Performing Arts. At SYCOM, music students work on top-of-the-line equipment (digital and analog) for mixing, editing, and electronic sound generating. Their musical material comes from research and creative projects, by arts and science people, in the university's other classes. Otherwise, the offerings at USF are of a standard variety, with general program areas in applied music, conducting, jazz studies, music education, music history, music theory and piano pedagogy. The school has 30 practice rooms and 20 pianos. It puts on 250 or more musical events for the Tampa community each year, including a new music/new media festival.

Winter Music Conference

For vocalists, songwriters, producers, disc jockeys *Metropolitan Miami — Fountainebleau Hilton Resort and Towers, 4441 Collins Ave., Miami Beach, FL 33140; 3450 NE 12 Ter., Fort Lauderdale, FL 33334* **Voice:** 954-563-6889 **E-mail:** WMC97@aol.com **Web Site:** http://www.members.aol.com/wmcconfac/home.html **Contact:** Louis Passenti, Bill Kelly, Co-Dirs. **Founded:** 1984 **Open:** Mid-Mar. **Admission:** Registration fee (all participants); showcase fee (performers); tape **Deadlines:** Mid.-Feb. for showcases **Cost:** $295 **Size-Attendees:** 2,000 **Handicapped Access**

TRENDS IN CONTEMPORARY club music change rapidly. The mission of the Winter Music Conference is to keep thousands of participants up to date on everything affecting the nightclub music market, from the mainstreaming of house music to the freestyle grooves now heard on crossover radio. Conference topics include house music, R&B, trance, reggae, trip-hop, rap/hip-hop, drum and bass, Latin dance/hip-hop, handbag, industrial, garage jungle and freestyle music. The ins and outs of the business and legal sides of music are presented in panel discussions covering such topics as brokering, publishing, licensing and more.

That's only the beginning; the conference features a workshop in remixing and editing, one in music and technology, and showcases of nightclub performers and expos of nightclub equipment, sound and lighting. To top it off: an international dealmaking expo and an awards banquet.

Georgia

Georgia State University School of Music

For instrumentalists, vocalists, composers, conductors *Downtown — University Plaza, Atlanta, GA 30303* **Voice:** 404-651-3676 **Contact:** Dr. Steven Winick, Dir. **Founded:** 1913 **Admission:** Application ($30), audition, diagnostic tests **Cost:** Per quarter-hour: $30 (resident), $69 (nonresident); no on-campus housing available **Financial Aid:** Loans; Scholarship; Work/Study **Size-Attendees:** 500 **Degree or Certification:** BM. MM, DMA **Handicapped Access**

LOCATED IN THE MAJOR southeastern commercial, industrial, financial and cultural center of Atlanta, Georgia State University is a comprehensive university. The School of Music is a professional training center offering studies in music education, performance, theory, history or literature. Students benefit from the presence of many members of the Atlanta Symphony on the faculty. The idea here is not only to prepare students for performing careers but to thoroughly ground them with ancillary skills, like teaching and entrepreneurship, that will help further their development for years to come. The school offers public concerts and lectures to the community. In the summer, GSU is home to a Summer Opera Workshop. The MM degree requires 50 to 58 quarter-hours of study.

Hambidge Center

For performers, composers, songwriters *Blue Ridge Mountains — P.O. Box 339, Rabun Gap, GA 30568* **Voice:** 706-746-5718 **Fax:** 706-746-9933 **E-mail:** jbarber@purple.tmn.com **Contact:** Judith Barber, Dir. **Founded:** 1988 **Open:** Year-round **Admission:** Application ($20), tape/score of recent work, resume, personal statement **Deadlines:** Jan. 31 (May–Oct.); Aug. 31 (Nov.– Apr.) **Cost:** $125/wk. **Financial Aid:** Fellowship **Size-Attendees:** 7

RESIDENT ARTISTS working in various disciplines live in the lovely private cottages at Hambidge Center in Nantahala National Forest. When artists are not working, they take advantage of Hambidge's beautiful setting, on 600 wooded acres in the Blue Ridge of northeastern Georgia. The center was established as a weaving industry in the 1930s and transformed in the 1970s into an artists' residency program and folk art gallery. The property and its 13 buildings are on the National Register of Historic Places. Pianos are available to composers in residence at the Hambidge Center and there are plenty of good practice places for performing musicians as well. Residents dine commun-

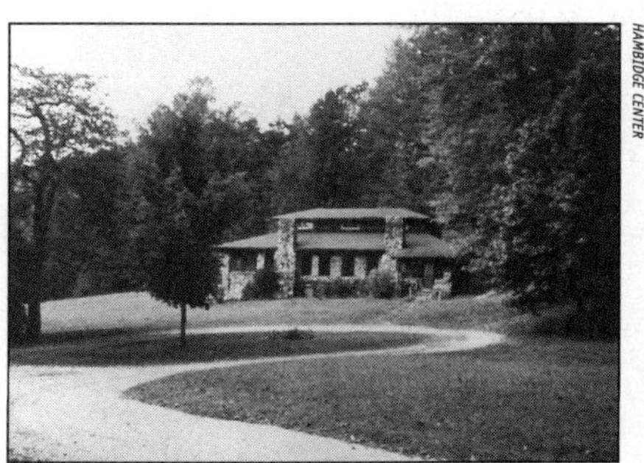

HAMBIDGE CENTER

The Rock House at Hambidge Center, Rabun Gap.

ally 5 nights a week during the summer season; winter residents must cook for themselves.

Southeastern Music Center

For instrumentalists *P.O. Box 8348, Columbus State University, Columbus, GA 31908* **Voice:** 706-568-2465 **Fax:** 706-568-2465 **E-mail:** Bullock_ William@ colstate.edu **Contact:** Dr. William J. Bullock, Exec. Dir. **Founded:** 1982 **Open:** July **Admission:** Application ($25), tape, letter of recommendation from current teacher **Deadlines:** May 31 **Cost:** $725 (resident), $835 (nonresident) **Financial Aid:** Scholarship; Fellowship; Work/Study **Size-Attendees:** 60 **Size-Class:** 10 **Handicapped Access**

Southeastern Music Center provides musicians aged 16 and up with a program of intensive study with leading artists. The center offers private instruction, masterclasses, guest and faculty concerts, student recitals and instruction in music theory. Limited enrollment permits students to work closely with the faculty. The center's summer program is held on the campus of Columbus State University. Chosen for its excellent facilities, the college offers ample classroom and practice space, concert and recital halls and air-conditioned student housing. Among the ensembles to participate in are the SMC Chamber Orchestra and the SMC String Orchestra. Faculty include Martha Gerschefski, who played cello under Stokowski in the American Symphony Orchestra, Ronald Wirt, former bassoonist of the Borealis Quintet and Charles Snead, who plays horn with the Tuscaloosa, Jacksonville and Macon orchestras.

Hawaii

University of Hawaii at Manoa

For instrumentalists, vocalists, composers, conductors *Near downtown — 2411 Dole St., Honolulu, HI 96822* **Voice:** 808-956-2175 **Fax:** 808-956-9657 **Contact:** Byron K. Yasui, Grad. Chair **Founded:** 1907 **Open:** Sept.–May **Admission:** Application ($10), audition, transcripts, letter of recommendation, interview **Deadlines:** May 1 **Cost:** $1,631 (resident), $4,825 (nonresident); $4,210 room and board **Financial Aid:** Loans; Scholarship; Work/Study **Size-Attendees:** 170 **Size-Class:** 20 **Degree or Certification:** BM, MM **Handicapped Access**

Located at the western end of the campus of the University of Hawaii at Manoa, the College of Arts and Humanities has a group of buildings including classrooms, studios, practice rooms, rehearsal halls, a listening facility, archives and the Mae Zeke Orvis Auditorium. The department's faculty includes many members of the Honolulu Symphony and offers the BM and BA degrees. It also runs a coordinated program with the College of Education to train musicians for teaching at the intermediate and high school levels.

One of the distinctive aspects of this music department is that it is the only one I could find that features the study of music of Pacific cultures. Ethnomusicology students can specialize in this genre at the University of Hawaii at Manoa. The campus is located on 300 acres in a residential area close to downtown Honolulu on the island of Oahu.

Idaho

Lionel Hampton School of Music

For instrumentalists, vocalists, composers, conductors *112 Morrill Hall, Moscow, ID 83844* **Voice:** 208-885-6243 **Contact:** Roger Wallins, Dean, College of Grad. Studies **Founded:** 1889 **Open:** Sept.–May **Admission:** Application ($25), audition/tape, transcripts, test scores **Deadlines:** Aug. 1 **Cost:** Free (resident), $5,380 (nonresident); $4,280 room and board **Financial Aid:** Loans; Scholarship; Work/Study **Size-Attendees:** 400 **Size-Class:** 25 **Degree or Certification:** BM, MM **Handicapped Access**

Since the late 19th century, music has been a key element of the academic program at the University of Idaho. Today, its Lionel Hampton School of Music is well respected in music education circles, training teachers for careers in elementary, secondary and college careers.

Students at the School learn by performing, listening to, analyzing and creating opera, orchestral, chamber and choral music. Emphasis is on the understanding of the musical style and techniques of all eras. The jazz program is also quite strong.

The university attracts over 9,000 students annually to its more than 125 programs.The main campus includes some 50 educational and residential buildings on 320 acres. The university also makes use of 8,000 acres of surrounding farm land and experimental forests.

Illinois

American Conservatory of Music

For instrumentalists, vocalists, composers, conductors *Downtown — 16 N. Wabash, Chicago, IL 60602* **Voice:** 312-263-4161 **Contact:** Patrick Riley, Dir. Grad. Programs **Founded:** 1886 **Open:** Sept.–May **Admission:** Application ($50), audition, transcripts, 2 letters of recommendation, interview, essay, video, portfolio **Deadlines:** Rolling **Cost:** $7,000; no on-campus housing available **Financial Aid:** Loans; Scholarship; Work/Study **Size-Attendees:** 160 **Degree or Certification:** BM, MM, DMA **Handicapped Access**

Members of the Chicago Symphony Orchestra and the Chicago Lyric Opera teach at the American Conservatory, located in the center of the city. The school, an independent institution, seeks to develop students as well-rounded performer-composer-listeners. The MM degree is offered with majors in performance, composition and theory. Students in the MME program are required to do extensive research. The DMA degree is offered with major fields of study in composition, performance and literature in piano, organ, voice and orchestral instruments.

There are many performance opportunities in choral music, opera and chamber music. General program areas include commercial music, jazz studies and musicology.

Preparedness for the marketplace is a major thrust at the school; the American Conservatory offers 5- and 8-week seminars on the music business, with intriguing titles like "Inside the Music Business," "Music Publishing" and "Public Relations."

Bloom School of Jazz

For anyone interested in playing jazz
Downtown — 520 N. Michigan Ave., Ste. 1230, Chicago, IL 60611 **Voice:** 312-527-9300 **Fax:** 312-527-9301 **E-mail:** dbloom1@mail.idt.net **Contact:** David Bloom **Founded:** 1975 **Open:** Year-round **Admission:** Application (no fee) **Deadlines:** Up to start of program **Cost:** $525 **Size-Attendees:** 100 **Size-Class:** 5 **Handicapped Access**

THE BLOOM SCHOOL OF JAZZ, perhaps Chicago's best-known jazz school, has been developing jazz players from beginner to professional since 1975. Many past students travel internationally with jazz greats like Johnny Griffin and Nicolas Payton. Both in private lessons and in classes the 8-week course covers basic and advanced concepts. Class topics include improvisation, arranging, composition, theory and ear training.

The school places a premium on the master-teacher experience. Working closely within the private study setting, students are encouraged to develop conscious control of all elements of performing from dynamics to rhythm to articulation and motivic development. Having thus helped students to lay the foundations, the Bloom School seeks to cultivate each performer's artistic voice. The school puts out a newsletter featuring news of its students and graduates and sends it to 800 important jazz venues and individuals.

Chicago's New Music Festival

For all performing musicians
Location varies — 660 South Michigan Ave., Chicago, IL 60605 **Voice:** 312-341-9112 **Fax:** 312-408-1827 **E-mail:** indie@indiefest.org **Web Site:** http://www.indiefest.org **Contact:** Leopoldo Lastre **Founded:** 1993 **Open:** Last wk. July **Admission:** $200 (registration); participants wishing to perform must submit materials for review **Deadlines:** Passes may be purchased up to the event; deadline for bands is mid-to-late Apr. **Cost:** $10 (submission fee) **Size-Attendees:** 2,000 (workshop); 11,000 (showcase) **Size-Class:** 100 **Handicapped Access**

NETWORKING IS CLEARLY a must in the music industry, and Chicago's New Music Festival is one place to do it in style. In 2 densely packed days including educational panels, a trade show, networking parties and showcases at more than a dozen clubs around town, you'll press a lot of flesh and hear a lot of tunes.

Virtually every corner of the popular music business is represented at CNMF (formerly the Independent Label Festival), so in addition to attending workshops and seminars, musician attendees can mill around getting quotes from CD manufacturers, swapping dates with other bands and drumming up business from local venues. Or they can shop for a label, an agent, an attorney or a promotion company. Bands compete hotly for showcasing opportunities at CHMF. The feeling is that if music is your career, this is one conference it helps to attend.

Northern Illinois University School of Music

For instrumentalists, vocalists, composers *65 mi. W of Chicago — School of Music, Northern Illinois University, Dekalb, IL 60115* **Voice:** 815-753-1551; 815-753-1552 **Fax:** 815-753-1759 **E-mail:** rholly@niu.edu **Web Site:** http://www.niu.edu/acad/music/index.html **Contact:** Paul Baver, Chair **Founded:** 1896 **Open:** Year-round **Admission:** Application ($30); audition/tape **Deadlines:** June 1 (fall), Nov. 1 (spring), Apr. 1 (summer); 1 mo. earlier for international applicants **Cost:** Per credit hour: $100 + $33/credit (3 times as much for nonresident); $1,700–$2,250 room and board **Financial Aid:** Loans; Scholarship; Fellowship; Stipend; Work/Study **Size-Attendees:** 350 **Size-Class:** 15 **Degree or Certification:** BM, BAMus, MM, Perf. Cert. **Job Placement:** Yes **Handicapped Access**

THE VERMEER QUARTET is ensemble-in-residence at Northern Illinois University's School of Music, making the school a top pick for string players bound for careers in chamber music. The Grammy-nominated ensemble is one of the most respected in America. Other faculty members include harpist Elizabeth Cifani, bass Myron Myers and double bassist Gregory Sarchet.

The jazz program, headed up by Ronald Carter, is particularly strong; NIU jazz ensembles have won multiple awards from *Downbeat* magazine. Students can perform in orchestral, choral, opera, music theater and world music events. Each year the university bestows Excellence in Teaching Awards on 3 faculty members from among 1,200 resident faculty university-wide. Since 1971, 8 of these award winners have come from the School of Music. NIU's 5,130-acre campus is just over an hour west of downtown Chicago, making it a reasonable commute from the obvious cultural attractions that city has to offer.

Northwestern University School of Music

For orchestral musicians, vocalists, composers *Suburban Chicago — 711 Elgin Rd., Evanston, IL 60208* **Voice:** 847-491-3141 **Fax:** 847-491-5260 **Web Site:** http://www.nuinfo.nwu.edu/music-school/ **Contact:** Wayne G. Gordon, Dir., Grad. Admission **Founded:** 1895 **Open:** Year-round **Admission:** Application ($40), transcripts, recommendations **Deadlines:** Feb. 1 (MMus); Jan. 1 (all others) **Cost:** $18,108; $8,955 room and board; summer session varies **Financial Aid:** Loans; Scholarship; Fellowship; Stipend; Work/Study **Size-Attendees:** 600 **Size-Class:** 10–15 **Degree or Certification:** MMus, DMus, Cert. Perf. **Job Placement:** Yes **Handicapped Access**

NORTHWESTERN UNIVERSITY School of Music is one of the oldest and most respected music schools in America. Established in 1895, the school is located on the shores of Lake Michigan in Evanston, just north of Chicago.

Superficially, Northwestern seems to be one more cookie cut out of the standard American music school mold. There are the standard degrees and courses offered, the usual statements of commitment to tradition and innovation. The secrets to Northwestern's extraordinary level of distinction, then, are without doubt its faculty and its size.

Northwestern is the primary teaching home of many distinguished members of the Chicago Symphony and as a result the school is a guaranteed draw for serious instrumentalists set on orchestral careers. Alumni have demonstrated an outstanding track record of success in the professional world.

With fewer than 600 students, plenty of individual attention is assured to students at Northwestern. What better outlook can a graduate student of oboe, for example, have when studying as one of just a handful in the studio of the legendary Ray Still? Still put in some 40 years as the principal oboist in what many believe has been the greatest wind section in what some believe is the greatest orchestra in America. Or how about Alex Klein, also on the faculty? Klein is the CSO's new principal oboist, a soloist of international renown and winner of virtually every major oboe competition in existence.

Performance opportunities abound at Northwestern. Students can play in chamber groups, choral ensembles or jazz groups or take part in musical theater productions. NWU is one of the best music schools west of the Mississippi.

Ragdale Foundation Residency

For performers, composers *Near Lake Michigan — 1260 N. Green Bay Rd., Lake Forest, IL 60045* **Voice:** 847-234-1063 **Fax:** 847-234-1075 **Contact:** Michael Wilkerson, Dir. **Founded:** 1976 **Open:** Jan. 2–Apr. 30; June 1–Dec. 15 **Admission:** Application ($20), recommendations, project description, tapes/scores **Deadlines:** June 1 (Jan.-Apr.); Jan. 15 (June–Dec.) **Cost:** $15/day **Financial Aid:** Loans; Fellowship **Size-Attendees:** 12

THE 2 MAIN STRUCTURES at the Ragdale Foundation Residency, its house and barn, were designed and built by Chicago architect Howard Van Doren Shaw in 1897, in the American Arts and Crafts style. The Shaw family included a number of writers, painters and sculptors who enjoyed staging musical and theatrical productions on the Ragdale grounds for the local community. In 1976, Shaw's granddaughter, the poet Alice Ryerson Hayes, created the Ragdale Foundation with the goal of turning the estate into a peaceful haven for artists of all disciplines.

Today, Ragdale is a year-round artists' residence, housing 12 artists at a time, including 8 writers, 3 visual artists and 1 composer. Residents at Ragdale are accepted for periods ranging from 2 weeks to 2 months.

Artists schedule their time as it suits them; the one element of imposed structure is the communal evening meal every night except Saturday. Artists are invited—but not required—to share their works-in-progress in informal performances. Some events, such as writing workshops and tours of the grounds, are open to the public.

Ragdale is an easy walk from upscale Lakewood, where shopping is plentiful and a good library is within reach. From Lakewood, trains leave hourly for downtown Chicago.

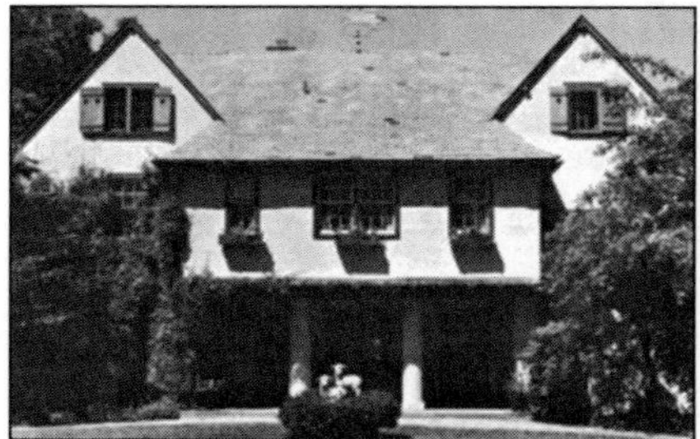
PAUL WHITING

Ragdale Foundation, Lake Forest.

Steans Institute for Young Artists

For string players, keyboardists, vocalists *Ravinia Festival grounds, near Chicago — 400 Iris Ln., Highland Park, IL 60035* **Voice:** 847-266-5106 **Fax:** 847-266-5063 **Contact:** Diane P. Dorn, Administrator **Founded:** 1988 **Open:** June–Aug. **Admission:** Application ($50 fee for piano and strings); tape for piano and strings, live audition for singers **Deadlines:** Jan. **Cost:** $2,000 for string players, keyboardists; vocalists on scholarship **Financial Aid:** Scholarship **Size-Attendees:** 60 **Handicapped Access**

FOR A LONG TIME, people associated with the Ravinia Festival (summer home of the Chicago Symphony) felt a need to establish a program for young artists. So in 1988, the Steans Institute for Young Artists welcomed its first class of pianists and string players, all of whom had already developed a superior technique and extensive repertoire. The idea was to give these young musicians a place to focus intensively on interpretation and performance. Robert Mann, founding first violinist of the Juilliard String Quartet, was artistic director for the first season. For the next 5 summers Walter Levin, first violinist of the now-disbanded LaSalle Quartet, led the faculty. In 1994 violinist Miriam Fried became faculty chairman. Zubin Mehta established the institute's vocal program in 1992; it concentrates exclusively on the genre of song.

The Steans faculty is absolutely top-of-the-line and includes violist Atar Arad, pianists Leon Fleisher and Menahem Pressler, violinist and conductor Peter Oundjian and the Tokyo String Quartet. It's an indication of the elite status of this program that the brochure features mile-long biographies of last year's *student* participants. The current music director of the Ravinia Festival is Christoph Eschenbach, music director of the Houston Symphony since 1988. He conducts regular masterclasses for both the instrumentalists and the vocalists at the institute. Steans is named for Lois M. Steans, a member of Ravinia's Women's Board.

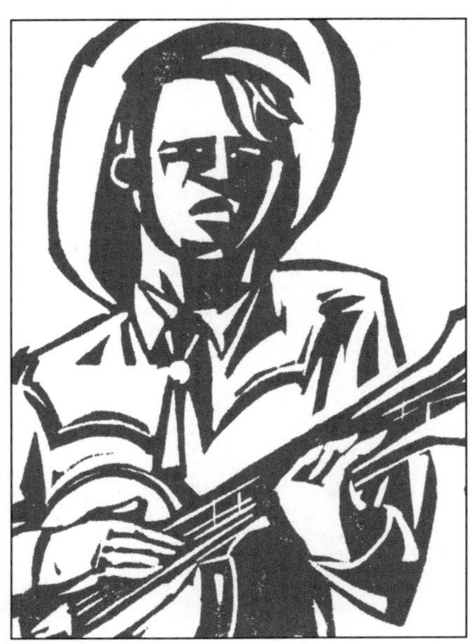

Indiana

Indiana University School of Music

For instrumentalists, vocalists, composers, conductors *Indiana University School of Music, Bloomington, IN 47405* **Voice:** 812-855-1582 **Fax:** 812-855-4936 **E-mail:** musicadm@indiana.edu **Web Site:** http://www. music.indiana.edu **Contact:** Gwyn Richards, Dir., Music Adm. **Founded:** 1910 **Open:** Year-round **Admission:** Application ($35), audition/tape, scores **Deadlines:** Mar. 1 (fall); Nov. 1 (spring) **Cost:** Per credit hour: $133 (resident), $388 (nonresident) **Financial Aid:** Loan, scholarship, fellowship, work/study **Size-Attendees:** 1,648 **Size-Class:** 1–100 **Degree or Certification:** AS, BME, BM, BS, BA, MA, MM, MS, DM, PhD, Artist Dip., Perf. Dip. **Handicapped Access**

INDIANA UNIVERSITY'S School of Music is one of the very largest and best regarded in the country. More than 1,400 students from around the world attend each year. The training offered is outstanding; one finds IU grads in virtually all of this country's major orchestras and opera companies. The school is particularly strong in voice and in strings. Up until his death, Josef Gingold turned out world-class violin soloists and chamber musicians.

The facilities of the School of Music include 4 buildings housing more than 110 offices and studios, 180 practice rooms, choral and instrumental rehearsal rooms, 3 recital halls and a music library with more than 380,000 books, scores, microfilms and periodicals and nearly 160,000 recordings. There is also a performance practice building with 80 soundproofed rooms.

The school is centered around the Musical Arts Center, a complex featuring an acoustically refined auditorium and a stage with capabilities that have yet to be rivaled at any other music school. Nearly 1,000 public programs presented yearly on the Bloomington campus include solo recitals, ensemble concerts and full-scale productions of opera and ballet.

Indiana University Summer Festival

For instrumentalists, vocalists, composers *Indiana University School of Music, Bloomington, IN 47405* **Voice:** 812-855-6025 **Fax:** 812-855-4936 **E-mail:** phillipl@indiana.edu **Contact:** Leonard Phillips, Dir., Special Programs **Founded:** 1965 **Open:** Mid-June–mid-Aug. **Admission:** Application ($25); audition tape **Deadlines:** Between Mar. 15 and June 1 (variable) **Cost:** $200–$600 **Size-Attendees:** 600 **Size-Class:** 20–30 **Degree or Certification:** BM, MM, DMA, PhD **Handicapped Access**

THE INDIANA UNIVERSITY at Bloomington School of Music seems to be the only school of music in the nation that offers a full program of study and performance with resident students and faculty during the summer season. Internationally renowned guest artists join the resident faculty and students in a great number of concerts and other productions.

The summer session features a lively series of chamber, orchestral, opera and musical theater presentations. During the summer session a full program of performance instruction, academic courses, masterclasses and workshops are offered. New or continuing degree students and visiting participants join forces for work with members of the regular IU faculty, as well as distinguished guests. In addition, there are special programs each year. In 1996 a retreat for professional violinists and violists, a natural horn workshop and a Latin American Composers' Project were offered.

Mary Anderson Center for the Arts

For performers, composers *Monastery 15 min. from downtown Louisville, KY — 101 St. Francis Dr., Mount St. Francis, IN 47146* **Voice:** 812-923-8602 **Contact:** Sarah Yates, Exec. Dir. **Founded:** 1989 **Open:** Year-round **Admission:** Application ($15), audio- or videotape, personal statement **Cost:** $350/wk. (some discounts available based on need) **Financial Aid:** Fellowship **Size-Attendees:** 6

FOUNDED IN 1989, the Mary Anderson Center for the Arts occupies 400 acres of rolling woodlands including a wildlife sanctuary, just 15 minutes north of Louisville, Kentucky.

The long and eclectic list of artistic disciplines at MAC embraces not only composers but fiction and nonfiction writers, jewelry makers, storytellers, architects and installation artists. Though the place is well equipped for most of the various artists who come, composers and performing musicians should be warned: MAC has neither pianos nor soundproofing on site, though arrangements can be made in cooperation with the music department at the University of Louisville.

Up to 6 MAC residents at a time live at MAC in private rooms at Loftus House, a large building that also serves as an administrative center and dining facility for the colony. All meals at the center are provided or their cost reimbursed. Public programs here include workshops, a children's summer art day camp and an arts festival, symposia and potluck dinners.

MAC has its origins in an arrangement between the Conventual Friars of Our Lady of Consolation Province, several of whom are artists, and a group of southern Indiana and Greater Louisville artists looking for a quiet place to work. Today, friars and artists work side by side here, enjoying the peaceful, contemplative atmosphere. That said, the center itself has no formal ties with the Catholic Church or the Franciscan Order.

Kansas

Blanche Bryden Sunflower Music Festival Institute

For chamber musicians *Washburn University, near downtown — 1700 SW College, Topeka, KS 66621* **Voice:** 913-231-1010 ext.1151 **Fax:** 913-357-4168 **E-mail:** zzsavl@acc.wuacc.edu **Web Site:** http://www.wuacc.edu/cas/music/ **Contact:** Kirt Saville, Chair, Dept. of Music **Founded:** 1993 **Open:** First 2 wks. June **Admission:** Application (no fee), tape **Deadlines:** Mar. 15 **Cost:** Free tuition, room and board **Financial Aid:** Full scholarship **Size-Attendees:** 26 **Handicapped Access**

Twenty-six students receive free tuition, room and board for the duration of this 1-week chamber music festival. Based at and administered by Washburn University, the festival focuses on the study and performance of chamber music repertoire. Two string quartets, 1 brass quintet, 2 woodwind quintets and 3 pianists make up the student body.

The faculty includes principals and members of the Boston, Chicago, Dallas, Detroit, London, New York Philharmonic and Pittsburgh symphonies. Highlights of the faculty list include Bryan Kennedy, horn professor at the University of Michigan; Charles Stegeman, concertmaster of the Pittsburgh Opera and Ballet; and Mark Tanner, instructor of viola at the University of Florida. Student ages range from 16 to 26.

Pittsburg State University Department of Music

For instrumentalists, vocalists, composers *1701 S. Broadway, Pittsburg, KS 66762* **Voice:** 316-235-4467, -4466 **Fax:** 316-235-7515 **E-mail:** lhoffman@pittstate.edu **Web Site:** http://www.pittstate.edu/music **Contact:** Dr. Keith C. Ward, Chair **Founded:** 1908 **Open:** Mid-Aug.–mid-May; June, July **Admission:** Open admission **Cost:** Per semester: $1,000 (resident), $3,000 (nonresident) **Financial Aid:** Loans; Scholarship; Stipend; Work/Study **Size-Attendees:** 85 **Size-Class:** 10–15 **Degree or Certification:** MME, MM Perf. **Job Placement:** Yes **Handicapped Access**

Formed in 1908, the department of music is one of 14 components of PSU's College of Arts and Sciences. From that time to the present, the department has functioned as a major educational and cultural resource for southeastern Kansas and the surrounding area.

The department includes a major complex of practice rooms, classrooms, large studios and a recital hall that is one of the best in the region. All of this is located in McCray Hall, home to 52 pianos, an electronic music studio, a 29-rank pipe organ, a practice organ, harpsichords and a collection of string and wind instruments. Many faculty hail from the Southeast Kansas Symphony.

Kentucky

University of Louisville School of Music

For instrumentalists, vocalists, composers *Belknap campus — University of Louisville, Louisville, KY 40292* **Voice:** 502-852-1623; 800-334-8635 ext. 1623 **Fax:** 502-852-0520 **E-mail:** lswheeoi@ulkyvm.louisville.edu **Web Site:** http://www.louisville.edu/music **Contact:** Linda S. Wheeler, Admissions **Founded:** 1932 **Open:** Year-round **Admission:** Application ($25), transcripts, letters of recommendation, test scores **Cost:** $2,570 (resident), $7,250 (nonresident); $1,500 room and board **Financial Aid:** Loans; Scholarship; Stipend; Work/Study **Size-Attendees:** 600 **Size-Class:** 30 **Degree or Certification:** BM, MM **Job Placement:** Yes **Handicapped Access**

THE SCHOOL OF MUSIC at the University of Louisville is probably the largest music school in the state, with some 50 faculty members and about 600 music majors. Housed on the Belknap campus of the university, the school of music has extensive facilities including a music library housing 50,000 titles, among which are the collected folksongs of Jean Thomas.

The school fits the standard music school mold in most respects, but in the music world, there is one thing for which the school is particularly well known: the University of Louisville Grawemayer Award in Music Composition. The Grawemeyer, perhaps the country's largest prize exclusively for composers, awards $150,000 to a different composer each year. The first person to receive the honor was Witold Lutoslawski in 1985.

Louisiana

University of New Orleans Jazz Studies

For instrumentalists, vocalists, composers, conductors *PAC Bldg., Rm. 108, New Orleans, LA 70148* **Voice:** 504-280-6039 **Fax:** 504-280-6098 **Contact:** Edward Peterson, Coord. **Founded:** 1989 **Open:** Late Jan.–mid May; late Aug.–early Dec. **Admission:** Application to the university, audition **Cost:** $1,181 (resident), $2,577 (nonresident) **Financial Aid:** Loans; Scholarship; Stipend; Work/Study **Size-Attendees:** 70–80 **Size-Class:** 15 **Degree or Certification:** BA, MM **Handicapped Access**

THE UNIVERSITY OF New Orleans has a great reputation in the jazz world. Ellis Marsalis is director of jazz studies, and the jazz faculty is otherwise star-studded with such teachers as Harold Battiste, Edward Peterson and Charles Blancq. The UNO department is small—usually about 70–80 students in all—and offers undergraduates a BAMus degree in 5 emphasis areas: performance, jazz performance, jazz arranging, music theory and composition and music history.

Through the university's College of Education, students may also seek a BA in music education with an emphasis in either vocal or instrumental teaching. The MM degree is available in performance, jazz studies, conducting or composition. Students may major in bass, piano, clarinet, saxophone, drums, trumpet, flute, trombone, guitar or voice.

Maine

Kneisel Hall Chamber Music School and Festival

For chamber musicians *Rural coast of Maine — Pleasant St., Rte. 15, Blue Hill, ME 04614* **Voice:** 207-374-2811; 207-374-2173 (summer) **Fax:** 207-374-2811 **Contact:** Seymour Lipkin, Art. Dir. **Founded:** 1902 **Open:** Late June–late Aug. **Admission:** Application ($50), tape, recommendations **Deadlines:** Apr. 1 **Cost:** $2,800 (all-inclusive) **Financial Aid:** Scholarship **Size-Attendees:** 50 **Size-Class:** 2–40 **Handicapped Access**

IN 1885 THE CELEBRATED Austrian violinist Franz Kneisel came to the U.S. to become the concertmaster of the Boston Symphony Orchestra. Here he formed the Kneisel Quartet, the first professional string quartet in this country's history. In 1902 Kneisel began bringing his chamber music students up to Maine for summer study at what is now known as Kneisel Hall. Some early Kneisel students were William Kroll, Joseph and Lillian Fuchs and Carl Stern. This is how Kneisel Hall became known as the cradle of chamber music teaching in America.

Today Kneisel Hall maintains its prominence as one of America's most prestigious chamber music programs. This is largely due to the leadership of former artistic director Leslie Parnas, acting director Roman Totenberg and current artistic director Seymour Lipkin. The superb faculty includes not only the Vermeer Quartet but also such chamber music luminaries as violinist Ronald Copes, violist Katherine Murdock and cellist Barbara Stein Mallow.

Pierre Monteux School for Conductors and Orchestra Musicians

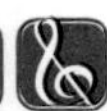

For orchestral musicians, conductors *Box 157, Hancock, ME 04640* **Voice:** 207-422-3931 **Fax:** 207-422-3280 **Contact:** Nancie Monteux-Barendse, Dir. **Founded:** 1947 **Open:** July **Admission:** Application ($75 for conductors, $40 for instrumentalists), tape, recommendations **Deadlines:** Apr. 1 **Cost:** $100 deposit; $400 housing/instrumentalists (no tuition); $1,800 housing and tuition/conductors **Financial Aid:** Loans; Scholarship; Stipend; Work/Study **Size-Attendees:** 60

FRENCH-BORN CONDUCTOR Pierre Monteux was the conductor of the famous riotous world premiere of Stravinsky's *Rite of Spring* in 1913. He conducted most major orchestras around the world, notably as the conductor of the Metropolitan Opera, the Boston Symphony, Amsterdam's Concertgebouw, the San Francisco Symphony and the London Symphony Orchestra. He was a major teacher of conductors, running a school in the French village of Les Baux-de-Provence until World War II, when he moved it to Hancock, Maine.

Beginning in 1943, the Hancock school was famous, bringing in major young conducting talents from around the world. Among Monteux's students were Erich Kunzel, David Zinman and Sir Neville Marriner.

At the time of Monteux's death in 1964, the Pierre Monteux Memorial Foundation was incorporated as a nonprofit organization, with Monteux's widow, Doris Monteux, as president. She decided to keep the school open. Charles Bruck, Monteux's former pupil and assistant, was named the school's director. When Bruck died in 1995 he was succeeded by Michael Jinbo, another Monteux protégé associated with the school.

The school runs from mid-June through mid-July, with a full orchestra of approximately 60 of whom 20 are also intermediate or advanced conducting students. The distinguishing feature of this program is that the conducting students learn to conduct by actually conducting a symphony through rehearsals and public concerts under the guidance of the master teacher. Work in sightreading and solfege is rigorous. The school presents a full concert every Sunday afternoon.

Maryland

National Orchestral Institute

 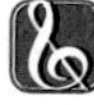 ***For orchestral musicians***

University of Maryland — 4321 Harwick Rd., Ste. 220, College Park, MD 20740 **Voice:** 301-403-8370 ext. 12 **Fax:** 301-403-8375 **Contact:** Donald Reinhold, Dir. **Founded:** 1988 **Open:** June **Admission:** Application (fee), audition, resume, letter of recommendation **Deadlines:** Audition Jan.–mid-Mar. **Cost:** Full scholarship for all participants **Financial Aid:** Scholarship **Size-Attendees:** 90 **Handicapped Access**

Designed for young musicians on the threshold of their professional careers, the National Orchestral Institute at the University of Maryland College Park offers full scholarships for an intensive 3-week training experience in orchestral musicianship. The average crop of players is selected through hundreds of auditions around the country.

Each week during the Institute, an acclaimed conductor-in-residence prepares and conducts a public concert. Participating conductors in 1996 were the Cleveland Orchestra's resident conductor Jahja Ling, Louisiana Symphony Orchestra music director James Paul and Marin Alsop, music director of several orchestras around the country. Concertmasters and principal players from major American orchestras lead sectional rehearsals and present masterclasses on repertoire required for professional auditions. Previous participants in the NOI have since won auditions with major orchestras and chamber ensembles. The faculty members mainly come from the first seats of the Baltimore and National symphony orchestras.

Peabody Institute

For all classically oriented musicians

1 E. Mount Vernon Pl., Baltimore, MD 21202 **Voice:** 410-659-8110; 800-368-2521 **Fax:** 410-659-8102 **Web Site:** http://www.peabody.jhu.edu **Contact:** David Lane, Dir. Admissions **Founded:** 1857 **Open:** Sept.–May **Admission:** Application ($45), audition/tape, transcripts, test scores **Deadlines:** Dec. 15 **Cost:** $18,700; $6,940 room and board **Financial Aid:** Loans; Scholarship; Fellowship; Work/Study **Size-Attendees:** 600 **Size-Class:** 10 **Degree or Certification:** BM, MM,DMA, Perf. Cert., Artists Dip., Grad. Perf. Dip. **Job Placement:** Yes **Handicapped Access**

The Peabody Institute of The Johns Hopkins University was the first conservatory of music to be established in America. It was founded in 1857 by George Peabody, America's great 19th-century philanthropist. A professional school within a university setting, Peabody offers some of the biggest names in teaching available in the mid-Atlantic region.

With almost a century and a half of history, the Peabody name has come to mean quite a lot. And with a small undergraduate and graduate population (the total is 500), it has chosen to focus its degree granting tightly to classical music performance only.

As a division of a prestigious university, Peabody shares with schools like Eastman, Yale and Oberlin the advantage of drawing double-degree aspirants and musicians hungry for a well-rounded and high-quality overall educational experience. Even for those who choose to specialize in music performance, liberal arts coursework is required.

Of particular interest to some musicians who may already have earned performance degrees of one kind or another is Peabody's special degree program in the recording arts and sciences. The program has excellent facilities and a distinguished faculty. (Alan P. Kefauver, director of recording at Peabody, has spent his career recording classical music greats around the world.)

Baltimore may not be New York, but arguably there's plenty to do and see for serious students of music. Some of the most eminent teachers have been trekking down here for years because for them, Peabody is worth the effort.

Rossborough Festival

For solo vocalists, keyboardists, cellists *Near Washington, DC — 4321 Hartwick Rd., Ste. 220, College Park, MD 20740* **Voice:** 301-403-8370 **Fax:** 301-403-8375 **Web Site:** http://www.intlcomp@umdacc.umd.edu **Contact:** Donald Reinhold, Festival Coord. **Founded:** 1971 **Open:** Mid-July **Admission:** Application (fee), for competition: tape, repertoire list **Deadlines:** Mar. 15 **Cost:** Varies **Size-Attendees:** 40 **Handicapped Access**

The University of Maryland's Rossborough Festival offers masterclasses, symposia, concerts and other events concurrently with major international competitions it holds on a rotating basis in piano, cello and voice. A member of the World Federation of International Music Competitions, the Rossborough Festival offers the William Kappell Piano Competition and Festival, the Leonard Rose Cello Competition and the International Marian Anderson Vocal Arts Competition and Festival. Approximately 40 international competitors are selected each year to compete for $50,000 in cash awards and prestigious concert engagements. Guest artists of international renown perform and lead masterclasses as part of these high-profile events.

Massachusetts

Audition and Performance Stress Reduction

For any type of performer *Boston Conservatory, 8 The Fenway, Boston, MA 02215; 51 Stuart St., Watertown, MA 02172* **Voice:** 617-924-6127 **Fax:** 617-924-7041 **E-mail:** obocanreed@aol.dom **Contact:** Dr. Stuart Dunkel, Dir. **Open:** Mid-Dec., mid-Apr. **Cost:** $15 **Size-Attendees:** 5–50 **Size-Class:** 20 **Handicapped Access**

Stuart Dunkel is a veteran professional oboist who has performed in every major Boston area orchestra, including the Boston Symphony, and who received his doctoral degree at the Juilliard School. In other words, he has been around. And as the author of a book on managing performance anxiety, he is an acknowledged guru in the field. These workshops are oriented to college-age students who need performance experience. They attract talented performers who would like to work their way through trouble with fear or confidence problems and who need to be educated on how to think through the performance experience in an empowering way. Based on phobia therapy, the 2-hour seminars stress successful attitudes in dealing with performance. Particular emphasis is placed on how to talk to oneself and how to tap into one's personal performing strengths.

Berklee College of Music

For instrumentalists, vocalists, composers, arrangers, songwriters *Back Bay — 1140 Boylston St., Boston, MA 02215* **Voice:** 617-266-1400; 800-421-0084 **Fax:** 617-536-2632 **E-mail:** admissions@berklee.edu **Web Site:** http://www.berklee.edu **Contact:** Admissions Office **Founded:** 1945 **Open:** Year-round **Deadlines:** Rolling; filing date of Mar. 1 for fall **Financial Aid:** Loans; Scholarship; Work/Study **Size-Attendees:** 2,850 **Size-Class:** 10–15 **Degree or Certification:** Bachelor of Music **Job Placement:** Yes **Handicapped Access**

FOUNDED IN 1945, Berklee is the world's largest independent music college and one of the very best for the study of contemporary (nonclassical) music. The college's 2,850 students and 300 faculty are very diverse; Berklee has the highest percentage of international graduates of any college in the U.S. Located in Boston's Back Bay neighborhood, Berklee's 11 buildings are set up for aspiring producers and engineers, housing 10 professionally equipped recording studios, more than 100 MIDI-equipped workstations and hundreds of synthesizers. The film scoring department includes 6 fully equipped film and video scoring and editing labs.

Faculty members include vibraphonist Gary Burton, singer/songwriter Livingston Taylor and trombonist Phil Wilson. Many of the music industry's best-known artists got their start at Berklee, among them Quincy Jones, Branford Marsalis, Pat Metheny and John Scofield.

Boston Conservatory

For instrumentalists, vocalists, composers *Close to Back Bay — 8 The Fenway, Boston, MA 02215* **Voice:** 617-536-6340 **Fax:** 617-536-3176 **Contact:** Richard Wallace, Dir. of Admission **Founded:** 1867 **Open:** Sept.–May **Admission:** Application ($60), audition/tape **Deadlines:** Mar. 1 **Cost:** $14,300; $6,680 room and board **Financial Aid:** Loans; Scholarship; Stipend; Work/Study **Size-Attendees:** 200 **Size-Class:** 10–15 **Degree or Certification:** MM in performance, MM in jazz (in collaboration with Berklee College of Music)

FOUNDED IN 1867, the Boston Conservatory offers training in music, dance and theater to more than 400 students. Music students at the undergraduate and graduate levels work with faculty members from among Boston's best-known ensembles. Boston Symphony players head many departments, as do other nationally known personal-

Versatility

After 29 years as drummer in the *Tonight Show* band, Ed Shaughnessy has devoted himself to teaching at clinics and workshops around the country. He says he enjoys his students' enthusiasm for jazz, but worries about the professional prospects that some will face.

"It was a lot easier when I started out. There were opportunities to work in apprentice-type situations. At 17, I was on the road on a band bus and I just learned as I went along. If you don't tell students it's harder to make a living today, you're being less than honest with them.

"I advise young people to be good all-round musicians, so they can get work playing in various styles. When I was a kid, Big Sid Catlet [a drummer who played a lot with Louis Armstrong] gave me that advice. Sid made sure he could read well, so he could be prepared for the lean times. If he needed work, he could go out and play Broadway shows or do studio work. I say the same thing to people today because after all, we know that jazz is a musical stepchild in this country. You have to be flexible enough to do other things to support doing what you love."

ities. John Adams, for example, teaches composition and theory.

With over 300 performances each year, students get a great deal of onstage experience during their course of study. They participate in orchestra, wind ensemble, jazz and choral ensembles, as well as pit ensembles for the dance, opera and musical theater mainstage productions at the school. Pianists work on solo playing and instrumental accompanying but can choose to expand their skills to work with dance and/or musical theater studio classes.

Boston University School for the Arts Music Division

For instrumentalists, composers *Near Kenmore Sq. — 855 Commonwealth Ave., Boston, MA 02215* **Voice:** 617-353-3341; 800-643-4796 **Fax:** 617-353-5331 **E-mail:** sfa_info@bu.edu **Web Site:** http://web.bu.edu/SFA **Contact:** Christopher Kendall, Dir. **Founded:** 1872 **Open:** Sept.–May **Admission:** Application ($50), audition, transcripts, letters of recommendation **Deadlines:** Rolling **Cost:** $643 (per credit); $1,200 (per year for applied lessons) **Financial Aid:** Loans; Scholarship; Fellowship; Stipend; Work/Study **Size-Attendees:** 650 **Size-Class:** 20–30 **Degree or Certification:** MM, DMA, Art. Dip., Perf. Cert. **Job Placement:** Yes **Handicapped Access**

THE BOSTON REGION is one of the liveliest musical centers in the nation, and the music division of Boston University's School for the Arts benefits from its location in the very heart of the city. The division's regular and adjunct faculty are drawn from the large number of topflight professional musicians in the area; the quality, diversity and sheer abundance of Boston's musical activities provide constant stimulation to students and faculty alike.

Most of the activities of the music division take place within the 6-story Commonwealth Avenue building that houses the School for the Arts. The building contains a 485-seat concert hall; music studios and practice rooms; 3 rehearsal halls for orchestra, wind ensemble, band and choral groups; a recording studio; and 3 electronic music studios. Opera rehearsal and coaching studios are housed across the street. With the opening of the Tsai Performance Center, the music division has a beautiful concert and rehearsal space for its major performing organizations.

Within the division, recitals are presented on a regular basis by faculty, seniors and graduate students; more than 400 performances are offered throughout the academic year. Phyllis Curtin runs the Opera Institute, and the Muir Quartet is BU's ensemble in residence.

Candidates for the MM may concentrate in performance, historical performance, composition, theory, history and literature of music or music education.

Brandeis Summer Music Festival

For keyboardists, string players, selected wind players *On the Brandeis University campus, near Boston — Rabb School of Summer, Special and Continuing Studies MS 084, 415 South St., P.O. Box 9110, Waltham, MA 02254* **Voice:** 617-736-3424 **Fax:** 617-736-3420 **E-mail:** summerschool@logos.cc.brandeis.edu **Web Site:** http://www.brandeis.edu/sumsch/Rabb.html **Contact:** Gwenn Smaxwill **Founded:** 1989 **Open:** First 2 wks. June **Admission:** Application ($50), audition/tape **Deadlines:** Early May **Cost:** $545 **Financial Aid:** Scholarship **Size-Attendees:** 40 **Size-Class:** 10–15 **Handicapped Access**

THE BRANDEIS SUMMER Music Festival offers young professionals, advanced music students and serious amateur musicians the opportunity to study chamber music in 1-on-1 and small group settings with members of the Lydian String Quartet. The Lydian is ensemble-in-residence at Brandeis and quite a well-known ensemble. Participants in the festival are encouraged to take creative reins, shaping their own musical ideas and ultimately their own performances. Preformed groups as well as individuals may apply. Participants can attend one or both of the 10-day sessions. The daily format includes coachings and rehearsals.

A variety of other events is offered, including masterclasses, classes on rehearsal technique, open rehearsals with the Lydians and concerts by participants. During free time the Brandeis campus and the attractions of the Boston area can be enjoyed.

Musicorda Summer String Program

For violinists, violists, cellists *Pioneer Valley, western MA — Mount Holyoke College, South Hadley, MA 01075; P.O. Box 557, South Hadley, MA 01075* **Voice:** 413-538-2590 **Fax:** 413-532-0607 **Contact:** Jacqueline Melnick, Adm. Dir. **Founded:** 1987 **Open:** Late June–mid-Aug. **Admission:** Application ($50; $75 after Apr. 1), audition/tape **Deadlines:** Apr. 1 **Cost:** $2,850 **Financial Aid:** Scholarship; Stipend; Work/Study **Size-Attendees:** 70 **Handicapped Access**

FOUNDED IN 1987 on the premise that string players need a special summer study environment, the Musicorda Summer String Program takes on some 36 violinists, 18 violists and 18 cellists from age 12 through graduate school each summer. The program focuses on solo and chamber music study.

The faculty includes some serious names in the business, like Paul Katz, the founding cellist of the Cleveland Quartet; James Buswell, a major violin soloist and teacher; and Marylou Speaker, principal second violinist in the Boston Symphony. There are 3 resident pianists, including Michael Adcock.

The program takes place in the context of more and more additional enterprises at Musicorda, such as the Festival Series, which presented the Turtle Island and St. Petersburg string quartets in 1995. Musicorda now also runs a children's string workshop, a young artists' series, and what they call the Musicorda Road Company.

The Road Company comes out of Musicorda's philosophy that training musicians means to prepare them to reach out to their communities with music. So the program sends solo performers and quartets out into the Mount Holyoke area for concerts in community centers, day camps, churches, libraries and museums.

In recent years, Musicorda has grown to become one of the hottest small festivals in western Massachusetts. In its first 10 years the festival, under the direction of founders Jackie Melnick and Terry Teraspulsky, has attracted a prestigious faculty, considerable community support, and a talented student pool from 42 states and 26 countries.

New England Conservatory

For instrumentalists, vocalists, composers, conductors *Back Bay — 290 Huntington Ave., Boston, MA 02215* **Voice:** 617-267-1120 ext. 430 **Fax:** 617-262-0500 **Contact:** Allison T. Ball, Dean, Enrollment Services **Founded:** 1867 **Open:** Sept.–May **Admission:** Application (fee), essay, resume/repertoire, recommendations, audition, test scores, transcripts **Deadlines:** Dec. 13 (fall); Nov. 1 (spring) **Cost:** $17,100; $8,000 housing **Financial Aid:** Loans; Scholarship; Fellowship; Work/Study **Size-Attendees:** 750 **Degree or Certification:** VM, DP, MM, GD, AD, DMA **Job Placement:** Yes **Handicapped Access**

MAJOR CULTURAL centers frequently have more than one music school, but in most cases, clear leaders stand out. In Boston, the competition is tough, but the New England Conservatory remains for many students the best place in Boston to study. You'll find NEC alumni in every major orchestra and opera company in this country, in well-known chamber ensembles, jazz ensembles and all manner of music-related work.

The facilities at NEC are right up there with those of all the other great conservatories. On its campus in Boston's historic Back Bay area, one finds a distinguished early music collection, computer and electronic music studios, a library containing more than 110,000 books and recordings, and several halls, including one of the most acoustically ideal concert spaces in the world.

The conservatory's Jordan Hall was built in 1903 and declared a national historic landmark in 1994. Its recent renovation was a major news event. Jordan's seating capacity of 1,019 provides performance space for NEC large-ensemble performances, faculty recitals and numerous professional concerts.

The faculty at NEC is indeed impressive. Saxophonist-composer Kenneth

Music as Service

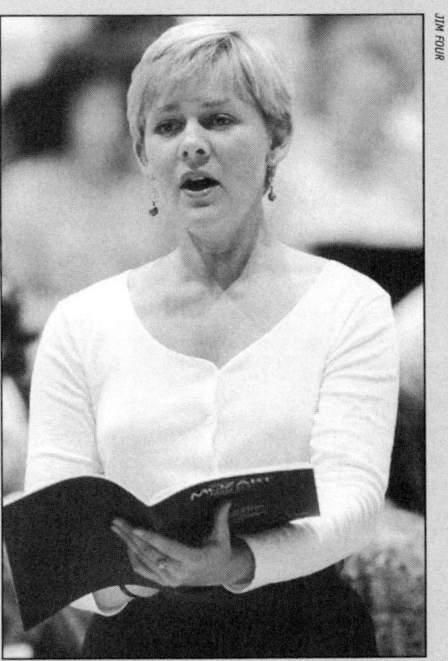

JIM FOUR

Barbara Bonney, soprano.

When soprano Barbara Bonney became an opera singer virtually overnight, no one was more surprised than she was. A University of New Hampshire junior in Salzburg studying German, she had left her cello back home in New Jersey because she couldn't afford the extra airline ticket to transport it.

"I told someone at the University of Salzburg that I was a musician and they said, 'Why don't you audition at the Mozarteum?' Since I didn't have my instrument, I just went there and sang some songs." Bonney was accepted, and very soon thereafter, she secured a repertory position in the Darmstadt City Opera. Over the next 4 years, she sang in more than 40 productions. "All this happened, and I had never made the conscious choice to sing."

Bonney had a lot of musicality going for her. "There are some singers who are blessed with amazing instruments and there are some, like me, who just manage to do something with what they've got." She adds that she's always been a good sightreader and a quick study with languages—both real assets for a singer.

Bonney has taught at Tanglewood and at Ravinia and leads workshops around the world. Teaching is instant gratification, she says. "Rather than fighting the ego trips up on stage with your colleagues, in a teaching context you know you are truly helping someone. And that's always been my goal. I feel that music is my calling because it is a very helpful, healing, useful tool."

As a child, Bonney was taken by the minister of her family's church to play guitar in nursing homes. "I've continued that sort of work though my life, performing for cancer patients, in hospices and that sort of thing."

In music, it's the human connection that matters most to Bonney. "That's why I like recital singing more than doing opera. In a recital, you can see people's faces responding to you; that sort of give-and-take makes the performance special. In an opera house, you can't see your audience. It's just dark out there."

Radnofsky appears on the long list of chamber music instructors. Paula Robison teaches flute; bassist Cecil McBee is one of 32 jazz studies professors.

Whether it is to the New York Philharmonic, the Artie Shaw Orchestra, the Metropolitan Opera Company or the *Tonight Show,* New England Conservatory students tend to go places, exciting places.

Smith Summer Workshops

For vocalists *Sage Hall, Smith College, Northampton, MA 01063; Western Wind, 263 W. 86 St., New York, NY 10024* **Voice:** 212-873-2848; 800-788-2187 **Fax:** 212-873-2849 **E-mail:** workshops@westernwind. org **Web Site:** http://www.westernwind.org **Contact:** William Zukof, Artistic Codir. **Founded:** 1981 **Open:** Late June–early July; early Aug. **Admission:** Refundable deposit ($100); open to all **Deadlines:** Late May **Cost:** $299 (5-day); $399 (8-day) **Financial Aid:** Scholarship; Work/Study **Size-Attendees:** 60–75 **Job Placement:** Yes **Handicapped Access**

DATING FROM 1969, the Western Wind Vocal Ensemble is one of the country's oldest a cappella vocal groups. And 20 years ago, when few people even knew this kind of music existed, Western Wind received a Grammy nomination for its recording of Revolutionary War songs. From the beginning, part of the group's mission has been to educate the public about the genre, and one way it accomplishes its goal is through its 2 workshops held each summer at Smith College. In the sessions, the group teaches singers of all levels about the rich and varied repertoire available to a cappella groups and shares technical tips on such skills as blending, phrasing, and singing in tune together.

Michigan

Alden B. Dow Creativity Center Residency Program

For all musicians *Northwood University campus — 3225 Cook Rd., Midland, MI 48640* **Voice:** 517-837-4478 **Fax:** 517-837-4468 **Founded:** 1978 **Open:** 8 weeks in summer **Admission:** Application ($10), recommendations, project description **Deadlines:** Dec. 31 **Financial Aid:** Stipend **Size-Attendees:** 4

IN THE OTHERWISE artistically competitive and creatively circumscribed world of residency programs in general, the open-ended appeal of the Alden B. Dow Creativity Center Residency Program is refreshing. Its brochure reads: "If you have an innovative idea that you think would work for you if you had time to develop it, this program could be a find."

Son of Dow Chemical Company founder Herbert Henry Dow, Alden B. Dow was an architect of distinction who studied and worked with Frank Lloyd Wright in the 1930s. Dow became friends with the founders of Northwood University when he helped design the school's Midland campus in 1959.

Out of appreciation for Dow's work and for his creative philosophy, Northwood created the Alden B. Dow Creativity Center in 1978. Since then, 4 residencies have been awarded there each year in diverse disciplines. Residents are invited to stay on the Northwood campus for fully paid 8-week periods. They live in large apartments and receive a $750 stipend to cover expenses.

Applicants are judged exclusively on the project idea they submit. Past participants have spent their residencies doing such tasks as looking into the politics of the art world, creating new math curricula and developing creative writing programs for use in prisons.

Training a Soloist

Pianist Vladimir Feltsman made big headlines with his dramatic arrival in the United States from Moscow in 1987, after many years and much difficulty trying to get permission to emigrate. As piano soloist, Feltsman is known not only for his prodigious technique, but also for the individuality and imaginativeness of his interpretations. He has appeared with every major American orchestra, under the most celebrated conductors of the world.

The soloist life, though, is not all it is cracked up to be, he says. "There is a lot of traveling, a lot of hotels and all of that kind of jazz. It's an interesting, full existence. But it's very far from the life some people imagine, with fast cars, and women throwing themselves at you."

Still, Feltsman has a highly desirable musical career, and he attributes his success largely to the Soviet Union of his youth. At the age of 6, Feltsman was tested for musical potential, along with hundreds of other talented 6-year-olds. He scored well and gained admission to the Moscow Special Music School, where he was to spend more than a decade immersed in musical study.

"Discipline and drive are musts in music. The difference between the Russia I grew up in and this country is that in Russia we were trained very rigorously right from the beginning. We had performance exams twice a year. If you didn't play well enough, they'd just kick you out. I don't have any nostalgia for this totalitarian approach, but it works. If you are very gifted but you don't get this kind of training, you don't really have the same chance of success." In America today, Feltsman says that talented young musicians get little or no institutional support. Instead, they have to depend on their families and private teachers to motivate and discipline them through the early years which, he feels, are the most critical of all.

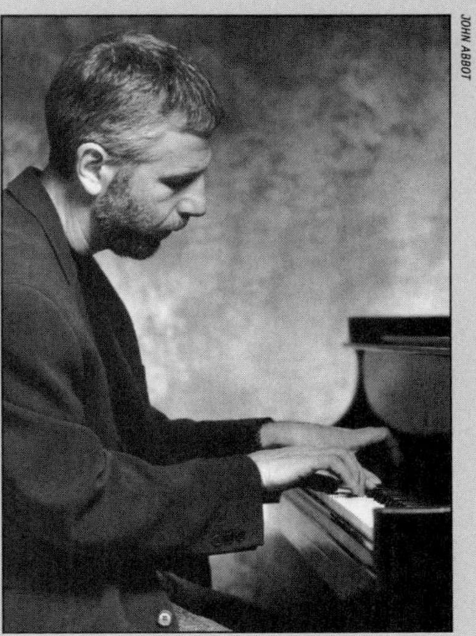
JOHN ABBOT

Vladimir Feltsman, pianist.

Irving S. Gilmore International Keyboard Festival

For keyboardists *SW Michigan — 100 W. Michigan Ave., Ste. 202, Kalamazoo, MI 49007* **Voice:** 616-342-1166; 800-34-PIANO **Fax:** 616-342-0968 **E-mail:** gilmoredh@aol.com **Contact:** David Hook, Exec. Director; Irma Vallacillo, Artistic Dir. **Founded:** 1991 **Open:** Biennial, even-numbered years, Apr.–May **Admission:** Private, noncompetitive search by search committee; interested players may submit tape for consideration **Cost:** Masterclasses free; housing provided by local families **Size-Attendees:** 70 **Handicapped Access**

The Irving S. Gilmore International Keyboard Festival is a biennial festival that celebrates keyboard music and the artists who play it. Concerts, masterclasses, lectures and public education programs add up to more than 150 events held in places like concert halls, churches, theaters and school gymnasiums in Kalamazoo and surrounding communities. The festival also helps develop the careers of classical pianists through the Gilmore Artist Award, a noncompetitive prize awarded every 4 years to an outstanding young pianist. Students at the festival come from the top music schools around the country. The festival is named after a Kalamazoo businessman and philanthropist who supported the careers of young musicians, especially pianists.

Minnesota

Bravo! Summer String Institute

For string players *Downtown — University of Minnesota School of Music, Minneapolis, MN 55455* **Voice:** 612-624-0846 **Fax:** 612-626-2200 **Contact:** Sally O'Reilly, Dir. **Founded:** 1989 **Open:** Mid-June–mid-July **Admission:** Application (fee), audition/tape **Deadlines:** Apr. 15 **Cost:** $750; $700 room and board **Financial Aid:** Scholarship; Fellowship **Size-Attendees:** 60–70 **Handicapped Access**

The Bravo! Summer String Institute was established to meet the needs of string players who want to spend a month in the summer focusing on their musical development. Each week, students receive a 1-hour private lesson, a technique and repertoire lesson, 2 chamber music coaching sessions and 3 chamber orchestra rehearsals. In addition to performance classes run by the faculty, Bravo! offers masterclasses with guest artists. In the past these have included Janos Starker, Fredell Lack and Adriana Contino. Student recitals are held twice each week and are attended by the public. Faculty recitals take place on Sunday afternoons. Bravo! emphasizes a collegial, noncompetitive atmosphere in which students may exchange information freely.

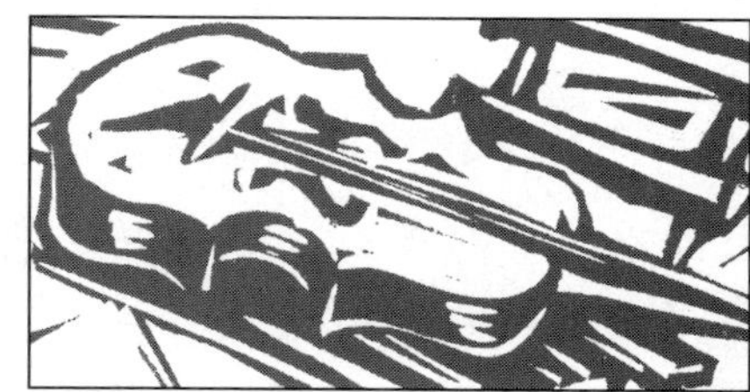

Montana

University of Montana Department of Music

For performers, composers *University of Montana, Missoula, MT 59812* **Voice:** 406-243-6880 **Fax:** 406-243-2441 **Contact:** Thomas Cook, Chair, Dept. of Music **Founded:** 1893 **Open:** Year-round **Admission:** Application ($30), audition, transcripts, test scores **Deadlines:** June 15 **Cost:** $2,251 (resident), $6,311 (nonresident); $3,367 room and board **Financial Aid:** Loans; Scholarship; Work/Study **Size-Attendees:** 165 **Degree or Certification:** BM, MM, BME, MME **Handicapped Access**

THE DEPARTMENT OF music at the University of Montana offers music degree candidates serious career preparation in teaching, music education administration, performing and composing. It is a small department, just 165 students, in the 11,000-student school. The campus is located in Missoula, an urban area in the western part of the state.

The BME degree meets the state's requirements for certification to teach music in the public schools. The graduate degree programs are the only graduate programs in music approved by the Board of Regents for the state institutions in Montana. Of significance to working teachers, the department offers the full MME program during the summer session. Performance groups include the University Choir, the Collegiate Choir, the Orchestra, the Marching Band, the University Band, the Jazz Band, the Wind Ensemble, the Opera Workshop and the Renaissance Ensemble.

Nebraska

University of Nebraska, Lincoln, School of Music

For instrumentalists, vocalists, composers *120 Westbrook Music Bldg., P.O. Box 880100, Lincoln, NE 68588* **Voice:** 402-472-6845 **Fax:** 402-472-8962 **E-mail:** cnynoff@unlinfo.unl.edu **Web Site:** http://www.unl.edu/wmus/wmb/wmb.hyml **Contact:** Colleen Nyhoff, Grad. Sec. **Founded:** 1894 **Open:** Year-round **Admission:** Application ($25), audition, transcripts, letters of recommendation **Deadlines:** Mar. 15 (fall), Dec. 1 (spring), May 1 (summer) **Cost:** Per credit hour: $99 (resident), $245 (nonresident); $3,145 room and board (per semester) **Financial Aid:** Loans; Scholarship; Fellowship; Stipend; Work/Study **Size-Attendees:** 320 **Size-Class:** 15–20 **Degree or Certification:** BM, BME, MM, DMA **Job Placement:** Yes **Handicapped Access**

THE SCHOOL OF MUSIC AT the University of Nebraska offers the traditional BM degree to students who complete 4 years of intensive study in music theory, composition, musicology or performance. Performers may pursue studies in chamber music, opera, jazz and choral music. It also offers a BFA in music theater to those looking toward careers in summer stock, repertory theater or dinner theater or on Broadway. All music majors and minors at the school must complete a 3-year sequence of courses called Comprehensive Musicianship, including basic courses in music theory, history and ear training.

The MM degree program has 3 possible areas of emphasis: performance, composition and music education. Students keen on body alignment will be glad to know that Nebraska is a major hub of Alexander Technique teachers and students, and the Lincoln campus offers Alexander classes.

Nevada

University of Nevada, Las Vegas

For instrumentalists, vocalists, composers, conductors *4505 South Maryland Pkwy., Las Vegas, NV 89154* **Voice:** 702-895-3114 **Fax:** 702-895-4194 **E-mail:** emerson@cfpa.nevada.edu **Contact:** Isabelle Emerson, Asst. Chair **Founded:** 1957 **Open:** Sept.–May **Admission:** Application ($40), audition, transcripts, test scores **Deadlines:** June 15 **Cost:** $1,800 (resident), $6,800 (nonresident); $5,000 room and board **Financial Aid:** Loans; Scholarship; Work/Study **Size-Attendees:** 265 **Degree or Certification:** BM, MM **Handicapped Access**

GRADUATE STUDENTS in the department of music at the University of Nevada at Las Vegas enjoy opportunities for professional performance and teaching, both through special departmental programs and in association with established organizations within the Las Vegas community.

Vocal students may participate in the school chorus and play minor roles with the Nevada Opera Theatre. Piano majors are given performance opportunities through the Fashion Show Mall. Outstanding instrumentalists are given the chance to perform with the Nevada Symphony and the Las Vegas Chamber Players.

The department's artist-in-residence program brings an artist to campus for a year to work with students and faculty. Jazz saxophonist Dan Menza was the first to serve in this capacity. Others have included cellist David Vanderkooi, jazz pianist Stefan Karlsson and conductor Takayoshi Suzuki. Ensembles in residence are the Sierra Winds and the Mariposa Trio.

New Hampshire

MacDowell Colony

For composers *S central NH, 40 mi. W of Manchester — 100 High St., Peterborough, NH 03458; 163 E. 81 St., New York, NY 10028* **Voice:** 603-924-3886 **Fax:** 603-924-9142 **E-mail:** macdowell@artswire.org **Contact:** Pat Dodge, Adm. Dir. **Founded:** 1907 **Open:** Year-round **Admission:** Application ($20), project description, 2 scores, with corresponding recordings **Deadlines:** Jan. 15; Apr. 15; Sept. 15 **Cost:** Artists are asked to pay what they can **Size-Attendees:** 30 **Handicapped Access**

WHAT DO AARON Copland's *Appalachian Spring,* Virgil Thomson's *Mother of Us All* and Leonard Bernstein's *Mass* have in common? They were all composed at the MacDowell Colony. Originally home to the composer Edward MacDowell, the colony is known the world over as one of America's most famous residential artists' retreats.

In 1906, such prominent Americans as Andrew Carnegie, Grover Cleveland

and J. Pierpont Morgan created a fund to help MacDowell (who was rather more noted then than now) and his wife, Marian, to establish the colony on their property in Peterborough, New Hampshire.

There are 28 very private artists' studios on the colony's 450 acres. Many of the studios are architecturally distinctive, designed by famous East Coast firms. Converted farmhouses and outbuildings form a social-administrative center, year-round housing and a dining hall.

More than 200 writers, composers, visual artists, photographers, printmakers, filmmakers, architects, interdisciplinary artists and various collaborating teams come to MacDowell from around the world each year. Composers' studios include a piano and a writing table.

MacDowell is both a retreat in which artists can work undisturbed and an intense social environment where, in the evening, residents come together not only for dinner but also for much discussion and informal, voluntary presentation of works-in-progress. The maximum length of residence at MacDowell is 2 months; the average stay is 6 weeks.

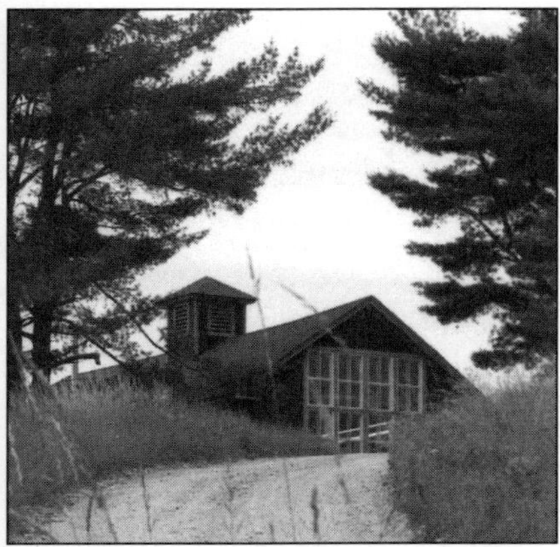

Firth Studio, MacDowell Colony, Peterborough.

New Jersey

JazzTimes Convention

For vocalists, composers *New York metropolitan area — Sheraton Meadowlands Hotel, East Rutherford, NJ 07073; 8737 Colesville Rd., 5th Fl., Silver Spring, MD 20910* **Voice:** 301-588-4119 ext. 23 **Fax:** 301-588-5531 **E-mail:** JTimes@aol.com **Contact:** Cheryl T. Goodman, Asst. Dir. **Founded:** 1984 **Open:** Early–mid-Nov. **Admission:** Registration **Deadlines:** May 31 (early registration) **Cost:** $219–$299 **Size-Attendees:** 1,000 **Handicapped Access**

JAZZTIMES IS ONE OF THE very top jazz publications. It comes out monthly and is packed with useful information for jazz lovers and for people working on all sides of the profession. One very special thing that the magazine does for its constituents is to put on one of the world's largest annual gatherings of jazz professionals, the JazzTimes Convention.

The convention began more than a decade ago as a relaxed meeting of a relatively small group of representatives from the business. Now it's a mega affair, and growing fast. Offerings run the gamut from how to run a jazz radio station fundraiser to improving your media profile to jazz in cyberspace. Showcases and similar produced events abound. An underlying thrust, year after year, seems to be working out a way to raise the public's awareness of jazz and finding ways for jazz to take more of the world's music market share.

Mason Gross School of the Arts

For instrumentalists, vocalists, composers, conductors *Rutgers University Department of Music, P.O. Box 270, Douglass Campus, New Brunswick, NJ 08903* **Voice:** 908-932-9302 **Fax:** 908-932-1517 **Contact:** Anneliese Callen, Dept. Coord. **Open:** Sept.–May **Admission:** Application ($40), audition/tape **Deadlines:** Mar. 1 (fall); Dec. 1 (spring) **Cost:** $5,389 (resident), $7,899 (nonresident) **Financial Aid:** Scholarship; Fellowship; Stipend **Size-Attendees:** 130 **Size-Class:** 10 **Degree or Certification:** DA, AD, MM, PhD, MA, MAT **Job Placement:** Yes **Handicapped Access**

A SEPARATE DEGREE-granting program associated with Rutgers University of the State University of New Jersey, the Mason Gross School of the Arts is usually just called Rutgers.

Graduate instruction is available in all orchestral instruments, keyboard, voice and choral conducting. Rutgers has a special graduate program in jazz that takes advantage of the archival materials in the Institute of Jazz Studies at Rutgers.

Rutgers is important not only because it offers graduate degrees in both classical music and jazz performance, but also because some members of its faculty are outstanding, including jazz bass player Larry Ridley, violist Michael Tree of the Guarneri Quartet, pianist Ilana Vered and composer Charles Wuorinen.

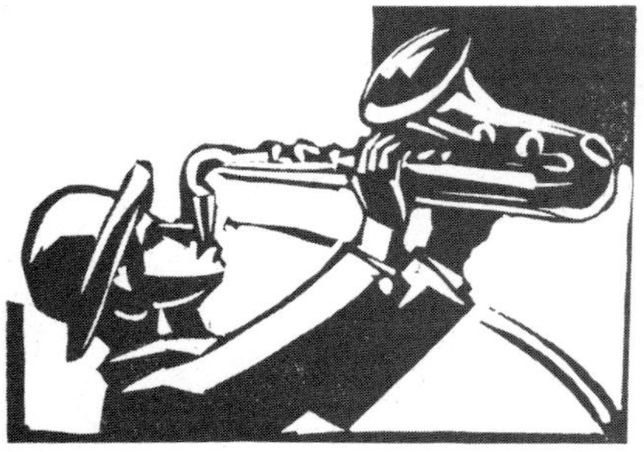

Westminster Choir College

For vocalists, organists, pianists, composers, conductors *101 Walnut Lane, Princeton, NJ 08640* **Voice:** 609-921-7100; 800-96-CHOIR **Fax:** 609-921-2538 **E-mail:** JonesH@Rider.edu **Web Site:** http://www.Rider.edu **Contact:** Heather Jones Sano, Dir. of Admissions **Founded:** 1926 **Open:** End Aug.–mid.-May **Admission:** Undergraduate: audition, transcripts, 2 letters of recommendation, test scores, personal statement, repertoire list; graduate: audition, resume, transcripts, personal statement **Deadlines:** Rolling **Cost:** $14,400; $6,300 room and board **Financial Aid:** Loans; Scholarship; Stipend; Work/Study **Size-Attendees:** 400 **Size-Class:** 15 **Degree or Certification:** BAMus, BM, MM, MME **Job Placement:** Yes

WESTMINSTER CHOIR College of Rider University is a center for music studies located in the heart of Princeton. At Westminster's core is a 4-year music college and graduate school that prepares men and women for careers in schools, universities, churches and various professional performing organizations. Programs include music theory and composition, music education, sacred music, voice, organ and piano performance and pedagogy, choral conducting, accompanying and vocal coaching.

Well known for choral excellence, the college has 7 major choirs providing students with extensive performing opportunities. The Symphonic Choir, composed of 200 upperclass and graduate students, regularly performs with the New York Philharmonic, the Philadelphia Orchestra and other major symphony orchestras. The 40-voice Westminster Choir performs throughout the U.S. and is the chorus-in-residence at the Spoleto Festival U.S.A. in Charleston, South Carolina.

New Mexico

Helene Wurlitzer Foundation

For composers *2½ hrs. N of Albuquerque — P.O. Box 545, Taos, NM 87571* **Voice:** 505-758-2413 **Fax:** 505-758-2559 **Contact:** Kenneth G. Peterson, Exec. Dir. **Founded:** 1954 **Open:** Apr.–Sept. **Admission:** Score and/or tape of recent work, project description **Deadlines:** Rolling **Size-Attendees:** 12 **Handicapped Access**

RICHARD DANIELPOUR and Daniel Brubaker are among the composers who have come to the Helene Wurlitzer Foundation of New Mexico to enjoy residencies of about 3 months, cooking and cleaning for themselves, setting their own schedules and partaking of complete solitude. This is a residency program for independent, self-motivated artists who want to get down to business. Its 12 studios are offered rent-free and utility-free to people involved in creative work of all kinds.

Wurlitzer accepts only inquiries made in writing and its waiting list has a way of stretching on for years. The program just may be worth waiting for, though; Taos's natural setting, with its mountains and dramatic skies, is food for the soul.

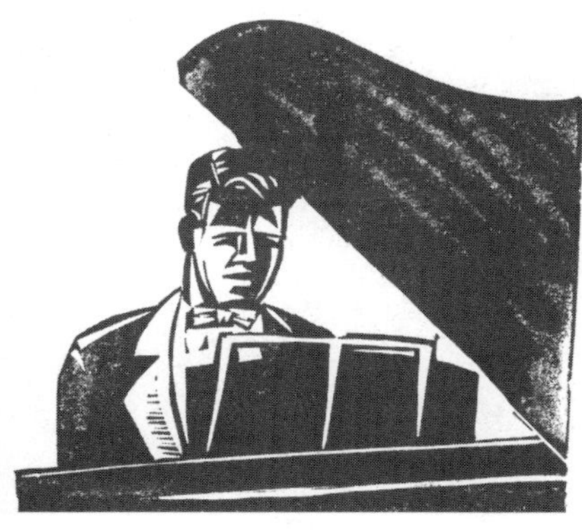

Taos School of Music

For chamber musicians *Taos Ski Valley — Hotel St. Bernard, P.O. Box 1879, Taos, NM 87571* **Voice:** 505-776-2388 **Fax:** 505-776-2388 **Contact:** Chilton Anderson, Dir. **Founded:** 1963 **Open:** June–early Aug. **Admission:** Application ($50) **Deadlines:** Mar. 1 **Cost:** Free **Size-Attendees:** 20 **Handicapped Access**

THE TAOS SCHOOL OF Music Chamber Music Festival and Program is a prestigious chamber music program located at the French-owned, family-style Hotel St. Bernard in New Mexico's Taos Ski Valley. A primary attraction of the program is that tuition, room and board are free.

Founded in 1963, Taos has been a training ground for members of such groups as the Alexander, Chester, Lark and Muir quartets and Musicians From Marlboro. Currently serving on the faculty are the American and the Takács string quartets, pianist Robert McDonald and the Guarneri Quartet's violist Michael Tree.

The program is an intensive 8-week session devoted solely to chamber music study. Students receive daily coaching, perform a great deal for one another and are encouraged to sightread as much as possible. Applying a narrow definition of chamber music, the festival takes only pianists and string players.

As summer programs go, the accommodations are exceptional. Students have private rooms in the hotel or the adjoining chalet, enjoy French cuisine, and have the full use of hotel facilities including amenities like its hot tub. The forests, streams, lakes and mountains of the surrounding Carson National Forest provide endless opportunities for hiking, climbing and fishing.

Because of the drama of its natural setting and the caliber of musicians it attracts, Taos has been the subject of feature stories on NBC's *Today* show and on National Public Radio's *Morning Edition*.

New York

Brooklyn Conservatory

For orchestral musicians, vocalists, composers, conductors *City University of New York, 2900 Bedford Ave., Brooklyn, NY 11210* **Voice:** 718-951-5286 **Fax:** 718-951-4502 **E-mail:** nhager@brooklyn.cuny.edu **Contact:** Nancy Hager, Dir. **Open:** Sept.–May **Admission:** Application ($35), audition (performance applicants), portfolio (composers), papers (musicology and performance practice applicants) **Deadlines:** Mar. 1 (fall); Nov. 1 (spring) **Cost:** $2,175 (resident), $3,800 (nonresident) **Financial Aid:** Scholarship; Stipend; Work/Study **Size-Attendees:** 2,000 **Size-Class:** 15–20 **Degree or Certification:** MA, MM **Job Placement:** Yes **Handicapped Access**

THE CONSERVATORY of Music of Brooklyn College, located on a handsome 26-acre campus in a residential section of Brooklyn, is not as well known as its Manhattan neighbors, Juilliard, the Mannes College of Music and the Manhattan School of Music. But here students may study with many of the same distinguished faculty members from those schools: prominent New York performers, composers, conductors, historians, critics and theorists. Instructional offerings feature a comprehensive curriculum in the major areas of study, special topics seminars, masterclasses, symposia, internships, guest artist appearances and a calendar of more than 150 performances by students and faculty.

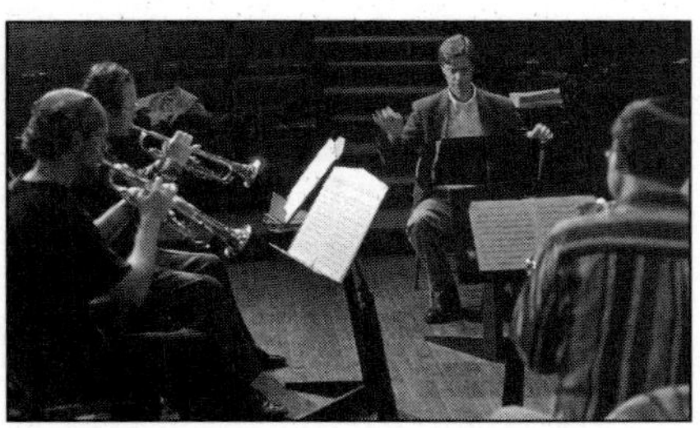

CATTRÍONA O'LEARY

Douglas Hedwig rehearsing members of the Brooklyn College Brass Ensemble.

Brooklyn Conservatory (as the school is informally known) can compete with New York's higher-profile schools. Its Performing Arts Center, for example, includes the 500-seat George Gershwin Theater, the 2,500-seat Walt Whitman Auditorium, the 170-seat Sam Levenson Recital Hall and a Workshop Theater.

And it doesn't hurt that Itzhak Perlman is on the faculty as a masterclass instructor. Top-drawer New York wind players like Charles Neidich also grace the list. Tania Leon teaches composition and conducting and directs the student Contemporary Players ensemble. Brooklyn Conservatory is part of the City University of New York (CUNY) system.

Byrdcliffe Arts Colony

For composers and performing musicians *The Catskills, 90 mi. N of New York City — 34 Tinker St., Woodstock, NY 12498* **Voice:** 914-679-2079 **Fax:** 914-679-1529 **Contact:** Katherine Berger, Coord. **Founded:** 1902 **Open:** Early June–late Sept. **Admission:** Application, tape and/or score of recent work, project description **Deadlines:** Mid-April **Cost:** June & Sept., $400; July & Aug., $500 **Financial Aid:** Scholarship **Size-Attendees:** 10 artists in residence

WOODSTOCK, AN internationally famous arts community, is home to the Byrdcliffe Arts Colony. Nestled in the Catskills some

90 miles from New York City, Byrdcliffe has offered residencies to visual artists, craftspeople, writers, musicians and theater artists since 1902. Famous musicians who have spent time at Byrdcliffe include Arnold Dolmetsch and Leon Barzin. Some other artists who have worked there are Isadora Duncan, Wallace Stevens and Chevy Chase.

For up to 16 weeks, 10 residents live in the Villetta Inn, a giant turn-of-the-century mountain lodge with a large common dining room and living room. Residents live in private rooms and work in separate, also private, studio space and cook their own meals in the communal kitchen.

Byrdcliffe is part of the Woodstock Guild, founded in 1940 to support study and practice in crafts, writing, music and theater. The Byrdcliffe estate is a National Register of Historic Places property.

Chamber Music at Mannes

For chamber musicians, including vocalists *Upper West Side — Mannes College of Music, 150 W. 85th St., New York, NY 10024; 949 West End Ave. #11C, New York, NY 10025* **Voice:** 212-749-4035, 212-580-0210 **Fax:** 212-749-4035 **Contact:** Nancy Garniez, Dir. **Founded:** 1984 **Open:** Year-round **Admission:** Registration ($20), phone interview, live audition **Deadlines:** Sept. 10 (fall); Jan. 20 (spring); June 10 (summer) **Cost:** $240 **Financial Aid:** Loans; Scholarship; Work/Study **Size-Attendees:** 45 **Size-Class:** 2–5 **Handicapped Access**

For serious New York chamber musicians of all levels, the Alaria Chamber Ensemble's Chamber Music at Mannes program has been a hit for years. Some of the students are enrolled at Mannes College of Music and others come from the local professional and semiprofessional chamber music community. All enter as individuals and are assigned to groups by Alaria members. Well more than half of the participants return each year, probably because the program makes a point to advance them meaningfully over time, through repertoire and focus of study.

Students may choose to focus on chamber music in general or specifically on sonata playing. In either case, all are required to perform in formal and informal contexts. Masterclasses are integral and the input of peers in these is regarded as critical to everyone's success in the program.

Alaria is a quartet that performs music of contrasting styles from the 15th century to the present day. The group's unusual instrumentation—violin, cello, recorder and keyboard—enhances this blend of old and very new. What the players tend to impart most is their philosophy of individual expression in chamber music playing.

"We are different because we feel an ensemble should not be homogeneous, but rather a coming together of separate, strong-minded individuals," says Alaria's Nancy Garniez. "We favor a very dynamic group interchange. The students are encouraged to have their own strengths musically and individually. We make no attempt to unify our approach." Nor does Alaria teach interpretation in the usual sense. Whereas many teachers dictate the best way to play things, Alaria attempts to draw out players' unique ideas.

This program is partially administered through the Mannes College of Music Extension Division, but is very much its own entity sustained by separate funds. Having carved out a distinctive pedagogical niche, the program is a true favorite of many local artists and listeners.

Chautauqua School of Music

For instrumentalists, vocalists *Rte. 34, 90 miles SW of Buffalo — P.O. Box 1098, Chautauqua, NY 14722* **Voice:** 716-357-6233, 716-357-6234 **Fax:** 716-357-9014 **Contact:** Richard Redington, Dir. **Founded:** 1889 **Open:** Late June–mid-Aug. **Admission:** Application ($25), audition/tape **Deadlines:** Mar. 1 **Cost:** $1,195 (instrumentalists), $1,670 (vocalists, keyboardists); $540 room, $665 board **Financial Aid:** Scholarship **Size-Attendees:** 85 instrumentalists, 35 keyboardists/vocalists **Size-Class:** 2–40 **Handicapped Access**

THE CHAUTAUQUA Institution, one of America's oldest and largest centers for the arts, education, religion and recreation, has been home base to the Chautauqua School of Music since early this century. The school trains singers and instrumentalists in musical theater, opera, orchestral repertoire and chamber music. Its resident faculty comes from such major music schools as Eastman, the Curtis Institute and Indiana University.

Chautauqua is a giant summer arts presenter, putting on major cultural events in virtually every genre. After high-quality instruction, immersion in the arts is a strong selling point to music students at Chautauqua. The institution houses nearly 7,000 people: students at the School of Fine and Performing Arts, students enrolled in Special Studies Programs and other visitors. All are free to attend a seemingly endless number of plays, films, opera, art exhibits and other presentations. It must be fun to mingle with residential visitors of world- famous stature and participate in the many and varied performance opportunities. Chautauqua has a residential symphony orchestra, an opera company, a ballet company, popular entertainment and distinguished visiting speakers and authors.

Also seductive to concertgoers and students alike is Chautauqua's physical setting. The 750-acre complex on the shore of Chautauqua Lake in southwestern New York State is a national historic district and a designated national landmark. It's really a Victorian minivillage, including such resort-style features as tennis courts, golf courses, hiking and biking trails, fishing spots and lots and lots of boats.

Eastman School of Music

For instrumentalists, vocalists, composers *Downtown — 26 Gibbs St., Rochester, NY 14604* **Voice:** 716-724-1060; 800-388-9695 **Fax:** 716-274-1088 **Web Site:** http://www.Rochester.edu **Contact:** Charles Krusentjerna **Founded:** 1921 **Open:** Year-round **Admission:** Application ($50), audition, recommendations, grades, scores **Deadlines:** Apr. 15 **Cost:** $17,850; $6,930 room and board **Financial Aid:** Loans; Scholarship; Fellowship; Work/Study **Size-Attendees:** 600 **Degree or Certification:** BM, MM, DMA, MA, PhD **Job Placement:** Yes **Handicapped Access**

GEORGE EASTMAN, founder of Eastman Kodak, established the Eastman School of Music in 1921 as the first professional school of the University of Rochester. Eastman, a self-confessed tin ear, nevertheless loved to listen to music and believed it to be a "necessary part of life."

Eastman is a big one. In 1994, *U.S. News and World Report* published a survey in which the school tied with Indiana University and the Juilliard School as having America's top master of music program. The Pulitzer Prize for music has gone to 5 Eastman graduates, the composers Domenick Argento, Gail Kubik, John LaMontaine, George Walker and Robert Ward. Some other alumni are Renee Fleming, Mitch Miller, Ron Carter and Chuck Mangione.

Eastman is prized for its faculty and its high overall musical standard of excellence. It's very strong both in classical music and in jazz. It is particularly attractive to musicians who want to take part in a thriving university, going for 2 degrees or just taking advantage of the broad range of studies such an environment can offer.

Eastman leads the pack in the vitally important area of progressive curriculum development. Facing up to the realities of today's musical marketplace, Eastman has pledged to deep-six up to one-quarter of its traditional course offerings by the year 2000, in favor of more entrepreneurial courses specifically geared to helping graduates prepare for today's work world.

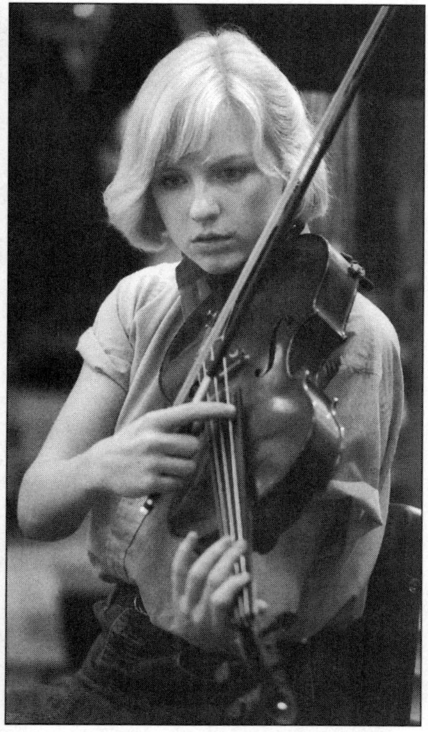

Lynn Rilling, viola student, Eastman School of Music, University of Rochester.

Juilliard School

For instrumentalists, vocalists, composers *60 Lincoln Center Plaza, New York, NY 10023* **Voice:** 212-799-5000 **Fax:** 212-724-0263 **E-mail:** juillpr@aol.com **Contact:** Joseph W. Polisi, President **Founded:** 1905 **Open:** Sept.–May **Admission:** Application ($75), audition **Deadlines:** Dec. 15 **Cost:** $13,600; $6,500 room and board **Financial Aid:** Loans; Scholarship; Fellowship; Stipend; Work/Study **Size-Attendees:** 680 **Size-Class:** 12 **Degree or Certification:** BM, MA, DMA, Perf. Cert. **Job Placement:** Yes **Handicapped Access**

The Juilliard School is widely regarded as the last word in music schools, period. Its reputation as a gateway to stardom is legendary. Juilliard turns out some of the country's best-known musicians. Composer Ellen Taaffe Zwilich, trumpeter Wynton Marsalis, and conductor Gerard Schwartz are just a few of its illustrious alumni. So are some 20 percent of players in the top 5 American orchestras and half of those in all of Lincoln Center's resident orchestras. Nevertheless, it's very important for prospective students to look at Juilliard just as coldly and carefully as they would at any other program.

Particularly for graduate students, Juilliard's primary advantage is the opportunity it affords to make key connections and to perform with professional ensembles while still in school. Few other schools draw such a consistently talented and driven body of students. Few others offer meaningful contact with the top musicians in the field.

Since coming on board in 1984, president Joseph Polisi has made strides toward making Juilliard a kinder, gentler place. During his tenure, Juilliard built a residence hall and created a student affairs office, psychological services, a newspaper and a student council. But don't kid yourself: Jailyard, as students affectionately call it, has always been highly competitive and it always will be. It's tough to get in, and it's tough to stand out.

For the stout of heart, though, Juilliard can make all the difference. Serious players, conductors and singers have numerous opportunities there to perform in New York's great halls, working closely with the top performers in the field.

One of America's most prestigious programs for training opera singers, the Juilliard Opera Center is a full scholarship program designed for advanced singers. Its curriculum allows musically qualified singers to enter at any stage of advanced development. The JOC has between 15 and 20 members, and applicants should be at least 21 years old. Faculty include many members of the Metropolitan Opera and the New York City Opera.

Juilliard's 3 regular symphonic performing ensembles, the Juilliard Orchestra, the Juilliard Symphony and the Juilliard Chamber Orchestra, give more than 30 performances each season at Lincoln Center and have appeared in Carnegie Hall as well. In addition to Otto-Werner Mueller, the school's director of orchestral studies, frequent guest conductors appear with the ensembles; among them have been Kurt Mazur, Zubin Mehta, Georg Solti and Leonard Bernstein. In recent years, Juilliard has placed new emphasis on career preparation for its students, acknowledging that even a Juilliard diploma is no guarantee in today's music market. Moving away from the traditional European music school tradition, Juilliard has now instituted a number of courses exploring career strategies and alternatives. This demonstrates that the school feels strongly its responsibility to assure its students success in the world beyond graduation.

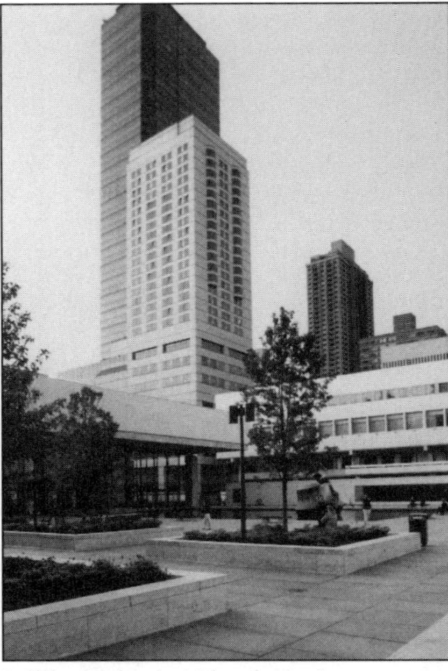

Juilliard School at Lincoln Center, New York City.

Options

Composer Arthur Bloom attended Juilliard Pre-College, Yale College, the Yale School of Music and the Aspen Music Festival and now he does it all, from composing for symphony orchestras to producing pop music.

"Crossing over" has brought Bloom artistic fulfillment and professional success, but he notes that classical musicians can be snobby about versatility.

"If I were working at Kmart, everyone would say, 'Oh, how honorable.' But when I arranged music for Michael Bolton, some of my colleagues told me I was selling my soul!"

Bloom stresses that musicians ought not to work in a vacuum. "Kids on the street use their $100 electronic synthesizers with more sophistication than you sometimes find in the electronic music studios at major music schools. Music technology has the half-life of yogurt. Pop music embraces this fact while classical music seems to deny it.

"Obviously, to write and orchestrate classically, you have to be exposed to serious training," Bloom says, "but don't let all the training keep you from having an open mind to everything else that's out there."

Le Mont Wind Chamber Music Seminar

For chamber wind players *Nyack College, Nyack, NY 10960; 158 Linwood Plaza, Ste. 227, Fort Lee, NJ 07024* **Voice:** 201-947-0312 **Fax:** 201-585-7060 **Contact:** Michele Miller, Exec. Dir. **Founded:** 1994 **Open:** Late May–mid-June **Admission:** Application ($15), audition/tape **Deadlines:** Feb. 15 **Cost:** $650 (room and board incl.) **Financial Aid:** Scholarship; Fellowship; Work/Study **Size-Attendees:** 12–15 **Size-Class:** 5 **Handicapped Access**

Clarinetist Charles Russo founded Le Mont in 1994 with his wife, the music publicist Michele Miller. Inspired by his own experiences as a student at Marlboro, Russo wants to create in Le Mont an intimate setting in which wind players can refine musical skills and explore styles and traditions in the genre. Originally located in the Berkshires, Le Mont has since moved to Nyack. Chamber music study, coachings, and masterclasses take place at Nyack College, with concerts held in various locations in town.

Amid the hundreds of programs emphasizing the string and piano literature, Le Mont stands out for specifically catering to wind players. Another distinctive feature of the program is that it focuses a good deal of energy on career management study. Masterclasses and informal sessions covering such topics as resumes and publicity, and the use of the Alexander Technique in dealing with physical tension, are all part of the package.

Charles Russo is one of the better-known clarinetists in New York. His long career includes historic appearances with the likes of Pablo Casals and Luciano Pavarotti. He has been guest soloist with such ensembles as the Juilliard, Guarneri and Emerson string quartets. Russo serves on the faculties of the Manhattan School of Music, the Hartt School, and SUNY Purchase. His previous appointments have been at Yale, Vassar and the New England Conservatory of Music.

Long Island Recorder Festival

For recorder players *New York Institute of Technology, P.O. Box 9029, Central Islip, NY 11722; 116 Scudder Pl., Northport, NY 11768* **Voice:** 516-261-8242 **E-mail:** ArcadianPr@aol.com **Contact:** Stan Davis, Coord. **Founded:** 1973 **Open:** Late June **Admission:** Application ($40) **Deadlines:** June 15 **Cost:** $270 (members), $300 (nonmembers); $290 (double), $320 (single) room and board **Size-Attendees:** 55–60 **Size-Class:** 10–12 **Degree or Certification:** In-service credit for educators

The Long Island Recorder Festival is for recorder players of all levels who are looking to learn and enjoy. The week-long workshop is held on the Central Islip campus of the New York Institute of Technology.

A typical LIRF day includes technique classes geared to varying degrees of proficiency. Each of the 3 advanced classes has a different emphasis. One concentrates on baroque, one on renaissance and one on contemporary technique. Other daily options include bass recorder ensembles, renaissance band, madrigal singing, phrasing in swing and jazz styles and renaissance dancing. Evening sightreading sessions finish each day. Instructors include past American Recorder Society president Marcia Bixler, *American Recorder*'s education editor Gene Reichenthal and LIRF workshop coordinator Stan Davis.

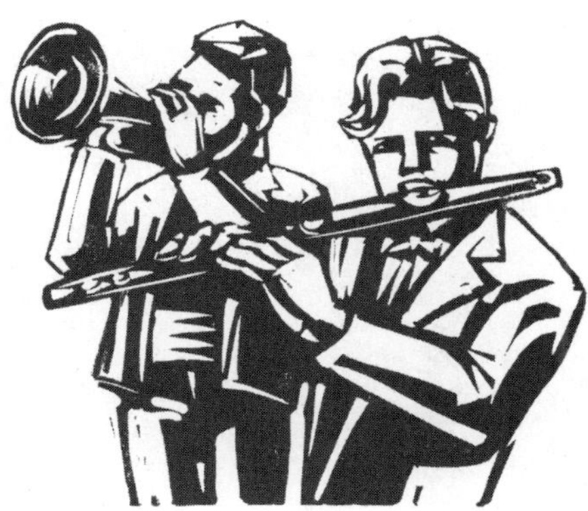

Magic Mountain Music Farm

For string players, occasionally wind players *RD 1, Box 48, Morris, NY 13808; 817 West End Ave., New York, NY 10025* **Voice:** 212-662-6634 **Contact:** Burton Kaplan, Dir. **Founded:** 1986 **Open:** May–Labor Day **Admission:** Application ($25) **Cost:** $1125 **Size-Attendees:** 11

PRACTICE HAS BEEN THE central focus of Burton Kaplan's Magic Mountain for more than a decade. Kaplan, professor of violin and viola at the Manhattan School of Music, refers to the 10-day sessions as practice marathon retreats, and musicians have sworn he has changed their musical lives for the better. Kaplan devotees turn up in orchestras and chamber groups everywhere.

The program is geared for violinists, violists and cellists, each of whom receives 4 lessons from Kaplan during the session. Two workshops per day feature ways to increase technical and artistic control. Additional daily consultations are available each afternoon. Solo performances are arranged whenever performers feel ready.

The main thing: 6 hours of practice is the goal for each marathoner. Every facet of the practice ritual is scrutinized, discussed and in many cases dramatically improved, with self-observation available through audio and video recordings.

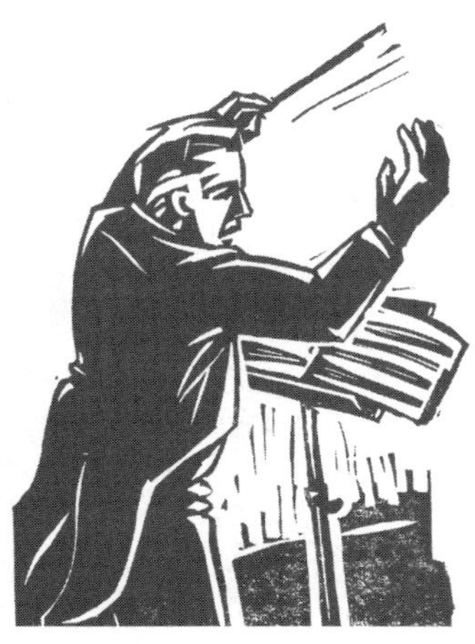

Manhattan School of Music

For instrumentalists, vocalists, composers *120 Claremont Ave. (Broadway and 122nd St.), New York, NY 10027* **Voice:** 212-749-2802 ext. 502 **Fax:** 212-749-5471 **Contact:** Lee Cioppa, Admissions Dir. **Founded:** 1918 **Open:** Sept.–May **Admission:** Application ($90), audition (video for international students) **Deadlines:** Dec. 16 (for Mar. auditions); Mar. 15 (for May auditions) **Cost:** $16,000; $9,000 housing **Financial Aid:** Loans; Scholarship; Fellowship; Work/Study **Size-Attendees:** 450 **Size-Class:** 15 **Degree or Certification:** BM, MM, DMA **Job Placement:** Yes **Handicapped Access**

THE MANHATTAN SCHOOL of Music is a leader among conservatories that offer training in both classical music and jazz. It started as a neighborhood school on New York City's Upper West Side some 75 ago, and has far exceeded anything its founder, Janet Schenck, could have imagined. Pablo Casals was among the first to contribute teaching and guidance at the school. (Casals's widow, Marta Casals Istomin, is now president of the school.)

The Manhattan School shares its neighborhood with the academic community of Barnard College, Columbia University, Union and Jewish Theological Seminaries, Columbia Teachers College and International House.

MSM does not languish in the shadow of Juilliard. In fact, the schools are close competitors in certain performance areas where faculty are particularly outstanding.

The Pinchas Zukerman Performance Program, for example, admits a limited number of violinists and violists. Mr. Zukerman gives each one 12 lessons per year. His associate, Patinka Kopec, works with students between lessons.

As is the case with most big conservatories, MSM offers masterclasses taught by visiting celebrities. Some recent participants are André Watts, Philip Glass and Yo-Yo Ma. MSM has 3 resident ensembles: the American String Quartet, the New Music Consort and the New York Wind Soloists.

Outreach is the new buzzword as music schools strive to equip graduates with the means to communicate the relevance of the art form to a wider audience. MSM is one of the few that can boast a long history of such efforts. In its first season, during the height of World War I, its students performed in camps and hospitals. This has been an ongoing tradition. Today, the spirit is alive with MSM programs like Music In Action, Music Teaches, Music Reaches and Music Heals.

Designed especially to address the professional needs of musical theater performers, the 3-week MSM Professional Musical Theater Workshop takes place in the month of June. The program features intensive hands-on training in many areas, including song and role selection for auditions, song coaching, audition techniques, acting through singing, voice lessons and career management.

MSM offers degrees in Jazz/Commercial Music, a program complemented by the MSM Summer Jazz Workshop. The workshop is for instrumentalists and vocalists who wish to pursue their studies in June and July, the height of New York's jazz festival season.

In affiliation with the JVC Jazz Festival/New York, special events feature JVC artists and other big jazz figures in performance demonstrations and panel discussions. Participants attend selected JVC Jazz Festival events free, and take part in an extended calendar of evening activities.

ENRIQUE DEL BURGO

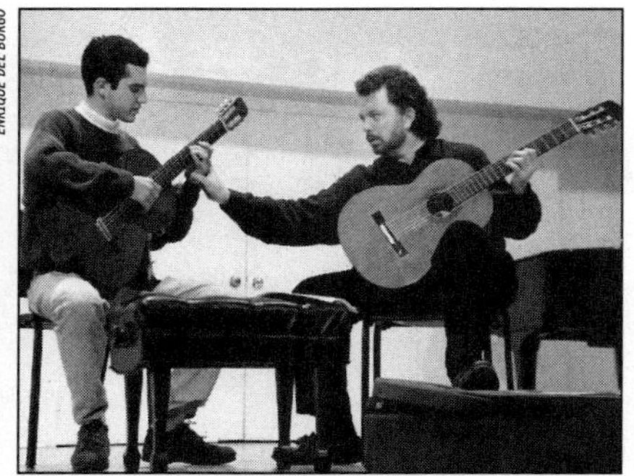

Manuel Barrueco, right, conducts a masterclass, Manhattan School of Music, New York City.

Mannes College of Music

For instrumentalists, vocalists, composers, conductors *Upper West Side — 150 W. 85th St., New York, NY 10024* **Voice:** 212-580-0210; 800-292-3040 **Fax:** 212-580-5281 **Contact:** Lisa C. Wright, Dir. Adm. **Founded:** 1916 **Open:** Sept.–May **Admission:** Application ($75), audition **Deadlines:** 4 wks. before audition date **Cost:** $15,520 **Financial Aid:** Loans; Scholarship; Work/Study **Size-Attendees:** 175 **Size-Class:** 1–100 **Degree or Certification:** BM, BS, MM, Dip. **Job Placement:** Yes **Handicapped Access**

Of New York City's 3 famous centers for the study of classical music—Juilliard, Manhattan and Mannes—Mannes is the small one, with fewer than 300 students. In large part because of its size, Mannes has come to be regarded as the special one among the 3 schools.

The school, housed in a charming Federal-style building on the Upper West Side, enjoys a reputation as a friendly and supportive place in the sometimes cutthroat world of major American music schools.

Deep and sustained educational involvement is possible between students and teachers at Mannes. Every name on the faculty is well known—including a number of first-chair New York Philharmonic and Metropolitan Opera Orchestra players—but absent are some of the superstar performers you see at other schools of this caliber. A teacher who's too busy touring to show up for regular lessons is not good in the end for much more than window dressing. Apparently Mannes recognizes this fact of life, engaging such artists more appropriately for masterclasses appearances.

The curriculum at Mannes is rooted in fundamentals, with strong emphasis placed on ear training, theory, harmony, dictation and analysis. It was at Mannes, after all, that Schenkerian analysis was pioneered, in the 1930s. Mannes College is part of the New School, a multifaceted university specializing in the arts, humanties and social sciences. Mannes students can take liberal arts courses in

Discipline

Viola and *virtuoso* are two words that do not often go together. For all its beauty of sound and soulfulness of expression, the viola is not always exactly dazzling. But, as Paul Neubauer has proved on many occasions, an instrument is no more or less virtuosic than the person playing it.

Neubauer seems like someone for whom everything has come easily. At 17 he won the prestigious Lionel Tertis Prize, beating out people twice his age. At 21, he became the youngest principal-chair string player in the New York Philharmonic's history. After 5 years he gave up that post to concertize as a soloist and chamber musician. He has been in high demand ever since. "I've been very lucky," he says.

But talk to Neubauer, and you learn that he's worked enormously hard for his success. A faculty member at the Juilliard School, he says, "I'm always surprised to find students who think that some teacher is going to solve every problem they have. I believe students need to do all the most important work themselves. I'm shocked when students say they don't have enough time to practice. I find this hard to believe. When I was in the New York Philharmonic, I'd be with my viola all day, and I'd still come home to practice."

Neubauer gets excited about students who show self-discipline and a measure of creative autonomy. The ones who are more aware of what they want musically are always the best students. Once a student can hear a sound or musical effect in his or her own mind, Neubauer feels the teacher can step in and make a difference, helping to show how to achieve musical goals with the instrument. "Your ear is the most important thing. It's when you don't hear anything, within yourself, that nothing happens.

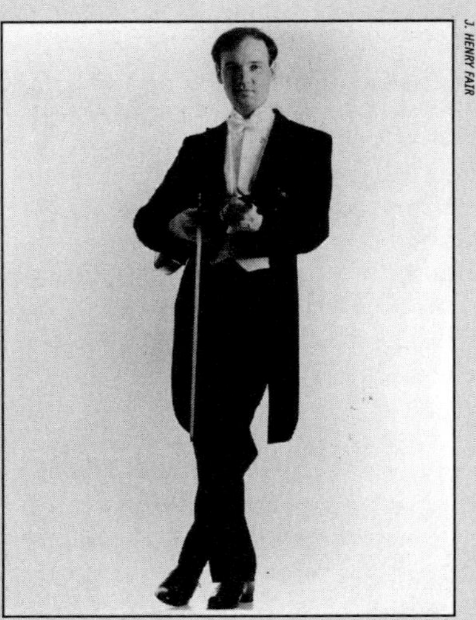
J. HENRY FAIR

Paul Neubauer, violist.

"I've always felt from my own experience, that learning never goes up in a straight incline. Progress will be flat for a long time (which can be frustrating) and all of a sudden there will be a jump when something just comes together somehow. It's a very personal, internal process."

Neubauer says that musicians should be prepared to stay motivated and to work hard through even the darkest times.

other New School divisions and interact with students at Parsons School of Design or the School of Dramatic Arts.

Mannes Jazz and Contemporary Music Program

For instrumentalists, vocalists, composers, arrangers *Greenwich Village — New School for Social Research, 55 W. 13th St., New York, NY 10011* **Voice:** 212-229-5896 ext. 302 **Fax:** 212-229-8936 **Web Site:** http://www.jazzcentralstation.com; http://www.NewSchool.edu **Contact:** L. E. Howell, Asst. Dir., Admissions **Founded:** 1986 **Open:** Last wk. Aug.– late Dec; 3rd wk. Jan.–2nd wk. May **Admission:** Application ($50), audition/tape, high school transcript or GED college transcript (if applicable), personal statement **Deadlines:** Apr. 1 (fall); Nov. 15 (spring) **Cost:** $14,580; $8,132 room and board; $150 registration fees **Financial Aid:** Loans; Scholarship; Work/Study **Size-Attendees:** 210 **Size-Class:** 10–12 **Degree or Certification:** BFA **Job Placement:** Yes **Handicapped Access**

SITUATED IN THE New School for Social Research in the heart of New York City's Greenwich Village, the Mannes Jazz and Contemporary Music Program affords talented students the opportunity to study with the masters of the art form. Faculty members are professional musicians who represent the past, present and future of jazz.

The course of study is based on small ensemble playing, and students also work intensively in the areas of composition, arranging and the business of music. Enrollment in the program has grown from 30 in 1986 to more than 200. Styles of music represented include classic jazz to bebop to Afro-Cuban to free jazz, the blues, world music and beyond.

Meadowmount School of Music

For string players *RFD #2, Box 2230, Westport, NY 12993; c/o Michigan State University School of Music, East Lansing, MI 48824* **Voice:** 518-873-2063, 517-349-6767 **Fax:** 518-962-2310, 517-349-6767 **E-mail:** carman@pilot.msu.edu **Contact:** Owen Carman, Dir. **Founded:** 1944 **Open:** Late June–mid-Aug. **Admission:** Application, tape, letter of recommendation **Deadlines:** Mar. 1 **Cost:** $1,500; $1,700 room and board **Financial Aid:** Scholarship; Work/Study **Size-Attendees:** 200 **Size-Class:** 1

IVAN GALAMIAN, icon of 20th-century violin pedagogy, believed that the ideal way to train violinists would be to spirit them off to an isolated place in the country with fresh air and time for practice without distractions. In 1944, he bought an old house in the Adirondacks and founded the now legendary Meadowmount School of Music. Many of today's leading violinists, violists and cellists have spent summers at Meadowmount, including Itzhak Perlman, Pinchas Zukerman, Kyung Wha Chung, Yo-Yo Ma and Joshua Bell. Since 1954 the school has operated under the aegis of the Society for Strings of New York City.

Following Galamian's death in 1981, the school endured a period of painful transition lasting several years. Today, thanks to the perseverance of Galamian's widow, Judith Galamian, and Meadowmount's new director, Owen Carman, the school is still very much on the map, continuing to enjoy its reputation as probably the most intense summer study environment available to young string players destined for solo and chamber music careers of distinction.

The Meadowmount daily schedule includes 5 hours of supervised practice and rehearsal. Weekly lessons, masterclasses and chamber music coachings prepare students for the 3 to 4 student concerts each week.

The staff includes Sally Thomas, violin teacher of guru status, and Margaret Pardee. Both were longtime teaching associates of Galamian. Five pianists provide accompaniment for concerts, and an in-house luthier keeps up with all the stressed-out fiddles.

Many of the students that arrive at Meadowmount (on the strength of taped auditions and teacher recommendations) come with a mix of prodigious, world-class talent and the often intensely complex personal issues that can accompany such gifts. For artists from the high-strung Michael Rabin to the more down-to-earth Yo-Yo Ma, Meadowmount has been a sanctuary of sorts, a place to withdraw from the world, to be understood and nurtured within the familiar context of hard work. Like a truly great instrumentalist, wrote Henry Roth in *The Strad* magazine, Meadowmount has a singular personality of its own, easily distinguishable from any other summer music school of its type.

Omega Institute for Holistic Studies

For all musicians *Hudson Valley, 90 mi. N of New York City — 260 Lake Dr., Rhinebeck, NY 12572* **Voice:** 914-266-4444; 800-944-1011 **Fax:** 914-266-3769 **Web Site:** http://www.omega-inst.org **Contact:** Andrea Johnson, Registrar **Founded:** 1977 **Open:** Spring–fall **Admission:** Varies **Deadlines:** 2 wks. in advance **Cost:** $200–$600 **Financial Aid:** Scholarship; Work/Study **Size-Attendees:** 50

OMEGA INSTITUTE IS a new-age center famous for its summer workshops. The themes are healing, recovery, self-help and spiritual discovery at Omega, where workshops run from 2 to 9 days in length. Music workshops include Healing with Spirit and Sound; Songmaking: Finding Our Own Song; and Shabda Yoga: the Mysticism of Sounds and Spirituality of Music. Recent music workshop teachers have included

Practicing

Ivan Galamian was very much concerned about his students at Meadowmount and elsewhere—their studies, their careers, their work habits. He is known to have called some of his "lazy" students early in the morning to tell them, "I'm glad I woke you up. Why aren't you practicing?" He believed in hard work. "Go home and practice!" was his standard remark. But he also believed that careers are not made in heaven: they are built with effort. "I tell them over and over: You have to push. You have to grow calluses on your head from pushing."

(From *Great Masters of the Violin* by Boris Schwarz, Simon & Schuster, 1983.)

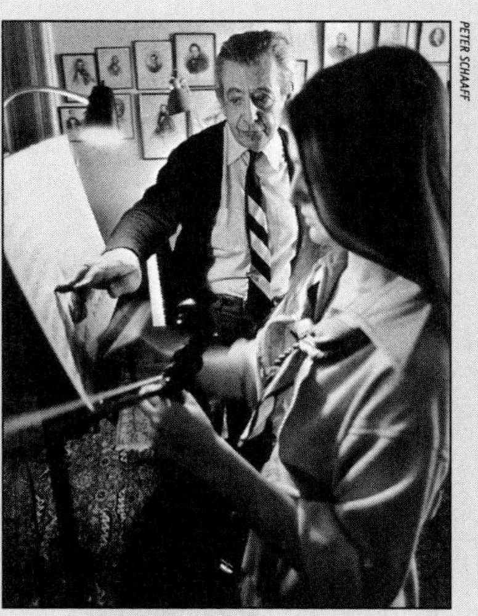

PETER SCHAAFF

The late Ivan Galamian instructs a student, Meadowmount School of Music, Westport.

Austin country music star Jimmie Dale Gilmore and Karl Hans Berger, a performer who blends African and Asian styles with Western classical forms and jazz. Accommodations at Omega range from simple, shared cabins to camping out. Meals are served in a large dining hall with a porch.

Pianofest in the Hamptons

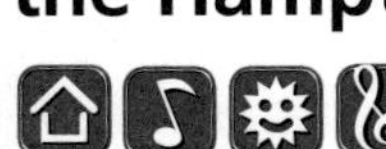

For pianists *100 miles E. of NYC — Southampton College, 239 Montauk Hwy, Southampton, NY 11969; P.O. Box 663, Southampton, NY 11969* **Voice:** 516-283-2044 **Fax:** 516-283-8754 **E-mail:** barbara.goldowsky@hamptons.com **Contact:** Paul Schenly, Dir. **Founded:** 1989 **Open:** Mid-June–mid-Aug. **Admission:** Application ($10), audition/tape **Deadlines:** Rolling until June 1 **Cost:** $1,500; $250/wk. room and board **Financial Aid:** Scholarship; Work/Study **Size-Attendees:** 10 **Handicapped Access**

Although it is one of America's smaller summer music festivals, Pianofest in the Hamptons has no difficulty attracting talented young pianists from all over the world. Most are in their twenties.

Pianofest boasts not only a world-class teaching staff but also a world-renowned string of beaches along the coast of New York's Long Island. Every summer, the dozen or so pianists practically leap at the chance to participate in 8 weeks of rigorous music training in such a beautiful setting.

The relaxed atmosphere, however, rather than detracting from, actually enhances the intensive musical efforts of both students and guest artists. In a world where the classical music job market has become increasingly cutthroat, Pianofest emphasizes support over competition among its participants, paying particular attention to accompanying skills and to the duo piano literature. Daily lessons are frequently attended by peers, and students are encouraged to give one another helpful feedback. Weekly masterclasses are run by director Paul Schenly, his faculty members Awadagin Pratt and Sergei Babayan and guest artists like André Watts, Richard Goode and Claude Frank. The classes are open to the public.

Quarters are not reputed to be terribly comfortable. Students practice in a private home crammed with pianos and lacking air conditioning and soundproofing. Of course, it can be argued, aspiring musicians can use all the character building they can get.

Southampton Chamber Music Festival

For instrumentalists, vocalists *Long Island University — 39 Montauk Hwy, Southampton, NY 11968; 6130 W. 87th St., #12R, New York, NY 10024* **Voice:** 516-283-4000 **Fax:** 212-496-5092 **E-mail:** bjbley@aol.com **Contact:** Annabel Gordon, Artistic Dir. **Founded:** 1994 **Open:** Last 3 wks. July **Admission:** Application, tape (suggested), resume/repertoire list **Deadlines:** June 1 **Cost:** Per weekend: $350 (room and board incl.); $250 (with meals only, for commuters) **Financial Aid:** Scholarship **Size-Attendees:** 40–45 **Handicapped Access**

Founded in 1994, Long Island's Southampton Chamber Music Festival seeks to inspire instrumentalists to make music as beautifully as their skill allows, and to present faculty concerts to the community. The program takes place over 3 consecutive summer weekends and is open to players of all ages and abilities. In 1995 the festival established the Marilyn Gordon Scholarship Fund to help musicians with financial needs to attend the workshops and concerts.

The Southampton Chamber Players, the resident ensemble of the festival, features a 20th-century work on each of its concerts. The ensemble members are cellist Annabel Gordon, pianist Jonathan Bley, violist Vincent Lionti and clarinetist Miriam Lockhart. To serve the festival's mission to make classical music seem less stuffy, performers talk to the audience about the music they will play, and play passages to listen for before each piece begins.

Yaddo

For composers *Foothills of the Adirondacks, less than 1 hr. N of Albany — P.O. Box 395, Union Ave., Saratoga Springs, NY 12866*
Voice: 518-584-0746 **Fax:** 518-584-1312
Contact: Candace Wait, Program Coord.
Founded: 1926 **Open:** Year-round, except certain weeks in Sept. **Admission:** Application ($20), resume, recommendations, score and recording of recent work **Deadlines:** Aug. 1 (Oct.–May); mid-Jan. (mid-May–Feb.) **Cost:** Voluntary $20/day contribution **Size-Attendees:** 35 summer; 15 winter **Handicapped Access**

WHAT (OR RATHER WHOM) do the MacDowell Colony and Yaddo have in common? Leonard Bernstein, Aaron Copland and Virgil Thomson. But that's not all. The 2 artists' retreats have been neck-and-neck for the whole of this century: they are the all-round most desirable residency programs for composers, writers, visual artists, choreographers, performance artists and video and filmmakers alike.

The property on which Yaddo is situated was purchased in 1881 by New York financier Spencer Trask and his poet wife, Katrina Trask, and named "Yaddo" by their young daughter (she was trying to say "shadow"). The Trasks held grand parties and salons there, and by 1900 they had turned the place into an artist colony. Their intent was to offer creative artists uninterrupted work time, comfortable living space and good artistic companionship. To this day, Yaddo succeeds brilliantly at doing precisely those things.

Almost 200 artists are invited to Yaddo each year, which is about one-fifth the number of artists who apply. As at MacDowell, the mood at Yaddo is intense and the primacy of work is taken very seriously.

Yaddo's "quiet" hours are between 9 a.m. and 4 p.m. and after 10 p.m. During these times, no visiting is allowed

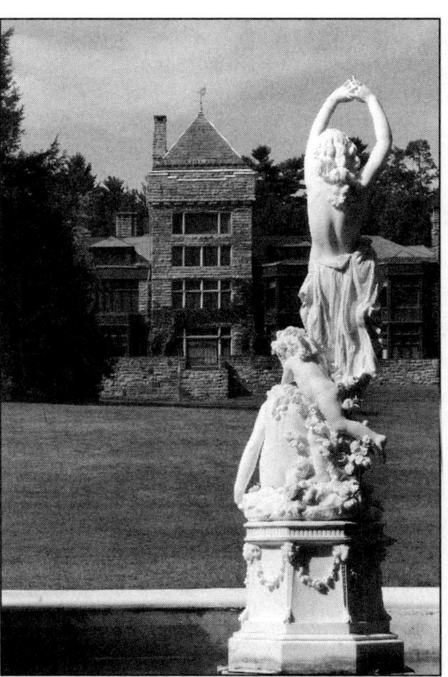
JOE LEVY

Yaddo mansion, Saratoga.

without invitation. There are no formal workshops at Yaddo, or readings or performances of any kind for that matter. And no accommodations can be made for spouses or friends or even pets at Yaddo. So be prepared to go it alone.

North Carolina

Appalachian State University School of Music

For instrumentalists, vocalists, composers, conductors *Appalachian State University, Boone, NC 28608* **Voice:** 704-262-3020 **Fax:** 704-262-6446 **E-mail:** harbinsonwg@appstate.edu **Web Site:** http://www.acs.appstate.edu/dept/music **Contact:** Dr. Arthur Unsworth, Dean **Founded:** 1899 **Open:** Year-round **Admission:** Acceptance to the university, live or tape audition **Deadlines:** June 1 **Cost:** $769 (resident), $4,011 (nonresident); $1,315 (housing/meal plan) **Financial Aid:** Loans; Scholarship; Fellowship; Work/Study **Size-Attendees:** 300 **Size-Class:** 20 **Degree or Certification:** BM, BS, MM **Job Placement:** Yes **Handicapped Access**

MUSIC EDUCATION is a strong thrust at Appalachian State University's School of Music, where half of the 300 music majors intend to teach professionally. Another popular major at the school is Music Industry Studies, a program that prepares graduates to work in a range of fields, from record producing to marketing to music administration.

Brevard Music Festival

For instrumentalists, vocalists, composers, conductors *Western NC — P.O. Box 312, 1000 Probart St., Brevard, NC 28712* **Voice:** 704-884-2011 **Fax:** 704-884-2036 **E-mail:** brevardmusic@pipeline.com **Web Site:** http://www/lightnin.brevard.edu/bmc **Contact:** John Candler, Pres.; David Effron, Artistic Dir. **Founded:** 1936 **Open:** Third wk. June–1st wk. Aug. **Admission:** Application ($50), audition/tape, recommendations, score and recording of original composition (if applicable) **Deadlines:** Early Feb. (vocalists); early Mar. (all others) **Cost:** All-inclusive: $2,400 (full session), $1,300 (half session) **Financial Aid:** Scholarship; Fellowship; Work/Study **Size-Attendees:** 360–370

FOR 7 WEEKS EACH summer, the tiny Blue Ridge Mountain town of Brevard enjoys the presence of more than 350 musicians aged 13 through postgraduate level, a faculty and staff of 120, and thousands of fans flocking to the area to attend Brevard Music Festival concerts at the Brevard Music Center. The focus is orchestral music, chamber music, choral music, accompanying, opera, composition and conducting.

BMF began in 1936 as the Davidson College Music School-Camp. In 1964 the conductor Henry Janiec began a long and fruitful tenure as artistic director, reorganizing the program and attracting such big names as pianists Gina Bachauer, Alicia de Larrocha and Van Cliburn and pop singers Andy Williams and John Denver. Janiec has retired, handing things off to David Effron.

The list of performing artists and resident faculty at Brevard includes some heavy hitters, like New York Philharmonic concertmaster Glenn Dicterow, piano virtuosos Vladimir Feltsman and Lee Luvisi and mezzo-soprano Frederica von Stade. About one-third of BMF students are from North Carolina.

Eastern Music Festival

For instrumentalists *Greensboro-Triad Area — Guilford College, 5800 W. Friendly Ave., Greensboro, NC 27410; P.O. Box 22026, Greensboro, NC 27420* **Voice:** 910-333-7450 **Fax:** 910-333-7454 **E-mail:** emf@nr.infi.net **Contact:** James C. Newlin, Exec. Dir. **Founded:** 1962 **Open:** Mid-June–Aug. 1 **Admission:** Application ($35), audition/tape **Deadlines:** Mar. 31 **Cost:** $1,940; $1,185 (room and board) **Financial Aid:** Scholarship; Work/Study **Size-Attendees:** 200 **Handicapped Access**

PEOPLE WHO ATTEND the Eastern Music Festival just seem to want to stick around. Such present-day EMF guest artists as Wynton Marsalis and such regular faculty members as Jennifer Combs, Chelsea Tipton and Rodney Mack came to the festival as students themselves years back. In fact, the average stay for EMF students is 11 consecutive years, which is virtually unheard of in this industry.

The 2.5-to-1 student-to-teacher ratio is surely one of the factors that makes EMF special for so many. Also, the program is noted for an atmosphere that is at once both professional and supportive. It eliminates competition by rotating seating within its 2 orchestras and programming them both with equally challenging music. And yet the standard for excellence is high and the competition for admission stiff. Live auditions are held in 28 states and 3 foreign countries. Over the years, the residencies of Marsalis, Claude Frank, Josef Gingold, Leonard Rose and the Guarneri String Quartet have become legendary.

A statement in the EMF brochure jumps off the page: "The life of a professional musician is about finding out what your best is, and then learning how to go beyond that. It's about turning weak points into strengths. It's about how to make Beethoven speak, and finding your own voice in the process. It's about respecting yourself and your colleagues, and finding self-worth through the hardest work of your life."

Glickman-Popkin Bassoon Camp

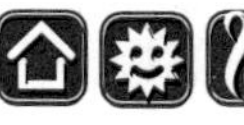

For bassoonists *Wildacres, P.O. Box 280, Little Switzerland, NC 28749; 740 Arbor Rd., Winston-Salem, NC 27104* **Voice:** 910-725-5681 **Contact:** Mark A. Popkin **Founded:** 1978 **Open:** Late May **Admission:** Application, $100 refundable deposit **Cost:** $440 (all-inclusive) **Size-Attendees:** 50

FOR NEARLY 20 YEARS, hordes of bassoonists have come together at Little Switzerland's Wildacres Retreat to revel and obsess over the joys and frustrations of bassoon playing and reed making.

Mark Popkin and Loren Glickman are key players on the greater New York bassoon scene, longtime friends and the coauthors of an important book on bassoon reed making. Popkin has been principal bassoonist of the New Jersey Symphony, the New York City Center Opera and the Mostly Mozart Festival Orchestra on tour. He has arranged wind music for Theodore Presser, designs and markets bassoon reed-making tools and teaches on the faculty of the North Carolina School for the Arts.

Glickman has performed as soloist with the Chamber Music Society of Lincoln Center, the Mostly Mozart Festival, the Casals Festival and on chamber and orchestral recordings on several prominent labels. He is also a composer and conductor of film scores and an important New York freelance contractor.

Famous guest artists-in-residence are always a hit at Glickman-Popkin. In 1995 they included David McGill, principal bassoonist of the Cleveland Orchestra, and John Hunt, bassoon professor at the Eastman School of Music. Bassoon makers, restorers and reed-business personalities show up with regularity as well.

Players are advised to shape up their lips ahead of time for the rigorous schedule. Each day begins with reed class, followed by studio class. After lunch, guest artists hold masterclasses, and at 4 p.m. students show their stuff in a recital followed by dinner and the evening class.

North Carolina School of the Arts

For instrumentalists, vocalists *200 Waughtown St., P.O. Box 12189, Winston-Salem, NC 27117* **Voice:** 910-770-3255 (school of music); 910-770-3291 (admissions) **Fax:** 910-770-3370 **E-mail:** rothkm@ncsavx.ncarts.edu **Web Site:** http://www.ncarts.edu **Contact:** Robert Yekovich, Dean, Music School **Founded:** 1963 **Open:** Late Aug.–late May **Admission:** Application ($35), audition, transcript, recommendations, SAT/ACT **Deadlines:** Rolling; auditions preferred before Mar. 1 **Cost:** $1,308 (resident), $9,159 (nonresident); $1,930 (room); $1,776 (meal plan) **Financial Aid:** Loans; Scholarship; Work/Study **Size-Attendees:** 30 **Degree or Certification:** BM, MM, College Arts Diploma **Handicapped Access**

Asked to name the most prestigious arts high schools in America, most people will name the North Carolina School of the Arts and Interlochen Arts Academy. Unlike Interlochen, however, the NCSA also accommodates undergraduate- and graduate-level students. In fact, NCSA, founded in 1965 as the first state-assisted residential conservatory in the nation, is really 5 professional schools in one. NCSA's is an interdisciplinary environment. Music students can benefit from working alongside dancers, filmmakers, actors and visual artists.

The MM program offers major studies in brass, conducting, organ, piano, saxophone, strings, woodwinds, guitar and voice, as well as chamber music performance, opera, and film music composition. Students also play in school orchestras and get a strong grounding in theory, ear training, the business of music and contemporary and electronic music.

Selected students are professionally engaged through apprenticeship programs and affiliations. Groups maintaining paying positions for NCSA students include the Western Piedmont Symphony, the Piedmont Opera Theatre and the North Carolina Symphony Apprenticeship Program.

The Intensive Arts program offers lessons, masterclasses, workshops and interdisciplinary electives during the 2 weeks following Thanksgiving break. During the summer, the school holds a 5-week session designed to give students individual attention with an emphasis on artistic and personal growth.

The school boasts many successful graduates, but in listing them it does not indicate which of those graduates attended the graduate school and which are alumni of the middle- and high-school programs. Many on the music

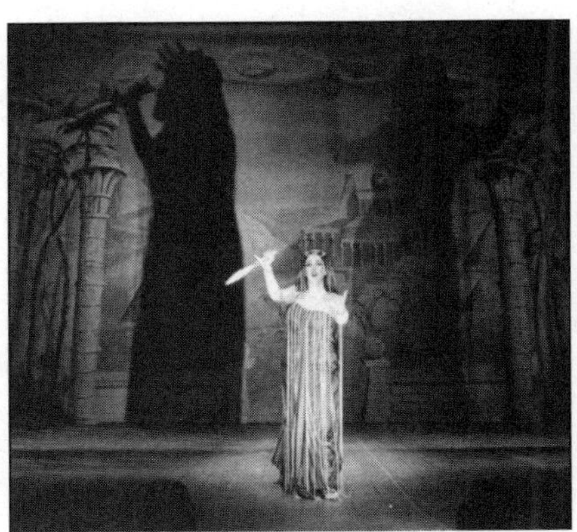

LENNY COHEN

The Impresario, as presented by the North Carolina School of the Arts.

faculty have put in long teaching careers at the school but are not especially well known otherwise.

Ohio

Baroque Performance Institute

For musicians interested in baroque music *Northern Ohio — Oberlin Conservatory, 77 W. College St., Oberlin, OH 44074* **Voice:** 216-775-8044 **Fax:** 216-775-8942 **E-mail:** Anna_Hoffman@qmgate.cc.oberlin.edu **Contact:** Anna Hoffman, Adm. Dir. **Founded:** 1971 **Open:** Last 2 wks. June **Admission:** Application ($75) **Deadlines:** End of May **Cost:** $660; $190 (double), $230 (single) **Financial Aid:** Scholarship **Size-Attendees:** 100 **Size-Class:** 15 **Handicapped Access**

RUN BY BAROQUE cellist and viola da gamba virtuoso Kenneth Slowik, the Oberlin Conservatory's Baroque Performance Institute is an internationally admired program in early music. Oberlin Baroque Ensemble members Lisa Goode Crawford, Michael Lynn, Marilyn McDonald and Catharina Meints lead a faculty that includes other well-known names in early music. The program comprises daily masterclasses and ensemble coachings, concerts, lectures, private lessons, recitals, student orchestra, chorus and baroque dance and gesture classes. Ready for use is the conservatory's enormous collection of harpsichords, organs and fortepianos, baroque violins, cellos, viols, flutes, oboes and bassoons. BPI welcomes musicians of all levels.

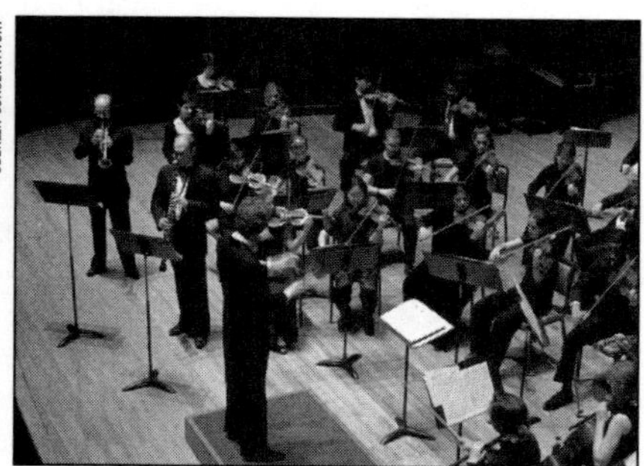
OBERLIN CONSERVATORY

In concert, Baroque Performance Institute, Oberlin.

Cleveland Institute of Music

For instrumentalists, vocalists, composers, conductors *Near downtown — 11021 East Blvd., Cleveland, OH 44106* **Voice:** 216-795-3107 **Fax:** 216-791-1530 **E-mail:** cimadmission@po.cwru.edu **Web Site:** http://www.cwru.edu/CIM/cimhome.html **Contact:** E. William Fay, Dir. of Admissions **Founded:** 1925 **Open:** Year-round **Admission:** Application ($60), audition, transcripts, letters of recommendation, examinations **Deadlines:** Oct. 15 (spring); Dec. 15 (fall) **Cost:** $15,540; $5,065 room and board **Financial Aid:** Loans; Scholarship; Work/Study **Size-Attendees:** 350 **Size-Class:** 15 **Degree or Certification:** BM, MM, DMA, Dip., Artist Dip., Prof. Studies Dip. **Handicapped Access**

THE CLEVELAND INSTITUTE of Music is to the Cleveland Orchestra what Northwestern University is to the Chicago Symphony Orchestra: the primary teaching venue in town. The faculty, headed by president (and active violinist) David Cerone, includes more than 30 members of the orchestra. As a result, CIM attracts a great many talented and promising students.

CIM stresses career preparation with several programs focusing on readiness. The Intensive Quartet Seminar, Chamber Music Festival and Apprenticeship Quartet Program are available to string students interested in chamber music careers. The school sponsors the biennial Cleveland International Piano Competition, the biennial Arts Song Festival, the summer Encore School for Strings and, in cosponsorship with Lyric Opera Cleveland, the summer Vocal Arts Apprenticeship Program. CIM also offers its students a 5-year double degree program in cooperation with nearby Case Western Reserve.

Not only is high-quality training available to orchestra players at CIM, but the chamber music opportunities are truly world-class. The school has 4 ensembles in residence: the Naumburg Award–winning Cavani String Quartet, the Cleveland Chamber Players, the Hecht-Shapiro duo piano team and the Weilerstein Duo. In addition, chamber music students can work with a long list of chamber music faculty, including the likes of Peter Salaff, founding violinist of the Cleveland Quartet and director of the string chamber music studies department.

Cleveland is a major center for early music, the home base of the service association Early Music America. Distinguished members of that community make the trek to the Oberlin Conservatory 30 miles away to teach, and some work at CIM, including keyboardists Janina Kuzma Ceaser and Karl Paukert and EMA executive director Beverly Simmons.

The vocal training program includes intensive study in art song, oratorio and opera. The sequence of opera courses focuses on the theory and practice of the various arts—musical, linguistic and dramatic—that come together in opera. The department puts on multiple performances of 2 fully staged productions each year, as well as a shorter program of opera scenes.

CIM was founded in 1920 and had as its first director the celebrated composer Ernest Bloch, who attracted other famous composers to the school, including Quincy Porter and Roger Sessions. During its formative years, CIM grew from a school with a collegiate enrollment of 25 students and 19 faculty to one with more than 350 students and 90 full- and part-time instructors. By limiting enrollment, CIM stands out for the personal attention it gives each student.

CIM is located in University Circle, a cultural, educational and scientific enclave situated about 3 miles east of downtown. Its 500 acres includes Case Western Reserve, numerous libraries, museums, hospitals, gardens, concert halls, churches and temples. It's the heart of the city.

Finding Your Own Way

Maxine Roach, violist in the jazz/classical crossover Uptown String Quartet, has done the music school thing. She went to Oberlin Conservatory and later studied for a year in Europe at a program called the Institute for Advanced Musical Studies (no longer in existence). There she studied with viola greats Paul Doctor, William Primrose and Heidi Castleman.

So what was the most meaningful influence on Roach's musical life? "In the end you have to just do it your own way," she says. "The greatest artists always end up being people who have done things on their own." Roach's father, Max Roach, is surely one example.

The conservatory experience was stimulating. But Roach's favorite part of coming up in music was listening to her father's friends, her teachers and her mentors tell stories, not all of them about music. "I loved listening to William Primrose talk about baseball," she says.

Encore School for Strings

For string players *Midway between Akron and Cleveland — Western Reserve Academy, 115 College St., Hudson, OH 44236; c/o Cleveland Institute of Music, 11021 East Blvd., Cleveland, OH 44106* **Voice:** 216-650-9744 **Web Site:** http://www.cwru.edu/CIM/cimhome.html **Contact:** David Cerone, Dir. **Founded:** 1985 **Open:** Late June–early Aug. **Admission:** Application ($250), tape **Deadlines:** Mar. 1 **Cost:** $3,000 (all-inclusive) **Financial Aid:** Scholarship; Work/Study **Size-Attendees:** 170 **Size-Class:** 1–10

WITHIN A 6-WEEK period of concentrated work, Encore seeks to guide advanced string players through individual study and in-depth chamber music work.

The school, administered by Cleveland Institute of Music president David Cerone, is located at Western Reserve Academy, a preparatory school in Hudson, Ohio. Hudson is a historic, New England-like town 8 miles northeast of Blossom Music Center, summer home of the Cleveland Orchestra.

A typical day at Encore starts with 4 hours of practice followed by private lessons, chamber music coachings, rehearsals, lectures or free time. There are concerts, masterclasses and recreational activities in the evenings.

Not only is Encore a summer offshoot of the Cleveland Orchestra, but it also boasts faculty associated with the Cleveland Institute. Highlights of the roster include violinists Jascha Brodsky and Victor Danchenko and Cleveland Orchestra principal violist Robert Vernon.

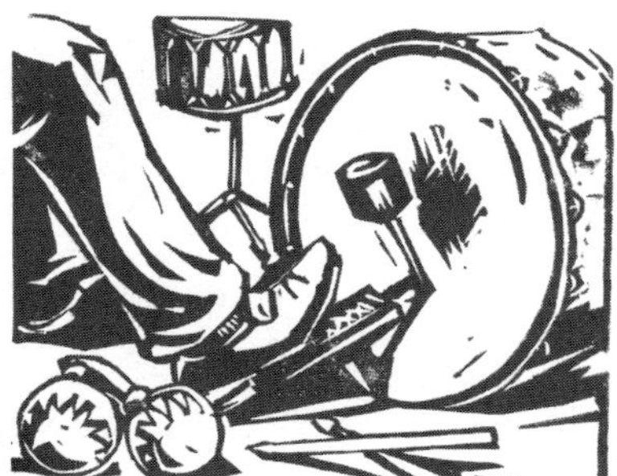

Glauser School of Music

For instrumentalists, vocalists, composers *Near Cleveland — Kent State University, Kent, OH 44242* **Voice:** 330-672-2172 **Fax:** 330-672-7837 **Contact:** Dr. John Lee, Dir. **Open:** Year-round **Admission:** Application, audition/tape, undergraduate degree in music **Cost:** $4,323 (resident), $8,511 (nonresident) **Size-Attendees:** 300 **Size-Class:** 15 **Degree or Certification:** MA, MM, PhD **Handicapped Access**

THE HUGH A. GLAUSER School of Music at Kent State University offers programs leading to undergraduate and graduate degrees for students seeking professional competence in instrumental or vocal music. Glauser's Center for the Study of World Musics has recently been established as a division of the school, and instruction is available there not only from Kent State University faculty, but from visiting scholars from a variety of Asian and African countries. The music education department is particularly strong, offering study in jazz, folk, musical theater, classical music and world musics. The Glauser School of Music is also home to Kent/Blossom Music, sponsored by Kent State University and the Cleveland Orchestra.

Grandin Festival

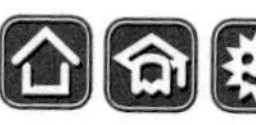  ***For instrumentalists, vocalists*** *Conservatory of Music, University of Cincinnati, Cincinnati, OH 45221* **Voice:** 513-556-9198 **Fax:** 513-556-0202 **Contact:** Barbara Honn, Sara Lambert Bloom, Artistic Dirs. **Founded:** 1994 **Open:** Last 2 wks. Aug. **Admission:** Application (no fee), tape, letter of recommendation **Deadlines:** May 15 **Cost:** $1,086 **Financial Aid:** Scholarship; Stipend **Size-Attendees:** 75 **Degree or Certification:** MMus, AD, DMA, BMus **Job Placement:** Yes **Handicapped Access**

THE GRANDIN FESTIVAL is a 2-week session offering study and performance of chamber music for voice and ensemble. Renowned guest artists coach ensembles alongside members of the Cincinnati College–Conservatory of Music faculty. The student core comprises CCM students and a limited number of advanced students and young professionals from outside CCM.

Oboist Sara Lambert Bloom runs Grandin with her colleague at CCM, the soprano Barbara Honn. Members of the resident faculty include pianist James Tocco, tenor Thomas Baresel and percussionist Allen Otte. Guest coaches have included clarinet virtuoso Charles Neidich, violinist James Buswell and singers Ruth Dobson and Warren Jones.

Grandin has a special place among summer chamber music programs because it specializes to such an extent in the type of literature studied. Given the caliber of the teaching at Grandin, this will continue to do a great deal to promote mixed voice and instrumental chamber music, some pieces of which are among the best on this earth.

Kent/Blossom Music

For instrumentalists, vocalists *Kent State University, P.O. Box 5190, Kent, OH 44242* **Voice:** 330-672-2613 **Fax:** 330-672-7837 **E-mail:** jlacorte@phoenix.kent.edu **Contact:** Jerome La Corte, Coord. **Founded:** 1968 **Open:** First wk. July–2nd wk. Aug. **Admission:** Application ($30), tape/audition **Deadlines:** Mar. 1 **Cost:** $100 participation fee (housing incl.) **Size-Attendees:** 40 **Handicapped Access**

A NATIONAL TRAINING center for professional musicians operated by Kent State University in cooperation with the Cleveland Orchestra and the Blossom Music Center, Kent/Blossom Music presents concerts by artist faculty and students for 6 weeks each summer. The educational focus is on chamber music, orchestral audition preparation and masterclass work.

Since 1968, some 1,750 young artists have come to Kent/Blossom for instruction from 200 teachers. The orchestra is conducted by Blossom Festival director Leonard Slatkin. Artist faculty groups include the Miami String Quartet, members of the Cleveland Orchestra and visiting artists from major orchestras and conservatories. Some students perform in the Kent/Blossom Chamber Players, which puts on free concerts at Kent/Blossom. Others play in the Blossom Serenades performances that precede Cleveland Orchestra concerts in the Blossom Music Center Pavilion.

Oberlin Conservatory of Music

For instrumentalists, vocalists, composers, conductors *77 W. College St., Oberlin, OH 44074* **Voice:** 216-775-8413 **Fax:** 216-775-6972 **E-mail:** conad-mail@ocvaxc.cc.oberlin.edu **Web Site:** http://www.oberlin.edu **Contact:** Michael Manderen, Dir., Conservatory Admissions **Founded:** 1867 **Open:** Sept.–May **Admission:** Application ($50), audition/tape, high school transcript, 2 recommendations from music teachers **Deadlines:** Feb. 15 **Cost:** $20,600; $2,970 room, $3,000 board **Financial Aid:** Loans; Scholarship; Work/Study **Size-Attendees:** 600 **Degree or Certification:** BM, MM **Job Placement:** Yes **Handicapped Access**

WHEN IT'S A MATTER OF music schools, good things almost always come in small packages. The Oberlin Conservatory of Music, with its student enrollment of just 600 and its location in an archetypical old-fashioned Midwestern small town, is surely among America's elite schools of music. Conservatory students get a lot of individual attention from faculty members, a number of whom are Cleveland Orchestra members. Several studios are particularly strong; Oberlin has a tradition of placing flute and oboe students in the world's best orchestras, for example, and the training in baroque performance at Oberlin is the best there is.

Oberlin is primarily undergraduate, but offers 5-year programs that yield graduate degrees in music education or conducting. This is worthy of note, as the school has turned out excellent music educators and such internationally acclaimed conductors as Michael Morgan and Robert Spano.

The conservatory is the soul of Oberlin College, whose total student count does not exceed 3,000. The campus is saturated with music, and for academic majors interested in taking lessons or doing a double degree with music, access is easy. Fun fact: Oberlin was the first music conservatory in America.

Ohio State University School of Music

For instrumentalists, vocalists, composers *Ohio State University, Columbus, OH 43210* **Voice:** 614-292-7664 **Fax:** 614-292-1102 **Web Site:** http://www.cgrg.ohio-state.edu/other/music/ **Contact:** Don Gibson, Dir. **Founded:** 1870 **Open:** Year-round **Admission:** Admission to university, audition, requirements vary by program **Deadlines:** Variable **Cost:** $4,942 (resident), $12,833 (nonresident) **Financial Aid:** Loans; Scholarship; Fellowship; Stipend; Work/Study **Size-Attendees:** 550 **Size-Class:** 20 **Degree or Certification:** MA, MM, PhD, DAM **Job Placement:** Yes **Handicapped Access**

AS ONE OF THE largest universities in the world, Ohio State University offers a wealth of resources on campus. In the midst of it all is the School of Music, offering professional training leading to degrees in performance, composition, music education, music history, music theory, jazz studies and conducting. The school has a full-time faculty of more than 60 professors.

In addition to the school's traditional merits—strong faculty, excellent facilities—the School of Music at Ohio State is distinguished by the special opportunities it holds out for interdisciplinary study. For example, scholars at the School of Music and in the psychology department conduct ongoing research in the area of music perception and cognition. And music students collaborate with students at the Advanced Computing Center for the Arts and Design on research in computer animation and graphics. Ohio State University School of Music alumni include the clarinet virtuoso Richard Stolzman, Metropolitan Opera soprano Barbara Daniels and Grammy-winning recording engineer Jack Renner.

Oklahoma

Oklahoma City University School of Music and Performing Arts

For instrumentalists, vocalists, composers, church musicians *2501 N. Blackwelder, Oklahoma City, OK 73106* **Voice:** 405-521-5351 **Contact:** Laura Mitchell, Dir. **Founded:** 1901 **Open:** Sept.–May **Admission:** Application ($20), audition, 3 letters of recommendation, test scores **Deadlines:** Aug. 15 **Cost:** $11,265 (all-inclusive) **Financial Aid:** Loans; Scholarship; Work/Study **Size-Attendees:** 275 **Degree or Certification:** BM, BME, MM **Handicapped Access**

SITUATED IN THE northwest section of Oklahoma City, the 60-plus–acre campus of Oklahoma City University has been run by the United Methodist Church (since the 3 branches of Methodism joined). The university was set up as a private school in 1901 by the Methodist Episcopal Church, working with the Oklahoma City Chamber of Commerce.

The school provides instruction for those interested in careers in performance, teaching and church music. A thorough theoretical and performance foundation is available for students planning graduate work. The school's major performance ensembles are the Chamber Choir, the University Orchestra, the Choral Union, the Surrey Singers, the Pep Band, the Kenesha Kids, the Jazz Ensemble, and the University Band, along with other vocal and instrumental ensembles. Besides classrooms, the Fine Arts building houses 2 auditoriums, 15 studios with electronic equipment, 25 practice rooms and an instrumental rehearsal room.

Oregon

Conducting Masterclass

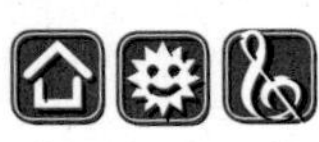 ***For conductors*** *University of Oregon — 1257 University of Oregon, Eugene, OR 97403* **Voice:** 541-346-5666; 800-457-1486 **Fax:** 541-346-5669 **Contact:** Dr. Thomas Somerville, Dir. **Founded:** 1970 **Open:** End June–mid-July **Admission:** Application (no fee), audiotape, videotape of rehearsal, resume **Deadlines:** Mar. 1 **Cost:** $950; $650 housing **Size-Attendees:** 40 **Handicapped Access**

TWENTY-EIGHT YEARS ago the Oregon Bach Festival was set up as a training ground for conductors. The festival has grown to become one of the most celebrated choral-orchestral music festivals in America. Under artistic director Helmuth Rilling, it presents such major works as the *St. Matthew Passion*, the *Missa Solemnis* and the *German Requiem*. Education is still at the core of the program, however.

The festival's Conducting Masterclass is intended mainly for conductors with a specialty in choral music, university conducting instructors, church music directors and choir conductors and community choir conductors, as well as masters- and doctoral-level conducting students. Masterclass time is balanced between seminars, rehearsals and work in the concert hall. In performance, participants conduct the festival choir, orchestra and soloists in the Discovery Series of lecture-concerts. Class work consists of 3 core seminars.

University of Oregon School of Music

For instrumentalists, vocalists, composers, conductors *1225 University of Oregon, Eugene, OR 97403* **Voice:** 541-346-3761 **Fax:** 541-346-0723 **E-mail:** gamartin@oregon.uoregon.edu **Contact:** Dr. Gary Martin, Assoc. Dean **Founded:** 1876 **Open:** Sept.–May **Admission:** Application ($50), audition, transcripts, 3 letters of recommendation, test scores **Deadlines:** June 1 **Cost:** $2,590 (resident), $10,300 (nonresident); $3,900 room and board **Financial Aid:** Loans; Scholarship; Work/Study **Size-Attendees:** 345 **Degree or Certification:** BM, MM, DMA **Handicapped Access**

THE SCHOOL OF MUSIC at the University of Oregon is housed in a complex that includes a 550-seat concert hall and a variety of state-of-the-art facilities, among them a music library equipped with interactive CD-ROM programs and a remote control–activated listening room. The 3 computer music studios at the school contain programs for an array of synthesis techniques, algorithmic composition, Midi sequencing and composition, as well as digital recording and editing in a fully automated mixing environment. The school offers advanced degrees in music history, music theory, conducting, piano pedagogy, composition, music education, performance and jazz studies. Faculty members include pianist Barbara Gonzalez-Palmer, musicologist Marian Elizabeth Smith and violinist Kathryn Lucktenberg. Since 1969 the school has conducted the annual Oregon Bach Festival during a 2-week period in late June and early July.

Pennsylvania

Curtis Institute of Music

For vocalists *Center City — 1726 Locust St., Philadelphia, PA 19103* **Voice:** 215-893-5262 **Fax:** 215-893-0194 **Contact:** Chris Hodges, Adm. Dir. **Founded:** 1924 **Open:** Sept.–May **Admission:** Application, audition **Deadlines:** Jan. 15 **Cost:** Full-tuition scholarship **Financial Aid:** Scholarship; Work/Study **Size-Attendees:** 15 **Size-Class:** 15 **Degree or Certification:** MM

Curtis Institute of Music, of course, is right up there with Juilliard when it comes to glittering alumni, a hallowed history, intense competition and great expectations all around.

But Curtis is different from Juilliard—and all the rest—because of 2 particular quirks. Curtis likes students young; it actually imposes an age limit on incoming students. This funnels perhaps some of the world's greatest—and youngest—prodigies directly into the school, especially because of Curtis's second distinguishing feature: it's free. It accepts students solely on the basis of talent and awards all students full-tuition scholarships.

Curtis does offer graduate degrees in one area: the MM program in opera. It requires a minimum of 33 credits and normally takes at least 2 years to complete. Each student receives at least 2 vocal coaching sessions per week. Each school year the Curtis Opera Theater generally stages 3 productions jointly with the Curtis Symphony Orchestra.

There is also the professional studies certificate in opera, available to incoming students without a prior music degree. The program parallels the opera masters program, except that no degree is awarded upon completion. The opera faculty includes voice coaches Susan Shiplett Ashbaker and Mikael Eliason and Danielle Orlando, principal opera coach.

Curtis was founded in 1924 by Mary Louise Bok (later Mrs. Efrem Zimbalist),

The Business of Music

Before 1986, when Gary Graffman became president and director of the Curtis Institute of Music, he enjoyed more than 3 decades as one of America's most celebrated piano soloists, performing in the most famous concert halls with the world's top orchestras, recording for the most popular record labels.

"For some of us, things have been relatively easy," Graffman says, adding that for the most famous musicians, business has a way of remaining relatively stable. A scholar and a collector of Oriental art, he says that in this respect the classical music world is like the art world: "When the market for Chinese pieces goes down, it affects 90 percent of the objects being sold; you can lose a lot of money on something you bought for $10,000. But the ups and downs have no effect on the top-of-the-line stuff. A $2 million plate will always be worth $2 million."

Many feel that Curtis, a tiny school known for its illustrious faculty and full scholarships for all, is America's best conservatory. But Graffman, himself a Curtis grad, says there are no guarantees for any music student anywhere. Four years ago, to help prepare Curtis students more fully for the realities that face all but a few, he instituted a course in the business of music, now a requirement for all seniors at the school.

a woman of vision with a great love of music. Since 1928 the school has maintained its famous scholarship policy and remains the only major conservatory to provide full tuition to all students regardless of their financial situation.

Duquesne University School of Music

For all musicians *School of Music, Duquesne University, 600 Forbes Ave., Pittsburgh, PA 15282* **Voice:** 412-396-6080; 800-934-0159 **Fax:** 412-396-5479 **E-mail:** jordanof@duq2.cc.duq.edu **Web Site:** http://www.duq.edu/music/music.html **Contact:** Nicholas Jordanoff, Dir., Music Admissions **Founded:** 1926 **Open:** Year-round **Admission:** Audition, written theory exam, oral musicianship test **Deadlines:** Mar. 15 (scholarship consideration); July 1 (acceptance) **Cost:** $16,412; $5,803 room and board **Financial Aid:** Loans; Scholarship; Fellowship; Stipend; Work/Study **Size-Attendees:** 350 **Size-Class:** 15 **Degree or Certification:** BM, BS, MM, Art. Dip. **Job Placement:** Yes **Handicapped Access**

Duquesne University School of Music is a large private music school. In addition to its full-time faculty roster of 25 well-known leaders in the fields of music therapy, technology, composition and performance, the 76-member adjunct faculty includes 25 members of the Pittsburgh Symphony Orchestra. Music has been a central part of Duquesne since its inception as the Pittsburgh Catholic College of the Holy Ghost in 1878. The School of Music opened its doors in 1926 and, as the years passed, it added new degree programs and established itself as a regional leader, particularly in music education, music therapy and sacred music. Because of the university's historic commitment to public service, the School of Music runs the Duquesne City Music Center, the area's largest community music school, bringing musical training to people of all ages and backgrounds throughout the Pittsburgh region.

Philadelphia Music Conference

For people interested in all styles of commercial music *Downtown — The Doubletree Hotel Philadelphia, Broad St. at Locust, Philadelphia, PA 19107; P.O. Box 29363, Philadelphia, PA 19125* **Voice:** 215-426-4109 **Web Site:** http://www.gopmc.com **Founded:** 1992 **Open:** Late Oct.–early Nov. **Admission:** Registration, fee **Deadlines:** Mid-Oct. **Cost:** $165 (discounts for early registration) **Size-Attendees:** 3,000

The Philadelphia Music Conference was founded in 1992 as the first conference to bring together people interested in all types of commercial music, with an emphasis on rock, hip-hop and acoustic music. Since then, PMC has become one of the fastest-growing music conferences in the country. Attendance is near 3,000, with about 15,000 coming to related nighttime events. The 1996 PMC hosted more than 40 seminars.

Quite a number of the bands showcased at PMC have gone on to sign major record deals. They include Anthrophobia, Divine Beings, the Nixons and

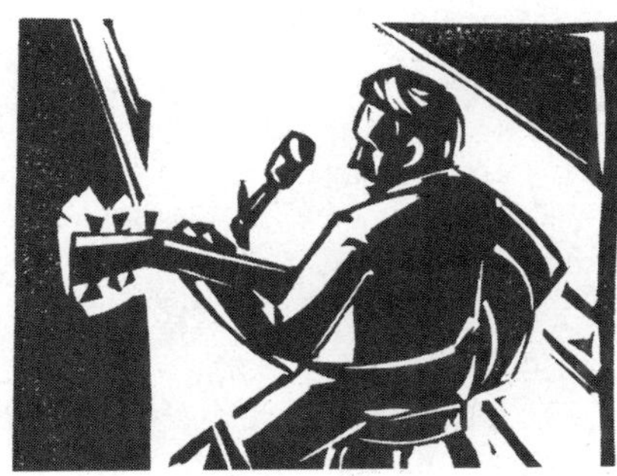

Pull My Daisy. In addition to exposure to reps from big labels, the conference affords learning opportunities. Classes have covered such topics as how to attract management and legal representation, starting and running your own independent label and the facts about advances, options and recoupment.

Quartet Program

For violinists, violists, cellists, pianists *Eastern Pennsylvania — Bucknell University, Lewisburg, PA 17837; 1163 East Ave., Rochester, NY 14607* **Voice:** 716-274-1592 (winter), 716-523-4911 (summer) **Fax:** 716-442-4282, 716-523-4910 **E-mail:** ccastleman@aol.com **Contact:** Charles Castleman, Dir. **Founded:** 1970 **Open:** Third wk. June–2nd wk. Aug. **Admission:** Application ($35), audition/tape **Deadlines:** Mar. 15 **Cost:** $2,795 **Size-Attendees:** 36 **Handicapped Access**

For nearly 30 years, the Quartet Program at Bucknell University has brought together musicians from around the world to learn to meet the demands of chamber music: how to adjust to colleagues under the conditions of a professional position and how to play better both as individuals and as ensemble members.

Thirty-six musicians participate in the 7-week program. Each gets a chance to participate in masterclasses and also to work up and perform at least 1 solo and 2 quartets. Coaches include violinist Pamela Frame, QP founder Charles Castleman and Jeffrey Irvine.

Quartet Program alumni have won top prizes at the Tchaikovsky, Brussels, Munich, Naumburg, Szeryng and Leventritt solo competitions and, in chamber groups, have won the Banff, Evian, Portsmouth, Munich, Naumburg, Fischoff, Coleman and Concert Artist Guild prizes. They work in top-ranked orchestras and ensembles around the world.

SummerTrios

For chamber musicians *Moravian College, 1500 Main St., Bethlehem, PA 18018; P.O. Box 1062, New York, NY 10025* **Voice:** 212-222-1289 **Fax:** 212-866-7129 **Contact:** Lily Friedman, Music Dir. **Founded:** 1991 **Open:** 1 wk. in July **Admission:** Application/deposit $75; tape (for placement only) **Deadlines:** June 15 (early payment discount by Apr. 1) **Cost:** $425–$850 (room and board incl.) depending on program **Financial Aid:** Work/Study **Size-Attendees:** 85 **Handicapped Access**

Of the hundreds of summer chamber music workshops that take place around the country, SummerTrios is the only one specifically geared to the chamber music pianist. Most of the others focus on the string quartet repertoire with a smattering of woodwinds and pianists. While most accept a handful of pianists, SummerTrios enrolls 25, serving amateurs, students and young professionals.

The camp runs for 1 week. Different programs accommodate players of varying levels of accomplishment. About half the groups are coached. There are good opportunities to improve sight-reading. Performing is optional. On the SummerTrios faculty are pianists Jan

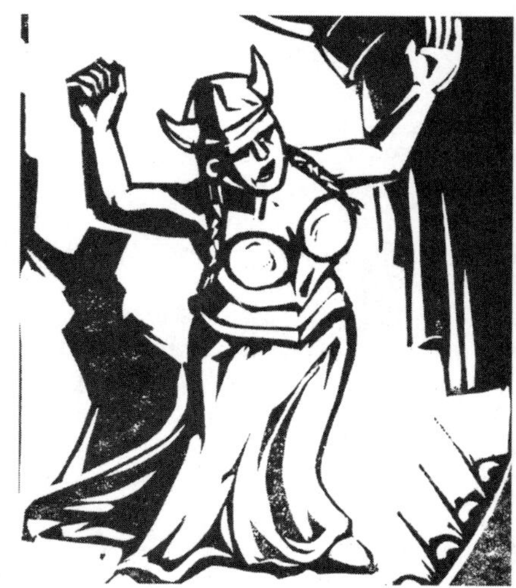

Deats, Benita Rose and SummerTrios director Lily Friedman, clarinetist Todd Palmer and violinist Suzanne Gilman.

The program takes place at Moravian College in a historic landmark district, in a building once used as a hospital by George Washington.

Walnut Street Theatre School

For vocalists *825 Walnut St., Philadelphia, PA 19107* **Voice:** 215-574-3550 ext. 510 **Fax:** 215-574-3598 **E-mail:** wstheater@aol.com **Contact:** William Roudebush, Dir. **Founded:** 1981 **Open:** Sept.–Dec.; Jan.–April; May–Aug. **Admission:** Audition (no fee) **Cost:** $265–$325 **Financial Aid:** Scholarship; Work/Study **Size-Attendees:** 10–15

Based in what claims to be America's oldest theater, Walnut Street Theatre School is a popular Delaware Valley theater training ground. Professionals teach 12-week sessions of classes to all levels of students.

The school has 3 divisions. The Discovery Division is for those eager to develop hidden talents that may lead to a career in theater or who simply want to acquire self- confidence and improve communication skills.

The Development Division is for people already working on a career in the theater who want to develop competitive industry skills. And the Master's Division is for experienced performers who embrace the continual need to learn.

Musical courses include Music Theatre Technique in the Discovery Division, Singing for the Musical Theatre in the Development Division, and The Music Theatre Studio in the Master's Division.

Rhode Island

Brown University Department of Music

For instrumentalists, vocalists, composers, conductors *Downtown — Brown University, Providence, RI 02912* **Voice:** 401-863-3234 **Contact:** Gerald Shapiro, Chair **Open:** Aug.–May **Admission:** Application ($40), test scores **Deadlines:** Jan. 1 **Cost:** $11,690; $2,245 room, $1,635 board **Financial Aid:** Loans; Scholarship; Work/Study **Size-Attendees:** 200 **Size-Class:** 1–100 **Degree or Certification:** BM, MMA **Handicapped Access**

Graduate degree programs are offered at Brown University's music department in the areas of composition, musicology and ethnomusicology. Faculty include the composer Gerald Shapiro, the ethnomusicologist Henry Kingsbury and music theorist James Baker. Beyond traditional applied study, numerous colorful opportunities exist for performers. For example, students may perform on the Balinese gamelon, with a Trinidadian steel drum ensemble or a Ghanian drumming and dancing group or in an old-time string band. The Brown University Orchestra, conducted by Paul Phillips, won the 1994 ASCAP-College Orchestra Award and has performed with Itzhak Perlman, Eugenia Zukerman, Dave Brubeck and other famous artists. Under the baton of Matthew McGarrell, Brown's Wind Symphony has toured London and Paris.

Tennessee

Academy of Gospel Music Arts

For aspiring songwriters and artists *Eight different cities, varying each year — 1205 Division St., Nashville, TN 37203* **Voice:** 615-242-0303; 800-GMA-3211 **Fax:** 615-254-9755 **E-mail:** GMATODAY@AOL.COM **Web Site:** http: //www.GOSPELMUSIC.ORG **Contact:** Lance Kaufman, Manager **Founded:** 1994 **Open:** Sept.–Apr. **Admission:** Anyone may register for the 2-day event **Deadlines:** Vary **Cost:** $100 (GMA members); $150 (nonmembers) **Size-Attendees:** 100–200 **Size-Class:** 50–75 **Handicapped Access**

A 2-DAY EVENT that takes place at various times and at various locations around the country, the Academy of Gospel Music Arts was developed to provide continuing education for Christian music performers and to raise the artistic standard of music in Christian churches and other venues. The program offers feedback, encouragement and mentoring to performing participants through artists-in-residence.

For each AGMA session, a different major industry talent joins the staff to share his or her expertise with participants. Guests have included Michael W. Smith and Charlie Peacock. The AGMA programs are administered by the Gospel Music Association, a membership organization serving artists, industry leaders, retail stores, radio stations, concert promoters and local churches involved in Christian music.

Crossroads Music Exposition

For bands, singer/songwriters, soloists *Downtown — P.O. Box 41858, Memphis, TN 38174* **Voice:** 901-526-4280 **Fax:** 901-527-8326 **Contact:** Corey Robertson, Managing Dir. **Founded:** 1991 **Open:** Mid-Aug.–mid-May **Admission:** Application ($20), tape, biography, photo **Deadlines:** Jan. 31 **Size-Attendees:** 1,000–2,000 **Handicapped Access**

CROSSROADS MUSIC Exposition is a cross-cultural music convention. Its purpose is to give dozens of young, unsigned performers the opportunity to perform for professionals in the music industry. Many popular genres are featured, such as blues and country, alternative rock, hard rock and gospel. Record companies, publishers, managers, attorneys and media from around the country gather to see the region's latest crop of new talent.

During the weekend-long event, there are panels and workshops in which various industry professionals offer instruction and advice. Each year, at least 1 band or artist gets signed to a major record deal as a result of the conference. A 501(c)(3) corporation, Crossroads generates revenue both through corporate sponsorships and through ticket sales.

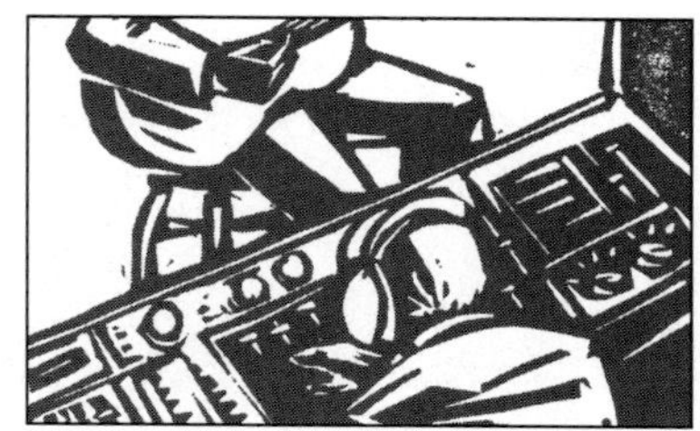

Gospel Music Week

For vocalists, songwriters *Renaissance Nashville Hotel and the Nashville Convention Center, Nashville, TN 37203; 1715 Division St. Nashville, TN 37203* **Voice:** 615-242-0303 ext. 223 **Fax:** 615-254-9755 **E-mail:** GMATODAY@AOL.COM **Web Site:** http://www.gospelmusic.org **Contact:** Marti Bushore, Customer Service **Founded:** 1964 **Open:** Last wk. Apr. **Admission:** Application (fee) **Deadlines:** Preregistration: mid-Apr. **Cost:** $275 (GMA members); $350 (nonmembers) **Size-Attendees:** 2,000 **Size-Class:** 300 **Handicapped Access**

HELD EACH APRIL in the Renaissance Nashville Hotel and the Nashville Convention Center, Gospel Music Week features 5 days of educational workshops, concert showcases and informational events. The purpose of the week is to nurture the growth and development of Christian music by bringing together all aspects of the industry, including not only performers, but also record companies, retail, radio, video, concert promotion and members of the press. Drawing an average of 3,000 participants nationwide, GMW offers educational programs on trends in Christian music and also features the final rounds of a national songwriting and talent competition.

GMW is a program of Gospel Music America, a service association based in Nashville. GMA's other well-known educational program is the Academy of Gospel Music Arts, a 2-day educational seminar held in 8 cities nationwide. Locations and details of the academy vary from year to year.

Nashville Songwriters Association Workshops

For songwriters *Loews Vanderbilt Plaza Hotel, Nashville, TN 37203; 15 Music Square W., Nashville, TN 37203* **Voice:** 615-256-3354 **Fax:** 615-256-0034 **Web Site:** http://songs. org/NSAI **Contact:** Events Coordinator, NSAI **Open:** Year-round **Admission:** Registration **Cost:** Varies **Size-Attendees:** 350 **Handicapped Access**

THE NASHVILLE Songwriters Association International is believed to be the largest nonprofit songwriters association in the world. Among the benefits of membership is being kept up to date on the various annual events and educational programs NSAI administers in Nashville. These include Song Camp 101, a 3-day songwriting retreat held in April and July, in which professional songwriters provide instruction in the craft of songwriting and in supercharging creativity and the lyrical and musical tools of the trade. Participants can follow up with Song Camp 102 in October.

NSAI's offerings don't end there. The Spring Symposium and the Summer Seminar are educational conferences that let registrants learn from and network with music industry professionals. NSAI's Nashville Workshop meets each week. The workshops feature guest speakers, song critiques and more. Regional workshops are held throughout the U.S. and in some foreign countries.

Sewanee Summer Music Festival

For instrumentalists, composers *Between Nashville and Chattanooga; University of the South campus — 735 University Ave., Sewanee, TN 37383* **Voice:** 615-598-1225 **Fax:** 615-598-1706 **Contact:** Martha McCrory, Exec. Dir. **Founded:** 1957 **Open:** Late June–July **Admission:** Application, tape, recommendations by teachers **Cost:** $1,750 (all-inclusive); private lesson $130 **Financial Aid:** Scholarship **Size-Attendees:** over 200 **Degree or Certification:** Cert. of Achievement **Handicapped Access**

BACK IN 1957, Sewanee Summer Music Festival was founded with the mission to encourage young people to enter the world of music performance. The festival admits students of all ages to participate in the program, which takes place at the University of the South's 10,000-acre campus.

Students are housed in dormitories, eat in university dining halls and make use of various other university facilities. Every participant is assigned to orchestra, chamber music and theory courses according to age and ability. Faculty members are drawn from symphony orchestras in the South, from Nashville's Blair School of Music, and from as far away as Brussels.

This is a serious, intensive program requiring discipline from all members. Everyone follows a tight schedule and accomplishes a lot in only 5 weeks. Sewanee is one of the region's major summer concert presenters.

A typical summer features performances by student ensembles as well as by such world-class groups as the Tokyo String Quartet.

Texas

Kerrville Songwriters School

For songwriters *Outdoor Theater, Quiet Valley Ranch, 5600 Medina Hwy., Kerrville, TX 78029; P.O. Box 1466, Kerrville, TX 78029* **Voice:** 210-257-3600; 800-435-8429 **Fax:** 210-257-8680 **E-mail:** kfest@hilcomet.com **Web Site:** http://www.fmp.com/~kerrfest **Contact:** Rod Kennedy, Dir. **Founded:** 1979 **Open:** Late May (School I); early June (School II) **Admission:** $144 preregistration (School I); $200 preregistration (School II), taped song, lead sheet (School II; must have completed School I in past 10 yrs.) **Cost:** $144 (School I); $200 (School II); free camping, 3 lunches included in both schools **Financial Aid:** Scholarship **Size-Attendees:** 30–60 **Handicapped Access**

FOR 3 DAYS EACH May, in the middle of the Kerrville Folk Festival, Nashville's Rick Beresford directs some of the nation's best songwriters in a curriculum designed to provide emerging and advanced songwriters with a chance to investigate, analyze and experience the craft and process of songwriting.

The program includes 18 hours of classes per school, 3 meals and camping on the Kerrville Music Foundation ranch. Besides Beresford, faculty for the school include Gail Davies and Dr. Dick Goodman.

Every evening, participants can attend events associated with the Kerrville Folk Festival and take advantage of the wealth of networking opportunities there. In fact, many choose to stay in town for the whole festival, which lasts some 3 weeks in all. Directly after the festival concludes in early June, graduates of Kerrville Songwriters School I can stay on to attend a follow-up session, School II.

Round Top

For instrumentalists *Halfway between Houston and Austin — P.O. Box 85, Round Top, TX 78954* **Voice:** 409-249-3129 **Fax:** 409-249-5078 **E-mail:** festinet@fais.net **Web Site:** http://www.rtis.com **Contact:** James Dick, Artistic Dir. **Founded:** 1971 **Open:** First wk. June–mid-July **Admission:** Application (no fee); audition/tape **Deadlines:** Early Mar. **Cost:** $85/wk. (general maintenance fee); scholarship covers tuition, room and board **Financial Aid:** Scholarship; Fellowship; Work/Study **Size-Attendees:** 110 **Handicapped Access**

WHEN THE PIANIST James Dick founded the International Festival-Institute at Round Top more than 25 years ago, the town of Round Top had a population of 99, the festival grounds consisted of 6 acres, and the program took place in an abandoned 4-room schoolhouse. Since that time, both the festival and the town have grown enormously.

Today Round Top enjoys 100 acres and 12 buildings. The site is admired for the personal touches Dick has added along the way, including his Tchaikovsky Gate, designed to imitate the one at Tchaikovsky's home in Russia. The main concert hall recalls features of the Lausanne (Switzerland) Cathedral.

The program is divided into 2 main sessions. The first focuses on orchestral and chamber music, with performances by the festival orchestra and seminars in orchestral auditions and musicology as well. Past conductors of the Festival Orchestra include Pascal Verot, Eiji Oue, Stefan Sanderling and Carl St. Clair. Violist James Dunham of the recently disbanded Cleveland Quartet, bassist James VanDemark and violinist Camilla Wicks are on the instrumental faculty. The ensemble in residence is the Dorian Wind Quintet.

The second session is for string quartets only. Only preformed groups are considered for admission. The faculty includes the Cavani String Quartet, cellist Martin Lovett and violinist Rostislav Dubinsky.

Every student accepted receives a major scholarship presented by the James Dick Foundation for the Performing Arts, covering tuition, room and board. A prizewinner in the Busoni, Tchaikovsky and Levintritt competitions, Dick has established Round Top as one of the more important summer training programs.

Southwest Texas State University Department of Music

For instrumentalists, vocalists, composers, conductors *601 University Dr., San Marcos, TX 78666* **Voice:** 512-245-3396, 512-245-2485 **Fax:** 512-245-8181 **E-mail:** rr14@swt.edu@internet **Contact:** Dr. Russell Riepe, Dir., Grad. Studies in Music **Founded:** 1899 **Open:** Mid-Jan.–mid-Dec. **Admission:** Application ($25), audition/tape, portfolio **Deadlines:** July 15 (fall, summer session II); Nov. 15 (spring); Apr. 15 (summer session I) **Cost:** Varies according to housing plan, etc. **Financial Aid:** Loans; Scholarship; Fellowship; Stipend; Work/Study **Size-Attendees:** 400 **Size-Class:** 35–40 **Degree or Certification:** MM **Job Placement:** Yes **Handicapped Access**

SOUTHWEST TEXAS State University is a multipurpose institution with an enrollment of 25,000 students, located in the small town of San Marcos in the Texas Hill Country. The beauty of the San Marcos River and the many cypress and pecan trees on campus add to the charm of the locale.

The Department of Music has 45 full-time faculty, and its 400 students may choose to major in performance, sound recording technology or music education. The department has 32 practice rooms, 3 organs, 20 practice pianos, 4 performance grand pianos, an electronic music studio, an opera laboratory and a piano laboratory. Performance groups include a concert band, jazz ensemble, choir, chamber ensemble and orchestra.

University of Texas at Austin School of Music

For instrumentalists, vocalists, composers *School of Music, University of Texas at Austin, Austin, TX 78712* **Voice:** 512-471-7764 **Fax:** 512-471-7836 **E-mail:** utmusic@www.utexas.edu **Web Site:** http://www.utexas.edu/cofa/music **Contact:** Stephen Wray, Grad. Adm. Coord. **Founded:** 1937 **Open:** Year-round **Admission:** Application ($50), audition/tape, transcripts **Deadlines:** Feb. 1 (Aug.–Dec.); Oct. 1 (Jan.–May); Feb. 1 (June–Aug.) **Cost:** $1,600 (resident), $4,200 (nonresident) **Financial Aid:** Scholarship; Fellowship; Work/Study **Size-Attendees:** 700 **Size-Class:** 10–20 **Degree or Certification:** MM, DMA, PhD **Handicapped Access**

Located in the fertile cultural environment of Austin, the University of Texas at Austin School of Music is fast becoming one of this country's very best music schools.

It's certainly one of the best endowed. The facilities, housed in its 6-story Music Building and Recital Hall, are impressive. Faculty salaries are highly competitive. And the school brings in quite a number of world-famous superstar guest artists and lecturers each year. The school's 350 undergraduates and 350 graduate students get ample attention, with a student-faculty ratio of 12 to 1.

Music students at UT Austin benefit from the school's place in the university as a whole, a giant school with some 50,000 students dispersed in 70 academic departments and programs of study. The School of Music collaborates for study projects and performance events with the other components of the College of Fine Arts at UT Austin, such as the Department of Radio-Television-Film, the Folklore Program, the African and Afro-American Studies Center and the Institute of Latin American Studies.

Utah

Brigham Young University Department of Music

For performers, composers *Near Salt Lake City — P.O. Box 2640, Provo, UT 84602* **Voice:** 801-378-3083 **Fax:** 801-378-5973 **Web Site:** http://www. byu.edu **Contact:** Mr. Barrus, Chair **Founded:** 1875 **Open:** Sept.–Aug. **Admission:** Application ($25), audition/tape, letter of recommendation, interview **Deadlines:** Feb. 15 **Cost:** Per semester: $1,315; $1,975 (non Latter-day Saints) **Financial Aid:** Loans; Scholarship; Fellowship **Size-Attendees:** 600–700 **Size-Class:** 25 **Degree or Certification:** BA, BM, BFA, MA, MM, PhD, DMA **Handicapped Access**

The Church of Latter-day Saints established Brigham Young University more than a century ago and maintains it today as an important center for religious, humanistic, scientific and professional study. The arts, including music, are integral to the school's overall approach to students' educational experience.

In many respects, though, the music department at this school resembles its counterparts around the country. It's equipped with the usual quota of rehearsal and performance spaces; theory and ear training are part of the standard course of study. As one might imagine in so religious an institution as this, there are more than the usual complement of pipe organs. A great many of the faculty are themselves Brigham Young University graduates. Non-alumni faculty include violist David Dalton and singer Marjo Burdette. The school is open to all, but Mormons get a tuition discount.

Park City International Music Festival and Summer Institute

For instrumentalists *1420 Meadowloop Rd., Park City, UT 84098; 1255 Park Ave., Park City, UT 84060* **Voice:** 801-649-5309 **Fax:** 801-645-8446 **Contact:** Leslie Harlow, Russel Harlow, Codirs. **Founded:** 1984 **Open:** Mid-July–mid-Aug. **Admission:** Application, optional tape ($25) **Deadlines:** May 20 **Cost:** $760; $440 housing **Financial Aid:** Scholarship; Fellowship; Work/Study **Size-Attendees:** 40–50 **Handicapped Access**

DESIGNED FOR professional-track young artists interested in orchestral and chamber music, the Park City International Music Festival and Summer Young Artists Institute is open to woodwind, piano, string and brass players. Each chamber ensemble receives 2 to 3 coachings per week, and woodwinds, strings and brass rehearse twice a week in the Festival Symphony Orchestra, performing 2 outdoor concerts during the 4-week program.

Students are encouraged to perform solo works for masterclasses and in student recitals. Chamber groups perform frequently in formal recitals and at various locations in the Park City community. Faculty artists have included violinists Charles Libove and Manuel Ramos and the pianist Timothy Hester.

Vermont

Manchester Music Festival

For instrumentalists *Mt. Equinox Valley — P.O. Box 1165, Center Hill and Elm Sts., Manchester, VT 05255* **Voice:** 802-362-1956; 800-362-1956 **Fax:** 802-362-0711 **Contact:** Michael Rudiakov, Dir. **Founded:** 1974 **Open:** First wk. July–2nd wk. Aug. **Admission:** Application ($40), audition/tape **Deadlines:** May 15 **Cost:** $1,200; $360 housing (no meals) **Financial Aid:** Scholarship; Stipend **Size-Attendees:** 25–35 **Size-Class:** 4 **Handicapped Access**

THE MANCHESTER Music Festival offers a 6-week summer program of intensive instruction and performance for 25–35 musicians aged 18 and up. The weekly schedule includes 1 private lesson and 3 chamber music coachings as well as masterclasses.

Opportunities to perform include the weekly Young Artists Concert Series and numerous community venues such as churches, hotels and private organizations. The festival is located in Manchester-in-the-Mountains, a year-round resort area in southern Vermont's Mt. Equinox Valley.

The Manchester Festival Orchestra, an ensemble of 15 former participants, tours throughout the year. The Manchester Chamber Players, MMF's resident ensemble, completed its fifth year of concerts in 1995. It is the ensemble-in-residence at Green Mountain College in Poultney.

Manchester's small faculty includes teachers from as far away as Iceland and Russia. Masterclass instructors include the cellist Nathaniel Rosen and the pianist Ilana Vered.

Marlboro Music

For string players, wind players, vocalists *Rural Vermont near Brattleboro — Box K, South Road, Marlboro, VT 05344; 135 S. 18th St., Philadelphia, PA 19103* **Voice:** 802-254-2394 (summer), 215-569-9497 (off-season) **Fax:** 215-569-9497 **Contact:** Philip Maneual, Manager **Founded:** 1951 **Open:** Late June–mid-Aug. **Admission:** Application (no fee), audition/tape **Deadlines:** Dec. 5 **Cost:** $4,500 (all-inclusive) **Financial Aid:** Scholarship **Size-Attendees:** 75 **Handicapped Access**

FOR CHAMBER MUSIC, Marlboro Music is *it*. For nearly half a century it has drawn a small—very elite—group of artists from all ages, backgrounds and parts of the world. Recent participants have included Donald Weilerstein, Leila Josefowicz and David Soyer. They come to make chamber music in a setting more or less opposite that of the concertizing norm. On the Marlboro College campus, which consists of an abundance of grassy hills and lots of old white buildings, participants are free from ordinary pressures. The emphasis is on rehearsal rather than on performance and the more spontaneous everything is, the better.

The Marlboro idea was the dream of violinist Adolf Busch, who founded the festival with his brother Herman, son-in-law Rudolf Serkin and colleagues Marcel, Louis and Blanche Moyse. Busch wanted Marlboro to be like a large family for its musicians. The festival is now run by a committee comprising Richard Goode, András Schiff and Mitsuko Uchida. Going strong today, the festival still lives up to that dream.

Raphael Trio Summer Chamber Music Workshop

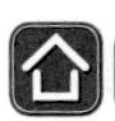 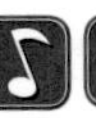 

For chamber musicians *Green Mountains, near Montpelier — Adamant Music School, Adamant, VT 05640; 175 W. 73rd St., #16D, New York, NY 10023* **Voice:** 802-229-9297, 212-362-0023 **Fax:** 212-362-3541 **Contact:** Daniel Epstein, Susan Salm, Codirs. **Founded:** 1982 **Open:** Late June– early July **Admission:** Application ($20) **Deadlines:** Feb. 1 **Cost:** $450; $250 room and board **Size-Attendees:** 35–40 **Size-Class:** 2–40

SUSAN SALM AND Daniel Epstein, pianist and cellist of the Raphael Trio, conduct 2 week-long sessions of music making every summer in Adamant. Their facility, a small music school with many spacious buildings, a concert hall, numerous pianos, practice studios and rehearsal spaces, is situated in the Green Mountains on 200 acres of secluded woodland.

Participants include a mix of professional players and advanced amateurs. Ensembles are formed at the beginning of the workshop and remain together for the entire program. The busy schedule includes daily coachings, masterclasses, seminars, lectures, sightreading sessions and informal concerts.

The atmosphere is casual. Meals are served family style, and participants help with chores both indoors and out. In addition to Salm and Epstein, the workshop's 10-person faculty includes clarinetist Todd Levy and violist Mary Ruth Ray.

Vermont Mozart Festival

For instrumentalists *P.O. Box 512, 110 Main St., Burlington, VT 05401* **Voice:** 802-862-7352; 800-639-9097 **Fax:** 802-862-2201 **Contact:** Betsy Whyte, Asst. Dir. **Founded:** 1974 **Open:** Mid-July– early Aug. **Deadlines:** June 1 **Cost:** $200; $250 room and board **Financial Aid:** Scholarship **Size-Attendees:** 15–20 **Handicapped Access**

SET IN VARIOUS locations in the Burlington area, the Vermont Mozart Festival has drawn crowds for decades. One of its primary venues is the Trapp Family Lodge in Stowe. A gracious 2,000-acre mountain retreat, the Lodge is owned and operated by the von Trapp family of *Sound of Music* fame. The Austrian-style lodge is surrounded by brilliant gardens, spectacular mountain views and hiking trails.

During the Vermont Mozart Festival's summer concert season, artists of the festival conduct 5-day workshops in Burlington for students of intermediate to advanced levels. The classes are a good opportunity for students to work closely with well-known musicians. In 1996, the festival offered 3: a string chamber music workshop with violinist Helen Kwalwasser, violist Ynez Lynch and cellist Alexander Kouguell; a piano workshop led by Daniel Epstein; and a trumpet workshop with trumpet soloist Scott Thornburg.

Winter Wonderland Workshop

For vocalists *West Brattleboro — All Souls Unitarian Church, Brattleboro, VT 05301; Western Wind Vocal Ensemble, 263 W. 86th St., New York, NY 10024* **Voice:** (212) 873-2848; 800-788-2187 **Fax:** 212-873-2849 **E-mail:** workshops@westernwind.org **Web Site:** http://www.westernwind.org **Contact:** William Zukof, Artistic Codir. **Founded:** 1981 **Open:** Feb. **Admission:** Refundable $100 deposit; open to all **Deadlines:** Mid-Jan. **Cost:** 3-day workshop $230; 1-day workshop $80 **Size-Attendees:** 60 **Job Placement:** Yes **Handicapped Access**

DATING FROM 1969, Western Wind Vocal Ensemble is one of the country's oldest a cappella vocal groups. And 20 years ago, when few people even knew this kind of music existed, Western Wind received a Grammy nomination for its recording of Revolutionary War songs. From the beginning, part of the group's mission has been to educate the public about the genre, and one way it accomplishes the goal is through its Winter Wonderland Workshops in Ensemble Singing, held each winter in Brattleboro.

Both 1-day and 3-day sessions are available. Here, singers of all levels learn about the rich and varied repertoire for a cappella groups and receive technical tips on such skills as blending, phrasing and singing together in tune.

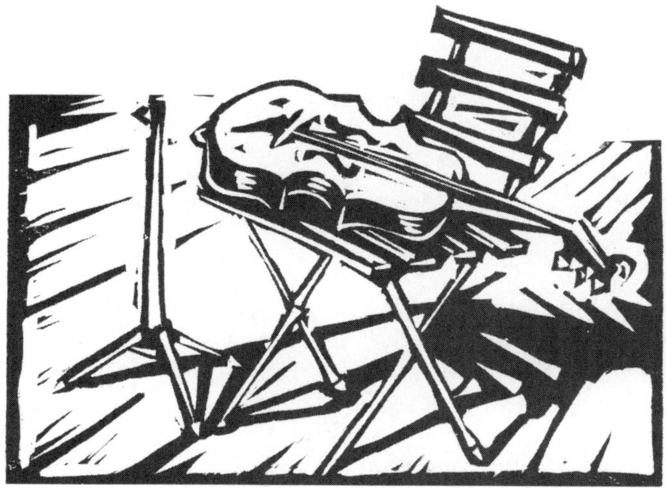

Yellow Barn Music School and Festival

For chamber musicians, composers *Near Brattleboro — R.D. Box 371, Old Rt. 5, Putney, VT 05346* **Voice:** 802-387-6637; 800-639-3819 **Fax:** 802-387-6637 **E-mail:** YBarn@aol.com **Web Site:** http://www.users.aol.com/ybarn **Contact:** Tova Malin, Exec. Dir. **Founded:** 1969 **Open:** Late June– early Aug. **Admission:** Application ($50), audition/tape, recommendations **Deadlines:** Mid–late Mar. **Cost:** $2,500 (all-inclusive) **Financial Aid:** Scholarship; Fellowship; Stipend **Size-Attendees:** 50–75 **Size-Class:** 2–40

Cellist David Wells and pianist Janet Wells had an intimate scale in mind when they founded Yellow Barn as a small cello workshop in 1969. The program was held in their Vermont country home with concerts and impromptu performances taking place in the attached, drafty old barn. Audiences, attracted by word of mouth, sat on rickety folding chairs; during intermission they drank fruit punch prepared by the Wells children. Participants studied with David Wells (then chair of the cello department at the Manhattan School of Music, now serving on the faculties of the Hartt School of Music and of the New England Conservatory).

Since those early days, the barn has been refurbished and the festival has evolved to include players of all instruments, mostly undergraduate and graduate students at major music schools. Every summer, 25 fully publicized concerts are attended by people from all over New England. Internationally known ensembles and teachers participate regularly, including the Alexander String Quartet and the New York Woodwind Quintet.

Despite growth and a wider public profile, Yellow Barn has remained surprisingly intimate and casual. As always, the feeling is supportive, the learning environment challenging but not competitive. Chamber groups include players of mixed experience level with the idea that all have much to learn and much to teach, and that music can be an excellent communication tool that can build bridges among people regardless of their differences.

Virginia

Ash Lawn–Highland Apprenticeship Program

For vocalists *James Monroe Parkway, Charlottesville, VA 22902* **Voice:** 804-293-4500 **Fax:** 804-293-8000 **Contact:** Judith Walker, Gen. Mgr. **Founded:** 1978 **Open:** Mid-June–mid-Aug. **Admission:** Application, resume, photo, nonreturnable cassette with 3 selections (one in English) **Deadlines:** Nov. 30 **Cost:** Free **Financial Aid:** Stipend **Size-Attendees:** 5

The Apprenticeship Program at the Ash Lawn-Highland Summer Festival is designed to develop and nurture young singers by taking them through all areas of opera production side by side with the festival's professional opera company members. Participants, who attend the program at no cost, actually take part in producing traditional opera of high quality and creating awareness of light opera forms including American music theater. They appear in a performance-oriented showcase featuring their musical ability and theatrical potential. They give solo recitals, concerts and outreach performances. And all are auditioned and some chosen for supporting roles in the company's own productions.

Among the topics covered in class and on the job are audition techniques, how to get an agent, the legal and ethical aspects of contracts, how to move, dance and act on stage and more.

Garth Newel Music Center

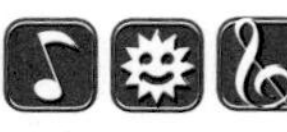
For chamber musicians *Halfway between Hot Springs and Warm Springs — Rt. 2, Box 565, Hot Springs, VA 24445; P.O. Box 240, Warm Springs, VA 24484* **Voice:** 540-839-5018 **Fax:** 540-839-3154 **Contact:** Luca DiCecco, Artistic/Admin. Dir. **Founded:** 1973 **Open:** July 4th weekend–Labor Day **Admission:** Application ($100 for students; free for professionals), audition/tape, resume **Deadlines:** Early spring **Cost:** Tuition, room and board provided **Financial Aid:** **Size-Class:** 4–10 **Handicapped Access**

THE GARTH NEWEL Music Center is best known for its Summer Chamber Music Festival, a series of 20 performances over 10 weekends from July 4 through Labor Day. Some 4,000 people attend each year, and a number of significant works have been commissioned and premiered by the festival.

Garth Newel is also home to a Summer Chamber Music Study Program, a competitive, full fellowship program that accepts only 14 students. In addition to daily private instruction, and ensemble coaching, participants have the opportunity to work and perform side by side with professionals in the Summer Chamber Music Festival Concerts.

As if that were not enough, Garth Newel is known as an extraordinary spot for musical gatherings, year-round. It offers a plethora of Holiday Weekend Retreats, famous not only for the fine music presented but also for the fine gourmet dining. A novel way to spend Thanksgiving or Christmas.

Also on a year-round basis, Garth Newel offers seminars and lectures, workshops (such as one on how to take orchestral auditions), classes in music literature and workshops for conductors and directors. The resident Garth Newel Chamber Players tour the area and sell their recordings and videos at the center. The newest Garth Newel enterprise: musical tours of Europe.

Virginia Center for the Creative Arts

For composers *SW VA, 160 mi. from Washington DC — Admissions Committee, Box VCCA, Sweet Briar, VA 24595* **Voice:** 804-946-7236 **Fax:** 804-946-7239 **E-mail:** vcca@artswire.org **Contact:** William Smart, Dir. **Founded:** 1971 **Open:** Year-round **Admission:** Application ($20), resume, recommendations, score and cassette/CD of a recent work **Deadlines:** May 15 (Sept.–Dec.); Sept. 15 (Jan.–Apr.); Jan. 15 (May–Aug.) **Cost:** Minimum contribution of $30 per day **Financial Aid:** Fellowship **Size-Attendees:** 24

OWNED BY NEARBY Sweet Briar College (for women), the Virginia Center for the Creative Arts is America's largest year-round artists' colony, and one of the most respected.

It's not easy to get in. As with MacDowell and Yaddo, applicants may try 2 and 3 times (or even more) before being invited for a residency. By all accounts, however, it's well worth the wait.

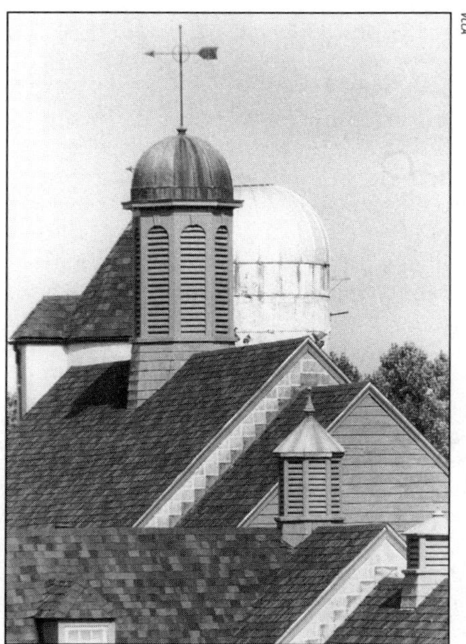
VCCA

Virginia Center for the Creative Arts, Sweet Briar.

The rhythm of life is much like that at MacDowell and Yaddo, including lunches delivered to the studio door and the no-socializing-during-quiet-work-time rules. In addition to uninterrupted time for work, VCCA offers 450 acres of lawns and woods to roam, as well as a swimming pool and all the excellent facilities available at Sweet Briar.

Though VCCA is much younger than either Yaddo or MacDowell—it was founded in 1971—it is clearly in the same overall league. It, too, is a place to which acceptance is a certain marker of success, and where meaningful creative relationships have a way of blossoming.

Washington

Centrum Artist Residency Program

For composers *On the Olympic Peninsula — P.O. Box 1158, Port Townsend, WA 98368* **Voice:** 360-385-3102 **Fax:** 360-385-2470 **Contact:** Marlene Bennett **Open:** Sept.–May **Admission:** Application ($10), resume, tape of recent work (with score if available), project description **Deadlines:** Oct. 1 for following year **Cost:** Free **Financial Aid:** Stipend

About 15 artists, usually including at least 1 composer, are selected each year for fully subsidized, month-long residencies at the Centrum Artist Residency Program. The residency package includes housing, studio space and a $300 stipend. Centrum leases space for its residencies from the State of Washington's Fort Worden State Park and Conference Center. Fort Worden is a 440-acre park located a few minutes from downtown Port Townsend on Washington's Olympic Peninsula. Resident housing is simple, in self-contained cottages within easy walking distance from beaches, tennis courts and miles of wooded hiking trails.

Cornish College of the Arts

For instrumentalists, vocalists, composers *710 E. Roy St., Seattle, WA 98102* **Voice:** 206-726-5016; 800-726-ARTS **Fax:** 206-720-1011 **Contact:** Sharron Starling, Asst. Dir. Admissions **Founded:** 1914 **Open:** Year-round **Admission:** Application ($35), audition/tape, transcripts, 2 essays **Deadlines:** Rolling **Cost:** $11,000; $7,000 room and board **Financial Aid:** Loans; Scholarship; Work/Study **Size-Attendees:** 150 **Size-Class:** 25 **Degree or Certification:** BMA **Handicapped Access**

The music department at Cornish College of the Arts has something of a hip profile. There are offerings in world music to help students prepare for musical life in a global context; music history coursework places an emphasis on relevance; and the music theater workshop gives students opportunities to perform anything from operatic scenes to pieces of solo performance art. Even the department's newest ensemble, the Cornish Millennium Players, has an aura of excitement, presenting side by side the works and performances of both students and faculty.

For those who don't fit into Cornish's established degree programs—in jazz, new music, classical music, composition, electro-acoustic music, MIDI and world music, the department encourages individualized programs. Ensembles-in-residence at Cornish include Sonora (new music), Gamelan Pacifica (Javanese and Balinese gamelan) and the James Knapp Big Band.

Women Conductors

Sometimes people fall into a profession not so much for love of the work itself as for the love of a particular early role model. It was that way for Rachael Worby.

"When I first saw Leonard Bernstein I was attending a Young People's Concert at Carnegie Hall. I must have only been 8 or 9, but I knew immediately that I wanted to be *him.* As I got older, I just had a desire to absorb the whole being of Leonard Bernstein: the poet, the composer, the pianist, the hip revolutionary with a social conscience, the American Jew on the stage. But I did not translate that feeling into an ambition to conduct, necessarily."

It was the early 1960s, a time when the idea of a woman conductor was unheard of anywhere in the world. So, Worby says, "I gradually allowed this notion of being Leonard Bernstein to go into a diminuendo."

Eventually, 2 women conductors, Antonia Brico and Sarah Caldwell, did manage to make it into the limelight. "The world had turned," says Worby, "and my consciousness turned with it. The idea of being a conductor reemerged, and somehow, in a parenthesized moment of positive self-esteem, I decided to go for it. I'm glad I did. You never dream of something unless somewhere inside, you believe you can make it happen.

"Then, of course, you spend many hours, years even, wondering if it's really true that you can succeed." Worby knocked on many doors before she found a conductor who would take on a female pupil. His name was Jacques Monod, and at the end of each lesson he made a ritual out of reminding Worby that in his opinion, women could not be conductors.

Worby continued working with Monod anyhow, and later she studied with Max Rudolph and Otto Werner-Mueller. In 1982 she became assistant conductor of the Spokane Symphony. Since 1986, she has been music director of West Virginia's Wheeling Symphony Orchestra. She is now also music director of Carnegie Hall's Youth Concerts with the American Composers Orchestra. (That's right: Bernstein's old gig.)

Today, a number of regional orchestras have women music directors, but Worby observes that women in conducting seem to have hit a glass ceiling. "Women in the field of conducting face the same issues that they do in other fields where they seek powerful leadership positions. Only in conducting, women are even more vulnerable because of the physical realities of the job. Think about it: everyone else is seated. You are standing. Not only are you standing, but you are also standing on a box on which you virtually tower over the players. Every violinist in the orchestra has been playing the violin for decades. And there you are, towering over them all, and a big part of your job includes telling them to play their violins or flutes or tubas in a different way: your way."

West Virginia

West Virginia University Division of Music

For instrumentalists, vocalists, composers, conductors *College of Creative Arts, P.O. Box 6111, Morgantown, WV 26506* **Voice:** 304-293-5511 **Fax:** 304-293-3550 **Contact:** Virginia Thompson, Dir., Grad. Studies **Founded:** 1897 **Open:** Sept.–May **Admission:** Application ($10), audition, transcripts, test scores **Deadlines:** Aug. 1 **Cost:** $2,192 (resident), $6,784 (nonresident); $4,434 room and board **Financial Aid:** Loans; Scholarship; Work/Study **Size-Attendees:** 300 **Degree or Certification:** BM, BME, MM, MME, DMA, PhD **Handicapped Access**

West Virginia University has shown a commitment to music since 1897, when it opened what is now its division of music.

Its faculty includes such artists as jazz and concert pianist James Miltenberger, Laureate Quintet French hornist Virginia Thompson and Pittsburgh Ballet and Opera oboist Cynthia Anderson.

Among the division's better-known alumni are Star Trek composer Jay Chattaway, Cincinnati Symphony bassoonist William Winstead and U.S. Navy Band flutist Margaret Baer.

The university is close enough to several metropolitan centers to afford students access to high culture. At the same time, Morgantown is just far enough away from the rest of the world to have one of the lowest crime rates in the nation, and some of the prettiest scenery a school could want.

Wisconsin

Apostle Islands National Lakeshore Artist-in-Residence Program

For performing musicians, composers *Sand Island — Rt. 1, Box 4, Bayfield, WI 54814* **Voice:** 715-779-3397 **Contact:** Kate Miller **Open:** Late June–mid-Sept. **Admission:** Application, resume, personal statement, 5-min. recording of composition or other performance **Cost:** Free **Size-Attendees:** 3

The Apostle Islands (there are 21 of them) are located in western Lake Superior, off Wisconsin's Bayfield Peninsula and spread out over a 750-square-mile area. The area is basically a nature preserve, with the exception of a few developed facilities, of which the Apostle Islands National Lakeshore Artist-in-Residence Program is one.

Without a doubt, AINL is the most rugged artist residency program in this book, taking brave performing and composing musicians out to secluded island cabins for 2–3-week periods in the summer. The program is free, but for some, the downside is without doubt the living sitution: there is no electricity and no running water and the nearest person (the park ranger) is 3 miles away by boat. Forget having a piano with you, unless you want to carry it there yourself.

If you're still interested given these kinds of accommodations, AINL will want to know 2 things about you: what you want to create during your residency, and whether or not you are physically and psychologically fit to survive it.

CANADA

Alberta

Music and Sound at Banff

For instrumentalists, vocalists, audio artists *75 mi. W of Calgary — 107 Tunnel Mountain Dr., P.O. Box 1020, Banff, AB T0L 0C0 Canada* **Voice:** 403-762-6180, 403-762-6188 **Fax:** 403-762-6345 **E-mail:** arts-info@banffcentre.ab.ca **Web Site:** http://www.banffcentre.ab.ca/ **Contact:** Isobel Moore Ralston, Artistic Dir./ Exec. Prod. **Founded:** 1933 **Open:** Year-round **Admission:** Application (no fee), nonrefundable deposit (C$48), tape, resume, letters of recommendation **Deadlines:** Varies by program **Cost:** C$43/day or C$300/wk.; C$33/day room and board **Financial Aid:** Scholarship; Stipend; Work/Study **Size-Attendees:** 300 **Handicapped Access**

A DIVISION OF THE Banff Centre for the Arts, Music and Sound at Banff is designed to support the music and audio professions in Canada by providing opportunities to Canadians (and Americans) in an international environment. The course offerings are cutting-edge, and participants are encouraged to investigate new concepts, including new technologies related to music. The major areas of study include not only masterclasses, ensemble programs and jazz programs but also interesting residencies, audio work/study programs and several intriguing special projects.

Banff has a distinguished instrumental faculty. In masterclass settings, the likes of flutist Samuel Baron, violist Karen Tuttle and cellist Aldo Parisot work intensively with students. Visiting artists in chamber music have included Laurence Lesser, Lorand Fenyves, Zoltán Székely and Kevin Fitz-Gerald. Banff has a choral workshop of up to 40 students led by Eric Ericson, professor of choral conducting at the Stockholm Conservatory of Music.

For more than 20 years, Banff has offered jazz instruction. The Jazz Workshop offers a solid foundation in the elements of jazz, at the same time imparting a holistic overall philosophy. The jazz program is headed by Hugh Fraser.

The Piano Technician Skill Development Residency is intended for piano technicians already active in the field and provides a chance for them to focus on developing particular areas of mastery. Another special project, The Art of Teaching, invites dedicated teachers with at least 5 years' professional experience to explore new and old pedagogical ideas.

Special residencies at Banff can be either long- or short-term and can be tailored to suit individual needs. Performers (including ensembles) can come to Banff to concentrate on personal artistic development in a self-structured context under the guidance of Banff faculty. Audio Product Development Residencies give professional artists the opportunities to give time and concentration to a recording effort such as the making of a master tape for a compact disc, radio program package or other mass distribution project.

Banff has 2 programs geared for audio professionals. In the Audio Associates program, audio engineers, sound designers and computer audio technicians work in collaboration with artists-in-residence. Residencies for Audio Assistants helps less experienced students gain fundamental knowledge through both work experience and small-group instruction.

The Banff Centre for the Arts is the heart of the Banff Center for Continuing Education, an institute that is dedicated to lifelong creative and professional development.

Red Deer College

For instrumentalists, vocalists, songwriters *Between Calgary and Edmonton — 56th Ave. and 32nd St., P.O. Box 5005, Red Deer, AB T4N 3G8 Canada* **Voice:** 403-342-3512 **Fax:** 403-347-0399 **E-mail:** ccooney @rdc.a6.ca **Contact:** Cheryl Cooney, Chair, Mus. Dept. **Founded:** 1973 **Open:** Sept.–Apr. **Admission:** Application (C$40 Canadian applicants; C$50 international applicants), audition/tape, theory placement test **Deadlines:** July 15 (fall); Nov. 15 (winter) **Cost:** Per semester: C$700; C$225–C$375 housing (no meals) **Size-Attendees:** 50 **Size-Class:** 15 **Degree or Certification:** 2-yr. diploma **Handicapped Access**

THE MUSIC PROGRAM at Red Deer College is a 2-year course of study that offers private instruction, as well as music theory, ear training, composition and merchandising. Graduates of the program go on to careers not only in performing, but also in promotions, recording engineering and other work in the music field. Students may focus on classical music, jazz, pop, country, folk or rock. Songwriting is encouraged and fostered. Faculty include Keith Mann in music merchandising, Ross Dabrusin in jazz piano and Sharon Braum in voice.

British Columbia

Capilano College Jazz Studies Program

For jazz musicians and educators *2055 Purcell Way, North Vancouver, BC V7J 3H5 Canada* **Voice:** 608-984-4951 **Fax:** 604-984-4985 **E-mail:** mreveley@claude.capcollege.bc.ca. **Contact:** Mike Reveley, Coord. **Founded:** 1974 **Open:** Sept.–Apr. **Admission:** Application (C$20), audition, theory test, interview, 2 letters of recommendation **Deadlines:** Early May **Cost:** C$1,200 per semester (incl. private lessons) **Financial Aid:** Loans; Scholarship; Work/Study **Size-Attendees:** 140 **Size-Class:** 20 **Degree or Certification:** BM, Dip. **Handicapped Access**

CAPILANO COLLEGE is something of a jazz industry, offering 4 music programs: a 2-year diploma in jazz studies, a 2-year BM transfer program degree and 4-year degrees both in jazz studies and in music therapy.

The program's stated mission is to produce graduates with a broad-based academic background and comprehensive abilities in music with jazz as the main focus. The idea is that jazz is an eclectic art form that draws on many different musical genres, and the more broadly educated the jazz musician, the better. Capilano also pushes students to complete their minor in teaching because having done so will increase their opportunities for employment.

The Jazz Studies Program supports 2 jazz choirs: Nite Cap and Capital Jazz.

Both have received top honors at Music Fest Canada and Festival Canada and have been guest performers at IAJE conventions in New Orleans and Boston. The studio vocal performance class, in which students develop their abilities as studio singers in a variety of styles, is taught by Corlynn Hanney, whose voice is familiar to Candians through her 20 years as studio singer for movies, records and commercials.

Capilano's Jazz Orchestra, conducted by Brad Turner, is another top-prize winner. Percussionists perform with this and a number of other ensembles. Guitarists and bassists have 2 ensembles of their own to develop sightreading, performance and interpretive skills. For composers and arrangers, courses include rhythm section scoring, 4-part writing and big band and vocal arranging.

Ontario

Country Music Week

For all involved in the country music industry *1997: Hamilton, ON; 1998: Calgary, AB; future sites TBA — Canadian Country Music Association, 3800 Steeles Ave. W., Ste. 127, Woodbridge, ON L4L 4G9 Canada* **Voice:** 905-850-1144 **Fax:** 905-850-1330 **Contact:** Sheila Hamilton, Exec. Dir. **Founded:** 1976 **Cost:** Registration, ticket prices set in May of each year **Size-Attendees:** 1,800 **Handicapped Access**

Country Music Week is one of the most important annual events on the Canadian country music scene. Run by the national service association Canadian Country Music Association, it usually draws in excess of 1,800 participants, catering as it does to the needs of a widely divergent population.

This conference features showcases and a keynote address. One year, for example, David Basskin (president of the Canadian Musical Reproduction Rights Agency) spoke on preparing for the future of country music, including changes in marketing, distribution, retailing and media. Aside from an awards luncheon, the CCMA annual meeting, a roundtable luncheon, a "guitar pull" and many other special events, the conference features a number of seminars. Seminar topics have included the publisher/songwriter mix, how to maximize your chances of being on television, making a date with a demo and a practical workshop for pickers.

Harris Institute for the Arts

For musicians and aspiring music professionals *Downtown — 118 Sherbourne St., Toronto, ON M5Q 2R2 Canada* **Voice:** 416-367-0178; 800-291-4477 **Fax:** 416-367-5534 **E-mail:** harrisi@interlog.com **Web Site:** http://www.ampsc.com/metronome/harris/index.html **Contact:** Stan Janes **Founded:** 1989 **Open:** Year-round **Admission:** Application, resume, transcripts **Deadlines:** Rolling **Cost:** C$9,760 (producing and engineering program); C$7,920 (recording arts management) **Financial Aid:** Loans; Scholarship **Size-Attendees:** 140 **Size-Class:** 6–25 **Degree or Certification:** PEP, RAM **Job Placement:** Yes

Harris Institute for the Arts is a world leader among music industry schools. Certified by Canada's Ministry of Colleges and Universities, it offers 1-year diploma programs. The recording arts management (RAM)

program covers the management functions within the music industry, including artist management, concert promotion, tour and venue management, music publishing, contracts, record distribution, print production and packaging, publicity and public relations.

The production/engineering program (PEP) covers the creative, technological and business aspects of music recording, including digital audio, music theory, signal processing, live sound, lighting and acoustics.

Both programs culminate in internship placement at companies and studios and with the formation of production and management companies. The Canadian music industry employs more than 70,000 people. The Harris Institute aims to prepare the recording, producing and arts management side of that workforce as pragmatically as possible.

Quebec

Domaine Forget

For instrumentalists, vocalists, composers *75 mi. NE of Quebec City — 398 Les Bains, Ste. Irénée, QB G0T 1V0 Canada* **Voice:** 418-452-8111; 888-DFORGET **Fax:** 418-452-3503 **Contact:** Elise Pare-Tousignant, Artistic Dir. **Founded:** 1977 **Open:** June–Aug. **Admission:** Application (C$40) **Deadlines:** None; 5% discount before May 1 **Cost:** C$425 (1 wk.), C$725 (2 wks.), C$1,020 (3 wks.) **Size-Attendees:** 15–75 **Handicapped Access**

THE DOMAINE FORGET Music and Dance Academy is regarded as one of Canada's leading centers of intellectual exchange and artistic development. The teaching staff includes some of Quebec's finest musicians and guest artists from around the world.

The academy is structured by consecutive week-long sessions, each with

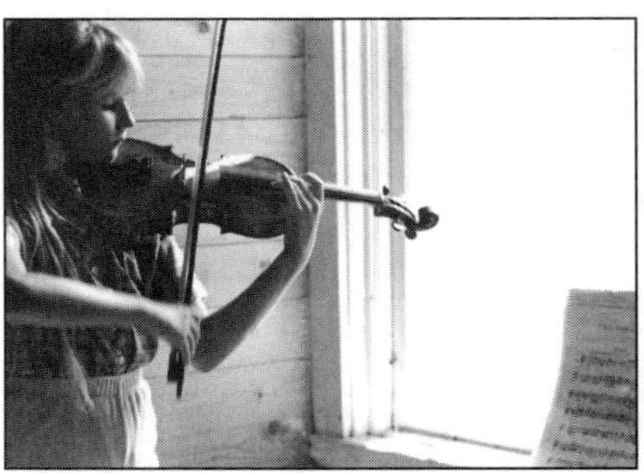
LE DOMAINE FORGET

Solo rehearsal at Domaine Forget Music and Dance Academy.

its own instrumental focus. There are symposia in all the major orchestral instruments as well as sessions in chamber music, orchestral music, orchestral conducting, band conducting, choral singing, a woodwind symposium, modern music and musical theater.

Domaine Forget is situated on a vast 150-acre estate overlooking the St. Lawrence River in Charlevoix County. Faculty represent the highest standards in their fields of expertise, including French horn virtuoso Herman Baumann, Metropolitan Opera principal oboist Elaine Douvas and Michel Donato, perhaps Canada's most famous jazz musician and recipient of the 1995 Oscar Peterson Award.

McGill Early Music Workshop

For baroque instrumentalists, vocalists *McGill University, 555 Sherbrooke St. W., Montreal, QB H3A 1E3 Canada* **Voice:** 514-398-4548 **Fax:** 514-398-8061 **E-mail:** hank@music.mcgill.ca **Contact:** Hank Knox, Dir. **Founded:** 1993 **Open:** Early June **Admission:** Application (deposit 15% of total cost) **Deadlines:** May 1 **Cost:** C$345 (participants); C$185 (harpsichord class); C$210 (accommodations) **Size-Attendees:** 40–50 **Handicapped Access**

THE EARLY MUSIC Workshop at McGill University offers classes to musicians at every level of advancement in harpsichord, baroque violin, baroque flute, baroque oboe, lute, voice, recorder, sackbut and continuo. There are masterclasses in the morning, as well as ensemble rehearsals in the afternoon. Private lessons may be arranged. The 10 faculty members include lutenist Francis Colpron, singer Valerie Kinslow and harpsichordist Kenneth Gilbert.

The harpsichord class is particularly popular and so is now open to auditors. The class usually focuses on a particular repertoire—for example, Book II of Frescobaldi's Toccatas—along with other 17th- and 18th-century repertoire.

Ensembles include a renaissance collegium, an early vocal music ensemble, a chamber orchestra and a baroque chamber ensemble. The final week of the program includes concerts and lectures by faculty, a concert by students and an outing in historic Montreal.

Musitechnic

For performers, composers, audio artists *451 St. Jean St., Montreal, QB H2Y 2R5 Canada* **Voice:** 514-845-4141 **Fax:** 514-845-2581 **Contact:** Joel Harbor, Student Advisor **Founded:** 1994 **Open:** Early Mar.–early June; early Sept.–early Nov. **Admission:** Registration (C$200), high school transcript/diploma or equivalent **Cost:** C$14,500 **Financial Aid:** Loans **Size-Attendees:** 150–200 **Size-Class:** 8–24 **Degree or Certification:** AEC in Sound Design **Job Placement:** Yes

FOUNDED IN 1994 to fill the specific needs of the Quebec music industry, Musitechnic is a private professional college aimed both at performing musicians and at techie-types who are looking to specialize in sound and audio. The school is located in Montreal, in the heart of most Canadian telecommunications activities.

Computer-assisted music technology is a major focus of the program. A thorough exploration of the latest technical and artistic facets of current hardware and software allows students to create, perform and record projects using the latest tools. The 18 courses in the computer-assisted sound design degree program are spread over 3 intensive sessions. The program has recently added a course in sound applications for the multimedia interactive scene. A certificate of Collegial Studies from the Quebec Education Ministry as well as a Musitechnic diploma are given to graduates. And sound design specialists, as they point out, are in high demand across the music industry.

Orford Arts Centre for Advanced Music Studies

For instrumentalists, vocalists *About 50 mi. N of VT — 3165 Chemin du Parc, Canton d'Orford, QB T1X 3W3 Canada* **Voice:** 819-843-3981; 800-567-6155 (Canada) **Fax:** 819-843-7274 **Contact:** Andrea Poulin, Admissions Officer **Founded:** 1951 **Open:** 4th wk. June–2nd wk. Aug. **Admission:** Application (C$45; C$55 if participating in competition), tape, 2 letters of recommendation, repertoire list **Deadlines:** Mar. 15 **Cost:** C$50–C$235/wk. (depending on program); C$225/wk. (single), C$250/wk (double) room and board **Financial Aid:** Scholarship **Size-Class:** 15

Now nearly half a century old, the Orford Arts Centre is eastern Canada's oldest summer school of music. Simultaneously with the activities that take place at the summer school, the Orford Arts Centre is home to a music festival of international repute, in which renowned artists, master teachers and budding talents take to the stage in more than 30 concerts.

The Orford Arts Centre is located in Mount Orford Provincial Park, amid 222 acres at the foot of majestic Mount Orford. Six pavilions grace its stunning surroundings. They are the Charles-Leblanc Pavilion, containing 33 studios for practice and class sessions; the Gilles Lefebvre Concert Hall, an intimate forum of exceptional acoustic quality that can seat up to 500; the Man and Music Pavilion, containing the Orford Arts Centre Visual Arts Exhibition and 13 rooms reserved for teachers; a building for dining and administration; and 2 residence halls.

Add to the physical surroundings an elite musical faculty, which has included visiting concertmasters from 4 great orchestras, the members of I Musici de Montreal Chamber Orchestra and other virtuosos from around the world. On the distinguished regular faculty are such famous musicians as clarinetist Charles Neidich, bassoonist Frank Morelli and oboist Theodore Baskin. For those who aspire to a solo career, Orford administers a competition. The winner gets a performance with I Musici de Montreal and a CD on the British Chandos label, distributed in 39 countries.

PART THREE

The Business of Music

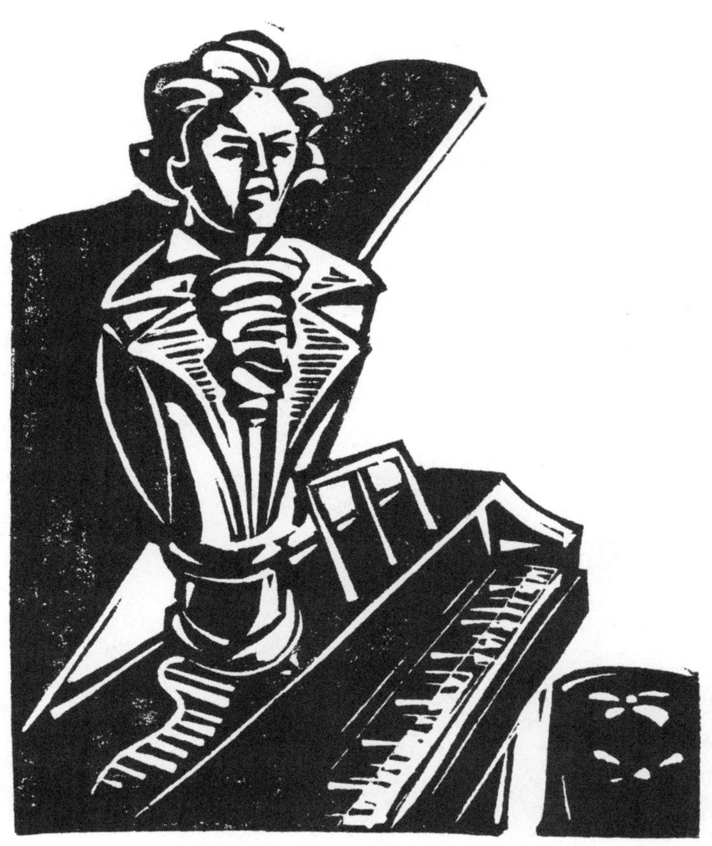

Financial Aid—The Inside Scoop

MUSICIANS DON'T CONCERN THEMSELVES ENOUGH with the important subject of grants and awards available to musicians. Consult some of the service associations listed in Part Two to find out what may be available to you.

Here, you can become a little more savvy about what to expect if you need financial aid to attend one of the programs listed in this book. Those programs described as offering financial aid are indexed as such.

Many music programs are nonprofit, and many are in need of financial aid themselves. Musicians who can pay full tariff or can make donations should do so. Apply for financial aid only after you make a conscientious effort to earn the tuition and travel money yourself.

At *Residential Programs* (music festivals and artists' colonies), expect anything from no financial aid at all (and high costs) to full financial support. Often this depends on the E word: endowment. Some offer aid analogous to collegiate "work/study." This may be meaningful work or it may be slave labor (bussing dishes or scrubbing pots). If you think this builds character or will someday find profound expression in your music, go for it.

Musicians' conferences are frequently inexpensive (this includes some of the best of them). Yet sometimes conferences are organizational extravaganzas, with gaudy and gilded rented facilities, overpaid celebrity keynote speakers, and "materials" fees for a lot of photocopied handouts with not much more than common sense printed on them but all bound up in a neatly labeled three-ring binder as a sort of souvenir of the conference itself. Beware of these excesses. Indeed, there may even be an inverse ratio here, with the simpler affairs providing more direct contact between teachers and students, offering the better value. If you do apply for financial aid at a conference, expect only partial help, and don't be surprised if the financial aid that's available is restricted to selected groups (regional, ethnic, gender) who are presumed to be in need.

Financial aid for music workshops and masterclasses is less common largely because so many workshops are inexpensive or meet only for short periods of time. At the bigger institutions (such as community music schools), prices may have risen to the point where asking for financial aid is reasonable. Not many of these programs offer work/study dollars, though, and scholarship money is generally very limited for any particular workshop in a broader program.

The subject of financial aid for graduate students in academic programs in music is arcane and deep enough for its own book. Most universities have both federal money and private money to hand out to qualified students. Carefully read the catalogue to see if there are scholarships provided specifically for any ethnic, geographical or gender group to which you swear allegiance. If the catalogue is unclear, request an annotated list of all scholarships offered and, if the university is within easy reach, go there for an exploratory talk with a financial aid officer. Leave no stone unturned.

Are loans worth the risk? First, be aware that loans are generally not available for workshops, masterclasses or conferences, and only rarely for festivals or other residential programs (where monthly charges can outstrip what you were paying to live at home in the city). By contrast, few people get through college or graduate school these days without taking on some debt for tuition. The theory is that the loan is an investment in your own future. If you won't bet on your own horse, why should anyone else? That's the rationalization; then there are the feelings. Some people simply hate to carry any debt, or hate the banks for charging usurious interest (though federally insured student loans have lower rates). Before you conclude that a loan is the right choice for you, take stock not only of your dollar resources but also of your attitude toward borrowing in general. Recent graduates of medical school at least have a chance of earning back the investment they made to get their degree. But people with a DMA in performance may be climbing a steeper slope to get out of debt. If the loan you are considering is substantial, be sure to take a good look at your overall financial needs now and expected in the years just after finishing the degree. Put the loan in context (mortgage, car payments, health insurance, kids) to see its relative value. If you believe you can handle it and really want that degree, by all means step up to the plate and swing away.

It's a true scandal that paying back student loans has become, in the words of Shakespeare's moody student, Hamlet, "a custom more honored in the breach than in the observance." No matter how unfair you may think the cold, cruel world out there may be to you and your fellow musicians, not paying back your federally or state insured loan(s) is hardly good citizenship, and what does it say to the even younger musicians coming along behind you? Under the Clinton administration, new legislation has empowered the government to aggressively prosecute student loan deadbeats. I say, "Hear! Hear! About time!"

Finally, I recommend that you keep your day job, to borrow a phrase from the theater world. The best financial aid you can give to your music habit is a paycheck. I dismiss the argument that a musical life and a paid working life are incompatible. Consider the precedents. Charles Ives was an insurance executive, Alexander Borodin a chemist, and so on. Okay, you get one point for countering with, "Yes but they all had wives at home folding laundry and cooking dinner." Still, the job creates benefits that go beyond the value of the paycheck. It gets you up in the morning into a structured day. It takes you out into the world and out of yourself. It makes you appreciate (and put to better use) the time you do assign to your music. Remember the old saying: "If you have all morning to write a letter, it will take you until eleven o'clock to find a pencil."

In sum, I'd say the best financial aid plan for a determined musician is to assume nothing, be open to anything, and learn to negotiate for a whopping fee at your first gig!

Grants, Fellowships and Awards for Musicians

Too few musicians are aware of the boosts they can get from foundations, corporations, prize-giving institutions and what remains of the National Endowment for the Arts and state and local arts agencies. What follows is a brief list of such bodies, known for their steadfast support of musicians. These entities have been known to fund anything from recitals to recording projects to educational outreach work. Many of them dispense funds through some of the service associations listed in Part Two. For a directory of foundations, see the Bibliography.

Amateur Chamber Music Players Foundation, 1123 Broadway, New York, NY 10010; 212-645-7424. Seeks to create and expand opportunities for participatory chamber music activity; awards fellowships, workshops subsidies and institutional grants to organizations in the U.S. and Canada.

Mary Flagler Cary Charitable Trust, 122 E. 42nd St., #3505, New York, NY 10168; 212-953-7700. Music program funds venturesome projects, especially new music.

Ford Foundation, 320 E. 43rd St., New York, NY 10017; 212-573-4606. In funding arts projects, Ford seeks to enhance creativity, strengthen arts institutions and expand the civic role of the arts.

North American Artists Foundation Recording Grants, 4750 N. Central Ave., Ste. 7N, Phoenix, AZ 85012; 602-234-1809. For composers and performing artists who wish to record nonstandard repertoire.

Pew Charitable Trusts, One Commerce Square, 2005 Market St., Ste. 1700, Philadelphia, PA 19103; 215-575-9050. Pew gives money to artists and organizations around the country, but has invested particularly heavily in the Philadelphia area arts community.

Setting Up Shop

UNLESS YOUR MUSIC IS ENTIRELY PRIVATE or totally a hobby, you are, like it or not, in business. Part time or full time, making big bucks or pennies, there are business, legal and tax consequences of your music habit. Here are some of the salient issues. See also the Bibliography in Part Four for books about managing your business affairs as a musician.

Marketing Your Skills

Self-Promotion or Working with a Manager, Agent or Publicist

I believe that most imaginative, organized and determined musicians can sell their own work. Nonetheless, there are the musician's perennial questions: "Should I get a manager? Should I engage a booking agent?

Do I need a publicist?" After numerous years in the music business I've heard scores of musicians ask these questions without having considered the necessarily preceding one: why would any of these folks want to represent my work? Let's do some arithmetic.

You've formed a string quartet. You've heard that Alice Tully Hall pays quartets $10,000 per concert. At $2,500 per person, that amounts to more than pocket change, if it books you. Tully is probably the top of the line unless you score an even bigger hit with Carnegie Hall or the Lincoln Center Great Performers series, and of course what's suitable for one presenter isn't suitable for another. Still, even at $2,500 per person, what would be in it for a manager? Fifteen per cent of $10,000 isn't pocket change either, and you tell him, or her, that your repertoire is full of dynamite pieces you can play all around the country. Why, if this presenter bites, then the next one, and so forth, we'll be raking in the dough.

But hold on there, pardner. What does it take in terms of labor and overhead to book your quartet? If the manager is lucky and well connected (already known and respected at the concert hall), one letter or phone call and a tape of your latest concert may do it. Much more likely is a protracted ordeal in which neither Tully's nor any other top-rank concert series says yes, and the weeks and months go by as the manager's in-box fills with rejection letters. Meanwhile the meter is running. Costs are mounting, and even if you do get engaged, the gig will bring in at best the 15 percent you and the manager hoped for in commission. And that payment may not come until after the concert, which could be months, or even more than a year, after the booking.

Is this any way to run a battleship? Of course not. And so most managers turn down all but the surest bets; that's why you see more pianists, violinists and sopranos than contrabassoon soloists on the rosters. Some will take on a few woodwind players. But more of them want players of mainstream solo instruments who can be relied upon to play standard repertoire. Why take on an oboist who plays Berio's *Sequenza* when you can take on a spaghetti-fed tenor instead and take in ten times the money? Fifteen percent of $35,000 ($5,250) or $350,000 ($52,500) will at least buy a cruise or a new Mercedes. The moral: Don't waste your time asking managers to do for you what you couldn't afford to do for other musicians if you were a manager yourself.

A manager can sometimes provide good advice about developing your repertoire for commercial purposes. The better managers know what presenters are looking for currently. Do not sign on with a manager unless you have had extensive conversations with him or her that convince you that the level of sensitivity to the musical qualities of your performing is high. Managers who are too busy to listen or who just don't like good music are not what you're looking for if you are a serious musician. If, on the other hand, you are cranking out *The Flight of the Bumblebee*, according to what your Juilliard teacher assured you is the shortest route to success, then your manager's musical sensitivity rating is a moot point. The manager's Rolodex is all that matters to you, and if the phone list has the right contacts on it, forge ahead.

Many musicians, particularly highly paid rock and country musicians, retain both managers and booking agents, the latter working specifically to keep the calendar straight. Again, consider the cut and crunch the numbers. Always go to managers first, and find out whether they handle booking as part of their services to artists.

Also find out if your potential manager will handle publicity. Frequently managers do not, especially in the very big time. The Cleveland Quartet, for example, was managed by ICM Artists.

If a journalist wants to do a profile on their twenty-seven years together, the PR firm of Shuman Associates will arrange interviews and send out a press kit. On the group's farewell tour, though, individual concert series presenting the quartet generated their own publicity for local and national consumption.

Selling your work by yourself is not easy either, and you may want to consider a middle path between representation and no representation. Sometimes, for a fee less than the 15 percent the manager might earn if the gig gets booked, a manager will act as a consultant or advisor, listening to your work, commenting, suggesting presenters to contact, and then stepping out of the way. If you expect to be sending tapes and press material to a selected set of presenters time and again (because you play for a niche market), it may be worthwhile to buy a manager's or consultant's services to help you set up your own Rolodex and network of contacts. Former presenters for the larger halls can sometimes provide this service.

In making important decisions about representation, remember that a number of membership organizations offer modest grants for consulting services to provide counseling for music groups with growing pains.

The How-To Bit

IT'S ALWAYS AMAZING TO THINK that in the markets with the fewest consumers (classical music and jazz, for example), the highest level of formal study is going on. Add to this the irony that for all this study, few institutions do a decent job of preparing classical and jazz musicians for the realities of the competitive world of work.

Meanwhile, in their hurry to learn about music simply by living the musical life, large numbers of rock, country and pop musicians skip college altogether in favor of getting right out onto the street. They engage in self-help from the start, picking up all manner of practical, inspiring how-to and success literature, seeking out mentors who will really do something for them. In other words, they forge ahead.

A gig is a gig. Essentially, all musicians ought to do just what the sensible rock, pop and country players do: hustle. And fortunately, hustling is not rocket science.

Buy a lot of 10" by 12" padded envelopes. Buy a Glue Stic. Get some shiny pocket folders. You're going to make yourself or your group a high-performance publicity packet.

Items to put in your packet include biographies and photos of you and/or your group, copies of favorable newspaper reviews or feature stories, and a brochure hyping your act whatever it may be. If at all possible, find a professional designer to do this one-time job for you. Amateurish-looking publicity can do a lot of harm.

Including a demo tape, or better yet a CD, can make all the difference, especially to those who may not already know you by reputation. Take the time and suffer the expense of making one if you do not already have one.

Preferably on a computer, you'll want to start an address list of venues in which you would like to appear. Clipped to the front of your publicity packet, include a brief cover letter addressed by name to the person specifically in charge of booking. The letter should state why you'd like to be engaged, what you can do, when and for how much.

After two to three weeks, follow up by phone. If time drags on and still there is no reply, ask for your packet to be returned. Keep a notebook and a file system so you'll know how each submission was treated.

Tools of the Trade

Your Instrument

One of the reasons classical music is regarded by some as elitist is that, historically, musicians of modest means have had a tough time gaining access to it. One key barrier is the cost of decent instruments.

While most professional-grade wind instruments fall into the "affordable" category (between $5,000 and $15,000), a stringed instrument good enough to play in a major orchestra costs more. Finding the "right" instrument can take years. But be forewarned: paying for it can take a lifetime. Fortunately, many orchestras lend money to players at low interest for the purchase of fine instruments.

Shipping and Postage

The availability of overnight mail for publicity and other correspondence does not mean you have to use it. Somehow the world kept turning for several billion years before FedEx came along. Priority mail at the post office, which as of 1997 was $3 for up to two pounds and gets a bright "Priority" sticker on it, is usually sufficient even when time is important. Priority moves as fast as or faster than first class, and in most areas of the country that amounts to overnight or second-day delivery. But there are exceptions, and it's not guaranteed. Nor can you track a priority mail package. Still, it's the best deal if guaranteed overnight delivery is not essential. UPS is next best. FedEx and Airborne Express, with the best services, are more expensive.

Cutting the Deal

Copyright

Of special concern to composers and songwriters is the matter of ownership. You establish copyright (legal ownership of your written work) by declaring it. Fortunately there are books, songwriters' organizations, classes and seminars on the topic of copyright, but the fact is that as soon as a composition is "fixed" (recorded or put down on paper), it is entitled to copyright protection. If you sing your song live it is not necessarily protected. So it's wise to tape the song and put a copyright notice on the tape including the date. Better yet, obtain copyright registration before performing the song in public. Registration costs $20. But be prepared to take a number: the U.S. Copyright Office processes more than half a million registrations every year, and it takes an average of two months to complete copyright registration.

Contracts

Once you've arrived at a verbal agreement with a club owner, university or other music presenter, you'll need to arrange for your manager to generate a contract for both parties to sign. If you are representing yourself, refer to the standard form offered by the American Federation of Musicians. The contract should cover not only who plays, what they play, when and for how much, but also any special considerations, such as who pays for travel and food and how heavy equipment will be transported. If a new client is reluctant to use a contract, press for one anyhow. And never forget to bring your copy of the signed document to the gig, just in case anyone needs any gentle reminders.

The Price Tag on Your Work

HOW MUCH IS YOUR WORK WORTH? Should you estimate its value on the basis of the amount of time you invested in practicing and, if so, what hourly rate makes sense? Should you surrender to your sense of the absurd and accept whatever the market tells you your work is worth? Is there any way to be reasonable about all this? You guessed it: the answer is Yes and No.

Presenters and musicians everywhere work from precedents, the "going rate." Nobody claims this is reasonable, but what else is there to do? There is no official pay scale for freelance musicians, although the American Federation of Musicians offers guidelines. Inside the studio music, orchestra and musical theater industries, where musicians are organized in unions that bargain collectively for them, yes, there are pay scales.

But for most musicians each project raises the same old question: How much is my work worth, and how can I negotiate for the highest payment? First, study the precedents. Attend a conference or two where the emphasis is on the business side of music, and don't be shy about asking for real numbers. Second, play poker. Whoever bids first in the negotiation is at a disadvantage. The next guy is bound to make a move to his advantage based on the first bid. ("Sorry, you're too high, or too low.") Rehearse with another successful musician. Set some limits ("I'll do it for no less than $X"), and stick to them.

Working for unreasonable pay helps no one, and usually a musician will do a shoddy job under these circumstances, and the presenter will complain, and the ripple effect through the business is bad news. A manager can be very helpful here, but as noted above few managers will help musicians sell anything that nets the manager just a few hundred dollars. Learn to be your own manager.

A simple formula will keep you sober and may help you to avoid underselling your ideas and skills. Set a gross income target. Calculate the number of billable hours per year for which you expect payment. Divide the gross income by the billable hours to get an hourly base rate. Add 33 percent to the base rate for fringe benefits and taxes you must pay for yourself as a self-employed musician. Assume about $5,000 for overhead costs (rehearsal space rent, instrument insurance and maintenance, phone). Divide the overhead by the billable hours, and add that to the base rate. The result is what you need to be paid per hour to hit the gross income target. Discuss your arithmetic with colleagues. If the precedents in your category of music support your figures, don't be shy about asking for this kind of pay. You'll be well armed to discuss payments with an employer if you know the market and can explain your own arithmetic.

Starting a Music Business

Incorporation

Why would a musical group incorporate? Not many need to. Incorporating gives a group its own legal status. Once incorporated, your group can now employ its members. It can pay salaries and expenses, and it can invest in other concerns. Incorporation can also bring protection against certain losses and liabilities. Of course, with incorporation you face legal fees and additional taxes and more complex bookkeeping and accounting.

What to do? Don't guess at it. See your lawyer and your accountant, and look for a musicians' conference featuring seminars on legal and business issues.

Taxes

If there is a more tedious subject, I don't know it. However, if you're serious about a musical career or if you think your freelance supplemental income may rise to the point where you can't avoid reporting it to Uncle Sam, then think of the costs of setting up a bookkeeping system and of laying a plan for minimizing your taxes as a basic business expense. Find a bookkeeper who is savvy about self-employment; learn to use a software program like Quicken (from Intuit) to put your checkbook register on the computer; and save/record those receipts as only a tax-hating maniac would. Every penny counts at the end of the year. Find an accountant who knows the ropes concerning deductions allowable for musicians, such as unreimbursed travel and meal expenses, stage clothing, music lessons, instrument repairs and so on. An accountant with only general experience, rather than some taste at least of the music world, may miss tax deduction opportunities for you. It's worth paying these number-crunching folks a few hundred bucks to set you up with easy-to-follow systems that will repeat year after year. If you work with appropriate professionals (whose fees are themselves deductible business expenses), you'll most likely cut your tax bill more effectively than if you muddle through on your own.

Several music guides and conferences recommend that you call the IRS to request this tax booklet or that. Generally with the IRS it's hard to get anyone to answer the phone and harder still to get help. Start with your accountant.

Investing for Your Future

As a full-time nonsalaried musician, in no matter what genre, you'll need a plan for the long term just as would any salaried employee in a corporation. Health insurance is one issue. A retirement plan is another. Systematic savings (for a rainy day or for an emergency) should be a third.

Certain musical organizations, such as the American Federation of Musicians, provide access to what they consider affordable health insurance. If you work for a certain minimum number of hours at union gigs, on Broadway for example, the AFM provides a no-frills health insurance policy free of charge. There is strength in numbers, and you may be able to get a better deal through an organization than on your own. In 1996 Congress passed health insurance reform legislation permitting individuals to set up tax-free health-care savings accounts, potentially a good idea for self-employed people. Research carefully.

The IRS allows various retirement plan payments (into specific accounts such as IRAs, SEP-IRAs and Keogh plans) for nonsalaried workers, providing tax deductions in the years when the contributions are made. See your accountant to discuss which plan is best for you.

For young people the news is good: even a small monthly investment will accumulate nicely by the time you hit 65 or so. (And keep in mind that as investments, good stringed instruments can appreciate wildly over the decades.) Those who are more advanced in age must invest more aggressively, and an investment advisor is likely to be a key player on your professional services team. For nonsalaried musicians the key in all of these decisions is discipline. From every check received, you'll have to set aside tax dollars (for estimated quarterly payments), and you should set aside savings/investment dollars, too. If you establish a plan, set up the accounts, keep the paperwork simple and adhere to the discipline, the system will flourish.

Now all you have to do is make music!

PART FOUR

Bibliography & Index

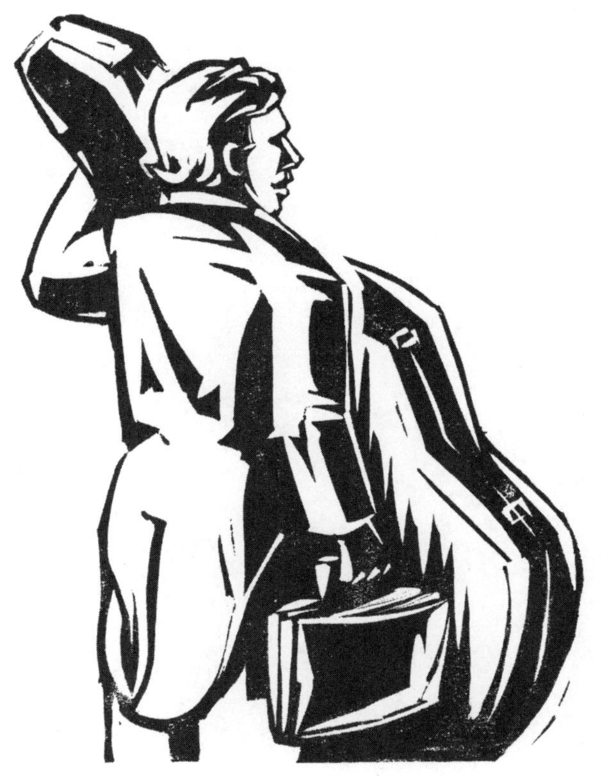

Bibliography

The Business of Music

The Billboard Guide to Music Publicity, by Jim Pettigrew Jr., Watson-Guptill Publications, 1515 Broadway, New York, NY 10036.

The Craft and Business of Song Writing, by John Braheny, Writer's Digest Books, 1507 Dana Ave., Cincinnati, OH 45207; 800-289-0963.

How You Can Break into the Music Business, by Marty Garrett, Lonesome Wind Corporation, P.O. Box 2143, Broken Arrow, OK 74013; 800-210-4416.

The Music Business, by David Naggar, Esq., and Jeffrey D. Brandstetter, Esq., DaJé Publishing, One Market, Spear St. Tower, 41st Fl., San Francisco, CA 94105.

Music, Money and Success, by Jeffrey and Todd Brabed, Schirmer Books, 1633 Broadway, New York, NY 10019.

Running Your Rock Band, by Bill Henderson, Schirmer Books, 1633 Broadway, New York, NY 10019.

This Business of Music, by M. William Krasilovsky and Sidney Shemel, Watson-Guptill Publications, 1515 Broadway, New York, NY 10036.

Your Own Way in Music, by Nancy Uscher, St. Martin's Press, 175 Fifth Ave., New York, NY 10010.

Directories and Resource Books

The A&R Registry, by Ritch Esra, SRS Publishing, 7510 Sunset Blvd., #1041, Los Angeles, CA 90046; 800-377-7411.

Directory of Independent Music Distributors, by Jason Ojalvo, Disc Makers, 7905 N. Rt. 130, Pennsauken, NJ 08110; 800-468-9353.

Music Directory of Canada, Norris-Whitney Communications Inc., 23 Hannover Dr., Ste. 7, St. Catherines, ON, L2W 1A3, Canada; 905-641-3471.

Music Publisher Registry, by Ritch Esra, SRS Publishing, 7510 Sunset Blvd., #1041, Los Angeles, CA 90046; 800-377-7411.

Musical America International Directory of the Performing Arts, K-III Directory Corporation, 1735 Technology Drive, Ste. 410, San Jose, CA 95110; 800-889-5799.

National Guide to Funding in Arts and Culture, Foundation Center, 79 Fifth Ave., New York, NY 10003.

Official Country Music Directory, Entertainment Media, P.O. Box 700, Rancho Mirage, CA 92270; 800-395-6736.

Peterson's Professional Degree Programs in the Visual and Performing Arts, Peterson's, P.O. Box 2123, Princeton, NJ 08543.

Songwriter's Market, Writer's Digest Books, 1507 Dana Ave., Cincinnati, OH 45207; 800-289-0963.

The Yellow Pages of Rock, The Album Network, 120 N. Victory Blvd., Burbank, CA 91501; 818-955-4000.

Index

General Index

A cappella singing, 82, 123
Academic programs, 10-11, 137; special advice on, 33-35. See also Academic Programs Index
Academy of Country Music, 28
Academy of Gospel Music Arts, 117
Accompanying, programs for, 103
Acoustic music, 113-14
Adams, John, 79
Adcock, Michael, 80
Administration of music, programs on, 39
AFM, 27
Agents, 139-41
Alaria Chamber Ensemble, 91
Alexander String Quartet, 48, 124
Alexander Technique, 85-86, 95
Alsop, Marin, 76
Amateur musicians' organizations, 27-32
Amateur musicians, 23; programs for, 49-50, 55
Amateur Chamber Music Players Foundation, 139
American Music Center, 28
American Federation of Musicians, 27, 31
American Society of Composers, Authors and Publishers, 31
American String Quartet, 97
American Composers Forum, 28
Anderson, Cynthia, 128
Applied music, 128
Apprentices, programs for, 52, 106-7, 124
Arad, Atar, 71
Arrangers, programs for, 39, 54, 78, 99, 130-31
Arranging, 68
Art song interpretation, 45
ASCAP, 31
Ashbaker, Susan Shiplett, 112
Associations and organizations, 28-31
Audio artists, programs for, 44, 129-30, 133
Auditions, programs on, 119, 124
Awards, 139
Babayan, Sergei, 101
Baker, James, 115
Bands, programs for, 85, 110-11, 111-12, 116, 118
Barer, Marshall, 43
Baresel, Thomas, 109
Baron, Samuel, 129
Baroque instrumentalists, programs for, 132-33
Baroque music, 47, 95; programs on, 106, 109-10
Baskin, Theodore, 134
Bassoonists, programs for, 104-5
Battiste, Harold, 74
Baumann, Herman, 132
Becoming a musician, career options, 17-23
Beresford, Rick, 118
Bixler, Marcia, 95
Black, Neil, 63
Blancq, Charles, 74
Bloch, Ernest, 45, 46, 107
Bloom, Arthur, 94
Bloom, Sara Lambert, 109
BMI, 31
Bok, Mary Louise, 113
Bonney, Barbara, 81
Booking agents, 139-41
Boston Symphony Orchestra, 73
Brass choirs, 47, 112
Brass players, programs for, 105, 121
Braum, Sharon, 130
Broadcast Music, Inc., 31
Broadcast Data Systems, 32
Broadway on Sunset, 28-29
Brodsky, Jascha, 108
Bruck, Charles, 76
Burdette, Marjo, 121
Burton, Gary, 78
Busch, Adolf, 122
Busch, Herman, 122
Business, starting up, 144-45
Business of music, 112, 135-45. See also Business of Music Index
Buswell, James, 80
Canadian Country Music Association, 29, 131

Canin, Stuart, 47
Career options, 94, 107; 94, 95, 107; becoming a musician, 17-23
Carillon playing, programs on, 39
Carman, Owen, 99
Carter, Ronald, 69
Casals, Pablo, 96
Castleman, Charles, 114
Catholic University of America, 59-60
Catlet, Big Sid, 78
Cavani String Quartet, 107, 120
Ceaser, Janina Kuzma, 107
Center for the Study of World Music, 108
Cerone, David, 106-7
Chamber music, 19-20. See also Chamber Music Index
Chamber Music America, 29
Chamber Music magazine, 29
Chancler, Ndugu, 48
Chicago Lyric Opera, 67
Chicago Symphony Orchestra, 67, 69, 73
Choral music, 20. See also Choral Music Index
Chorus America, 29
Christian music, 117
Christian Music Networking Guide, 30
Christian musicians, programs for, 116
Church music, 39, 53-54, 88
Church musicians, programs for, 110-11
Cifani, Elizabeth, 69
Cleveland Chamber Players, 107
Cleveland Orchestra, 109
Colpron, Francis, 133
Combs, Jennifer, 104
Comet, Catherine, 46
Commercial music, 19, 67, 113-14
Community outreach, 40, 47, 49, 56-57, 62, 80, 81, 113
Conductors, programs for, 39, 41, 42, 57-58, 64, 65, 66, 71, 74,75, 80, 88, 90, 97-99, 103, 106-7, 109-10, 111, 118, 125, 128,132
Conferences, 10. See also Conferences Index
Contracts, 143
Copes, Ronald, 75
Copyright, 143
Country music, 21, 48, 116, 130, 131
Cross-cultural music, 116
Curtin, Phyllis, 79
Cypress Lake Center for the Arts, 61
Dabrusin, Ross, 130
Dallas Symphony Orchestra, 73
Dalton, David, 121
Danchenko, Victor, 108
Davidson College Music School-Camp, 103
Davies, Gail, 118
Davis, Stan, 95
de Coteau, Denis, 47
Deats, Jan, 114-115
Delay, Dorothy, 51
Detroit Symphony Orchestra, 73
Diaz, Andres, 61
Dick, James, 119
Dicterow, Glenn, 53, 103
Disc jockeys, programs for, 64
Discipline, 98
Djerassi, Carl, 44
Donato, Michel, 132
Dorian Wind Quintet, 119
Douvas, Elaine, 132
Dow, Alden B., 82-83
Dramatists Guild, 32
Dreyfus, Karen, 53
Dubinsky, Rostislav, 119
Dunham, James, 119
Dunkel, Stuart, 77
Early music, 81, 107, 132-33
Early Music America magazine, 29
Early Music America, 29, 107
Eastman, George, 92
Eddy, Timothy, 63
Effron, David, 103
Electro-acoustic music, 126
Electronic music, 48, 73, 79, 81, 105, 118
Eliason, Mikael, 112
Emerson String Quartet, 51
Epstein, Daniel, 123
Ericson, Eric, 129
Eschenbach, Christoph, 71
Ethnomusicology, 50, 66, 115
Exchange programs, 39
Fellowships, 139
Feltsman, Vladimir, 83, 103
Festivals, 11; special advice on, 35-36. See also Festivals Index
Film music composition, 105-6
Financial aid, 13, 137-39. See also Financial Aid Index
Fleisher, Leon, 71
Flutists, programs for, 109-10

Folk Alliance, 29-30
Ford Foundation, 139
Frame, Pamela, 114
Fraser, Hugh, 129
Fried, Miriam, 71
Friedman, Lily, 115
Gaddini, Eugenio, 49
Galamian, Ivan, 99, 100
Garth Newel Chamber Players, 125
Gerschefski, Martha, 66
Gilbert, Kenneth, 133
Gilman, Suzanne, 115
Gilmore, Irving S., 84
Gingold, Josef, 71
Glickman, Loren, 104-5
Goldmark, Rubin, 53
Gonzalez-Palmer, Barbara 111
Goode, Richard, 122
Goodman, Dick, 118
Gospel music, 21; programs on, 116
Gospel Music Association, 30, 116
Gospel Music America, 117
Grace, Susan, 53
Graffman, Gary, 112
Grants, 139
Grawemeyer Award in Music Composition, 74
Guitar, 47; programs for, 105
HaLevy, Libbe S., 43
Hampton, Bonnie, 47
Hampton, Lionel, 67
Hanani, Yehuda, 61
Handicapped access, 13. See also Handicapped Access Index
Hanney, Corlynn, 131
Heath, Albert "Tootie," 48, 49
Heath, Fenno, 55
Hecht-Shapiro duo, 107
Hedwig, Douglas, 90
Hester, Timothy, 121
Honn, Barbara, 109
Horne, Marilyn, 46
Icons, 10-11, 12
Improvisation, 68
Improvisation for Strings (workshop), 49
Incorporation, 144
Independent Label Festival, 68
Information: display format, 11-13; gathering, 13-14
Institute of Jazz Studies, 88
Instruments, purchasing, 142
Insurance, personal, 145
Insured loans, 138
International Bluegrass Association, 30
International Festival of Arts and Ideas, 55
International Musician, 31
Investments, personal, 145
Irvine, Jeffrey, 114
Istomin, Marta Casals, 96
Janiec, Henry, 103
Jazz, 20, 78. See also Jazz Index
Jinbo, Michael, 76
Johns Hopkins University, 76-77
Jordan Hall, 81
Kaplan, Burton, 96
Katz, Paul, 80
Kaufman, Kevin, 43
Kefauver, Alan P., 77
Kennedy, Bryan, 73
Kerrville Folk Festival, 119
Keyboardists, programs for, 70-71, 77, 79-80, 84
Kingsbury, Henry, 115
Kinslow, Valerie, 133
Kitsopoulos, Maria, 61
Klein, Alex, 70
Klinghoffer, William, 48
Kneisel, Franz, 75
Kouguell, Alexander, 123
Krigbaum, Charles, 55
Kwalwasser, Helen, 123
Leeper, Doris, 60-61
Lehmann, Lotte, 45
Leon, Tania, 90
Levin, Walter, 71
Levy, Todd, 122
Libove, Charles, 121
Ling, Jahja, 76
Lipkin, Seymour, 75
Liturgical music. See Church music
Livingston, Taylor, 78
Loans, 138; insured student, 138
London Symphony Orchestra, 73
Lovett, Martin, 119
Lowenthal, Jerome, 46
Lucktenberg, Kathryn, 112
Lutoslawski, Witold, 74
Luvisi, Lee, 103
Lydian String Quartet, 79-80
Lynch, Ynez, 123
MacDowell, Edward, 86-87

Mack, Rodney, 104
Madden, Edward J., 40
Madrigal singing, 41-42, 95
Mallow, Barbara Stein, 75
Managers, 139-41
Manhattan String Quartet, 55
Mann, Keith, 130
Mann, Robert, 71
Marsalis, Ellis, 74
Mary Flagler Cary Charitable Trust, 139
Masterclasses, 11, 137. See also Masterclasses Index
McBee, Cecil, 82
McDonald, Robert, 89
McInnes, Donald, 46, 62
McKenna, John, 48
Mehta, Zubin, 71
Melnick, Jackie, 80
Metropolitan Opera Orchestra, 97
Miami String Quartet, 109
Milhaud, Darius, 45
Miller, Michele, 95
Miltenberger, James, 128
Modern music, 132
Monteux, Pierre, 75-76
Moravian music, 115
Moravian College, 114
Morelli, Frank, 134
Moyse, Blanche, 122
Moyse, Louis, 122
Moyse, Marcel, 122
Mueller, Otto-Werner, 94
Muir Quartet, 79
Murdock, Katherine, 75
Music education, 81, 83. See also Music Education Index
Music history, 42, 45, 50, 54, 64, 65, 67, 79, 110, 126
Music literature, 42, 53, 65, 79, 125
Music technology, 58-59, 64, 113, 129; computer-assisted, 133
Music therapy, 113, 130-31
Musical tours of Europe, 125
Musical comedy orchestration, 115
Musical America International Directory of the Performing Arts,18
Myers, Myron, 69
Nashville Songwriters Association International, 30
National Academy of Recording Arts and Sciences, 30
Neidich, Charles, 90, 134
Neubauer, Paul, 98
New Music Consort, 97
New York Philharmonic, 73, 97
New York Wind Soloists, 97
New York Woodwind Quintet, 124
Nightclubs, 64
North American Artists Foundation Recording Grants, 139
Oberlin Baroque Ensemble, 106
Oboe players, programs for, 69-70, 109-10
Olivier, Rufus, 48
Opera, 20, 81. See also Opera Index
OPERA America, 30-31
Oral History, American Music Project, 58
Orchestral music, 19. See also Orchestral Music Index
Oregon Bach Festival, 111
Oregon Wind Ensemble, 111
Organists, programs for, 39, 55, 57, 67, 88, 105, 128
Orlando, Danielle, 112
Otte, Allen, 109
Oundjian, Peter, 71
Palmer, Todd, 115
Panetti, Joan, 57
Pardee, Margaret, 100
Parisot, Aldo, 129
Parnas, Leslie, 75
Paukert, Karl, 107
Paul, James, 76
Peabody, George, 76-77
Percussion, 47, 111-12
Perlman, Itzhak, 90
Peterson, Edward, 74
Pew Charitable Trusts, 139
Pianists, programs for, 45-46, 64, 67-68, 73, 86, 88, 101, 105-6, 114, 118, 121, 128; training, 83
Piano accompanying, 79, 88, 101
Pit ensembles, programs for, 79
Pittsburgh Symphony Orchestra, 73, 113
Polisi, Joseph, 93
Popkin, Mark, 104
Practicing, 100
Pratt, Awadagin, 101
Pressler, Menahem, 71
Pricing your work, 143-44
Pritchard, Eric, 61
Professional musicians, 21-23
Professional musicians' organizations, 27-32
Program selecting, 32-33

Publicists, 139-41
Publicity packets, 141-42
Purchasing instruments, 142
Radnofsky, Kenneth, 81-82
Ramos, Manuel, 121
Ray, Mary Ruth, 122
Recorder players, programs for, 95
Recording media, 45, 77, 79, 132
Reichenthal, Gene, 95
Renaissance ensembles, programs for, 85, 133
Residential programs, 10, 137. See also Residential Programs Index
Ridley, Larry, 88
Rilling, Helmuth, 111
Roach, Maxine, 107
Robison, Paula, 82
Rock music, 20-21, 116, 130
Rome, Benjamin T., 59
Rose, Benita, 115
Rosen, Nathaniel, 122
Rosenberg, Laura, 42
Rosenberg, Richard, 42
Russo, Charles, 95
Sacred music, 88, 113
Salaff, Peter, 107
Salm, Susan, 122
Sarchet, Gregory, 69
Saxophone players, programs for, 105-6
Schenck, Janet, 96
Schenly, Paul, 101
Schiff, András, 122
Schoenberg, Arnold, 45, 50
Scott, Jo Ryman, 40
Selling your work, 141
Serkin, Rudolf, 122
SESAC, 32
Shaker music, 115
Shapiro, Gerald, 115
Shaughnessy, Ed, 78
Shipping and postage, 142
Sightreading, 76, 89, 95, 131
Simmons, Beverly, 107
Slatkin, Leonard, 109
Slowik, Kenneth, 106
Smith, Marian Elizabeth, 112
Snead, Charles, 66
Society for Strings of New York City, 99
Solfege, 76
Song Camp, 117
Songwriters Guild, 31
Songwriter's Market, 18
Songwriters, programs for, 130. See also Composition Index
Sound recording technology, 118
Southampton Chamber Players, 102
Southeast Kansas Symphony, 73
Speaker, Marylou, 80
Starting up business, 144-45
Steans, Lois M., 71
Stegeman, Charles, 73
Stoeckel, Gustav, 56
Stoeckel, Ellen Battell, 56
String improvisation, 49
String players, programs for, 49, 55, 71-72, 79-80, 80, 84, 96, 99, 105-6, 106-7, 108, 114, 121
Student loans, 138
Sweet Briar College, 125-26
Tanenbaum, David, 47
Tanner, Mark, 73
Taxes, 144-45
Teraspulsky, Terry, 80
Thomas Jean, 74
Thomas, Michael Tilson, 62-63
Thomas, Sally, 100
Thompson, Virginia, 128
Thornburg, Scott, 123
Tipton, Chelsea, 104
Tocco, James, 109
Tokyo String Quartet, 71
Totenberg, Roman, 75
Trapp Family Lodge, 123
Tree, Michael, 88, 89
Tsai Performance Center, 79
Tuttle, Karen, 129
Uchida, Mitsuko, 122
Unions and other labor organizations, 31-32
University of Maryland College Park, 76, 77
VanDemark, James, 119
Vered, Ilana, 88, 122
Vermeer Quartet, 69, 75
Vernon, Robert, 108
Vivona, Peter M., 41
von Stade, Frederica, 103
Washburn University, 73
Weilerstein Duo, 107
Wells, David, 124
Wells, Janet, 124
Western Wind Vocal Ensemble, 82, 123
Wicks, Camilla, 119
Wilson, Phil, 78

Wincenc, Carol, 63
Wind ensembles, programs for, 79, 85
Wind players, programs for, 79-80, 95, 96
Wirt, Ronald, 66
Wolfe, Paul, 63
Wolfram, William, 53
Women conductors, 127
Woodstock, 90-91
Woodwind players, programs for, 105-6, 121, 132
Worby, Rachael, 127
Workshops, 137; 10. See also Workshops Index
World Federation of International Music Competitions, 77
Wuorinen, Charles, 88
Wurlitzer, Helene, 89
Yale School of Music, 56
Young musicians, programs for, 48-49, 56-57, 70-71, 73, 76, 84, 112-13, 121
Zukerman, Pinchas, 96

Music Programs

Academy of Gospel Music Arts, 116
Alden B. Dow Creativity Center Residency Program, 82-83
American Conservatory of Music, 67-68
Apostle Islands National Lakeshore Artist-in-Residence Program, 128
Appalachian State University School of Music, 103
Arkansas State University Department of Music, 41-42
Ash Lawn-Highland Apprenticeship Program, 124
Aspen Music Festival and School, 51-52
Atlantic Center for the Arts, 60-61
Audition and Performance Stress Reduction, 77-78
Baroque Performance Institute, 106
Berklee College of Music, 78
Blanche Bryden Sunflower Music Festival Institute, 73
Bloom School of Jazz, 68
Boston Conservatory, 78-79
Boston University School for the Arts Music Division, 79
Brandeis Summer Music Festival, 79-80
Bravo! Summer String Institute, 84
Brevard Music Festival, 103
Brigham Young University Department of Music, 120-21
Broadway on Sunset, 28-29, 43
Brooklyn Conservatory, 90-91
Brown University Department of Music, 115
Byrdcliffe Arts Colony, 90
Capilano College Jazz Studies Program, 130-31
Central City Opera, 52
Centrum Artist Residency Program, 126
Chamber Music at Mannes, 91
Chautauqua School of Music, 92
Chicago's New Music Festival, 68
Christian Artists' Seminar in the Rockies, 52-53
Cleveland Institute of Music, 106-7
Close Encounters with Music, 61
Colorado College Summer Conservatory and Music Festival, 53
Conducting Masterclass, 111
Cornish College of the Arts, 126
Country Music Week, 131
Crossroads Music Exposition, 116
Curtis Institute of Music, 112-13
Djerassi Resident Artists Program, 43-44
Domaine Forget, 132
Duquesne University School of Music, 113
Eastern Music Festival, 104
Eastman School of Music, 92-93
Encore School for Strings, 108
Fairbanks Summer Arts Festival, 40
Folk Alliance Annual Conference, 29-30, 59
Garth Newel Music Center, 125
Georgia State University School of Music, 65
Glauser School of Music, 108
Glickman-Popkin Bassoon Camp, 104-5
Gospel Music Week, 117
Grandin Festival, 108-9
Hambidge Center, 65-66
Harris Institute for the Arts, 131-32
Hartt School of Music, 54
Headlands Center for the Arts, 44
Helene Wurlitzer Foundation, 89
Hot Springs Music Festival, 42
Indiana University School of Music, 71-72
Indiana University Summer Festival, 72
Irving S. Gilmore International Keyboard Festival, 84
JazzTimes Convention, 87
Juilliard School, 93-94

Kent/Blossom Music, 109
KentMusic, 55
Kerrville Songwriters School, 118-19
Kneisel Hall Chamber Music School and Festival, 75
Le Mont Wind Chamber Music Seminar, 95
Lionel Hampton School of Music, 67
Long Island Recorder Festival, 95
MacDowell Colony, 86-87
Magic Mountain Music Farm, 96
Manchester Music Festival, 121-22
Manhattan School of Music, 96-97
Mannes College of Music, 97-99
Mannes Jazz and Contemporary Music Program, 99
Marlboro Music, 122
Mary Anderson Center for the Arts, 72-73
Mason Gross School of the Arts, 88
McGill Early Music Workshop, 132-33
Meadowmount School of Music, 99-100
Mills College Music Department, 45
Music Academy of the West Summer School and Festival, 45-46
Music and Sound at Banff, 129-30
Musicians Institute, 46
Musicorda Summer String Program, 80
Musitechnic, 133
Nashville Songwriters Association Workshops, 117
National Orchestral Institute, 76
New Arts Festival, 61
New England Conservatory, 80-82
New Haven Festival Masterclasses, 55
New World Symphony, 62-63
Norfolk Chamber Music Festival, 56-57
North Carolina School of the Arts, 105-6
Northern Arizona State University School of Performing Arts, 41
Northern Illinois University School of Music, 69
Northwestern University School of Music, 69-70
Oberlin Conservatory of Music, 109-10
Ohio State University School of Music, 110
Oklahoma City University School of Music and Performing Arts, 110-11
Omega Institute for Holistic Studies, 100-101
Orford Arts Centre for Advanced Music Studies, 133-34
Park City International Music Festival and Summer Institute, 121
Peabody Institute, 76-77
Philadelphia Music Conference, 113-14
Pianofest in the Hamptons, 101
Pierre Monteux School for Conductors and Orchestra Musicians, 75-76
Pittsburg State University Department of Music, 73
Quartet Program, 114
Ragdale Foundation Residency, 70
Raphael Trio Summer Chamber Music Workshop, 122
Red Deer College, 130
Rome School of Music, 59-60
Rossborough Festival, 77
Round Top, 119
Samford University School of Music, 39
San Francisco Conservatory of Music, 46-47
San Francisco State University Department of Music, 47-48
Sarasota Music Festival, 63
Sewanee Summer Music Festival, 118
Smith Summer Workshops, 82
Songwriters Guild of America Workshops, 48
Southampton Chamber Music Festival, 101-2
Southeastern Music Center, 66
Southwest Texas State University Department of Music, 119-20
Stanford Jazz Workshop, 48-49
Steans Institute for Young Artists, 70-71
SummerTrios, 114
Symphony at Sea, 49-50
Taos School of Music, 89
UCLA Department of Music, 50
University of Alabama School of Music, 39
University of Alaska Fairbanks Music Department, 40
University of Arkansas Department of Music, 42
University of Colorado at Boulder College of Music, 53-54
University of Colorado at Denver Department of Music, 54
University of Delaware Department of Music, 58-59
University of Hawaii at Manoa, 66

University of Louisville School of Music, 74
University of Miami School of Music, 63
University of Montana Department of Music, 85
University of Nebraska, Lincoln, School of Music, 85-86
University of Nevada, Las Vegas, 86
University of New Orleans Jazz Studies, 74
University of Oregon School of Music, 111-12
University of South Florida Department of Music, 64
University of Texas at Austin School of Music, 120
Vermont Mozart Festival, 123
Villa Montalvo Artist Residency Program, 50-51
Virginia Center for the Creative Arts, 125-26
Walnut Street Theatre School, 115
West Virginia University Division of Music, 128
Westminster Choir College, 88
Winter Music Conference, 64
Winter Wonderland Workshop, 123
Yaddo, 102-3
Yale Institute of Sacred Music, 57
Yale School of Music, 56, 57-58
Yellow Barn Music School and Festival, 124

Residential Programs

Alden B. Dow Creativity Center Residency Program, 82-83
Apostle Islands National Lakeshore Artist-in-Residence Program, 128
Ash Lawn-Highland Apprenticeship Program, 124
Aspen Music Festival and School, 51-52
Atlantic Center for the Arts, 60-61
Baroque Performance Institute, 106
Brandeis Summer Music Festival, 79-80
Bravo! Summer String Institute, 84
Brevard Music Festival, 103
Byrdcliffe Arts Colony, 90-91
Central City Opera, 52
Centrum Artist Residency Program, 126
Chautauqua School of Music, 92
Close Encounters with Music, 61
Colorado College Summer Conservatory and Music Festival, 53
Conducting Masterclass, 111
Djerassi Resident Artists Program, 43-44
Eastern Music Festival, 104
Encore School for Strings, 108
Garth Newel Music Center, 125
Glickman-Popkin Bassoon Camp, 104-5
Grandin Festival, 108-9
Hambidge Center, 65-66
Hartt School of Music, 54
Headlands Center for the Arts, 44
Helene Wurlitzer Foundation, 89
Hot Springs Music Festival, 42
Indiana University Summer Festival, 72
Irving S. Gilmore International Keyboard Festival, 84
Kneisel Hall Chamber Music School and Festival, 75
Long Island Recorder Festival, 95
MacDowell Colony, 86-87
Magic Mountain Music Farm, 96
Marlboro Music, 122
Mary Anderson Center for the Arts, 72-73
McGill Early Music Workshop, 132-33
Meadowmount School of Music, 99-100
Music and Sound at Banff, 129-30
Musicorda Summer String Program, 80
New Arts Festival, 61
New World Symphony, 62-63
Norfolk Chamber Music Festival, 56-57
North Carolina School of the Arts, 105-6
Omega Institute for Holistic Studies, 100-101
Orford Arts Centre for Advanced Music Studies, 133-34
Pianofest in the Hamptons, 101
Pierre Monteux School for Conductors and Orchestra Musicians, 75-76
Quartet Program, 114
Ragdale Foundation Residency, 70
Raphael Trio Summer Chamber Music Workshop, 122
Round Top, 119
Sarasota Music Festival, 63
Sewanee Summer Music Festival, 118
Southampton Chamber Music Festival, 101-2
Stanford Jazz Workshop, 48-49
Steans Institute for Young Artists, 70-71
SummerTrios, 114
Taos School of Music, 89
Vermont Mozart Festival, 123
Villa Montalvo Artist Residency Program, 50-51

Virginia Center for the Creative Arts, 125-26
Yaddo, 102-3
Yellow Barn Music School and Festival, 124

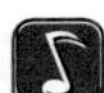

Workshops

Audition and Performance Stress Reduction, 77-78
Baroque Performance Institute, 106
Bloom School of Jazz, 68
Brandeis Summer Music Festival, 79-80
Brevard Music Festival, 103
Broadway on Sunset, 43
Chamber Music at Mannes, 91
Chicago's New Music Festival, 68
Crossroads Music Exposition, 116
Domaine Forget, 132
Garth Newel Music Center, 125
Irving S. Gilmore International Keyboard Festival, 84
Le Mont Wind Chamber Music Seminar, 95
Magic Mountain Music Farm, 96
Manhattan School of Music, 96-97
McGill Early Music Workshop, 132-33
Musicians Institute, 46
Nashville Songwriters Association Workshops, 117
New Arts Festival, 61
Norfolk Chamber Music Festival, 56-57
Northwestern University School of Music, 69-70
Omega Institute for Holistic Studies, 100-101
Pianofest in the Hamptons, 101
Pierre Monteux School for Conductors and Orchestra Musicians, 75-76
Quartet Program, 114
Raphael Trio Summer Chamber Music Workshop, 122
Smith Summer Workshops, 82
Songwriters Guild of America Workshops, 48
Southampton Chamber Music Festival, 101-2
Stanford Jazz Workshop, 48-49
Symphony at Sea, 49-50
Vermont Mozart Festival, 123
Walnut Street Theatre School, 115
Winter Wonderland Workshop, 123

Conferences

Academy of Gospel Music Arts, 116
Chicago's New Music Festival, 68
Christian Artists' Seminar in the Rockies, 52-53
Country Music Week, 131
Crossroads Music Exposition, 116
Folk Alliance Annual Conference, 59
Gospel Music Week, 117
JazzTimes Convention, 87
KentMusic, 55
Philadelphia Music Conference, 113-14
Winter Music Conference, 64

Academic Programs

American Conservatory of Music, 67-68
Appalachian State University School of Music, 103
Arkansas State University Department of Music, 41-42
Aspen Music Festival and School, 51-52
Berklee College of Music, 78
Boston Conservatory, 78-79
Boston University School for the Arts Music Division, 79
Brigham Young University Department of Music, 120-21
Brooklyn Conservatory, 90
Brown University Department of Music, 115
Capilano College Jazz Studies Program, 130-31
Chamber Music at Mannes, 91
Cleveland Institute of Music, 106-7
Cornish College of the Arts, 126
Curtis Institute of Music, 112-13
Duquesne University School of Music, 113
Eastman School of Music, 92-93
Georgia State University School of Music, 65
Glauser School of Music, 108
Grandin Festival, 108-9
Harris Institute for the Arts, 131-32
Hartt School of Music, 54
Indiana University School of Music, 71-72
Indiana University Summer Festival, 72
Juilliard School, 93-94
Lionel Hampton School of Music, 67
Manhattan School of Music, 96-97
Mannes College of Music, 97-99

Mannes Jazz and Contemporary Music Program, 99
Mason Gross School of the Arts, 88
Mills College Music Department, 45
Musicians Institute, 46
Musitechnic, 133
New England Conservatory, 80-82
North Carolina School of the Arts, 105-6
Northern Arizona State University School of Performing Arts, 41
Northern Illinois University School of Music, 69
Northwestern University School of Music, 69-70
Oberlin Conservatory of Music, 109-10
Ohio State University School of Music, 110
Oklahoma City University School of Music and Performing Arts, 110-11
Peabody Institute, 76-77
Pittsburg State University Department of Music, 73
Red Deer College, 130
Rome School of Music, 59-60
Samford University School of Music, 39
San Francisco Conservatory of Music, 46-47
San Francisco State University Department of Music, 47-48
Sarasota Music Festival, 63
Southwest Texas State University Department of Music, 119-20
UCLA Department of Music, 50
University of Alabama School of Music, 39
University of Alaska Fairbanks Music Department, 40
University of Arkansas Department of Music, 42
University of Colorado at Boulder College of Music, 53-54
University of Colorado at Denver Department of Music, 54
University of Delaware Department of Music, 58-59
University of Hawaii at Manoa, 66
University of Louisville School of Music, 74
University of Miami School of Music, 63
University of Montana Department of Music, 85
University of Nebraska, Lincoln, School of Music, 85-86
University of Nevada, Las Vegas, 86
University of New Orleans Jazz Studies, 74
University of Oregon School of Music, 111-12
University of South Florida Department of Music, 64
University of Texas at Austin School of Music, 120
West Virginia University Division of Music, 128
Westminster Choir College, 88
Yale Institute of Sacred Music, 57
Yale School of Music, 57-58

Festivals

Ash Lawn-Highland Apprenticeship Program, 124
Aspen Music Festival and School, 51-52
Baroque Performance Institute, 106
Blanche Bryden Sunflower Music Festival Institute, 73
Brandeis Summer Music Festival, 79-80
Bravo! Summer String Institute, 84
Brevard Music Festival, 103
Central City Opera, 52
Chautauqua School of Music, 92
Colorado College Summer Conservatory and Music Festival, 53
Conducting Masterclass, 111
Eastern Music Festival, 104
Encore School for Strings, 108
Fairbanks Summer Arts Festival, 40
Garth Newel Music Center, 125
Glickman-Popkin Bassoon Camp, 104-5
Grandin Festival, 108-9
Hot Springs Music Festival, 42
Indiana University Summer Festival, 72
Irving S. Gilmore International Keyboard Festival, 84
Kent/Blossom Music, 109
Kerrville Songwriters School, 118-19
Le Mont Wind Chamber Music Seminar, 95
Long Island Recorder Festival, 95
Manchester Music Festival, 121-22
Marlboro Music, 122
Meadowmount School of Music, 99-100
Music Academy of the West Summer School and Festival, 45-46
Music and Sound at Banff, 129-30
Musicorda Summer String Program, 80

National Orchestral Institute, 76
New Arts Festival, 61
New Haven Festival Masterclasses, 55
Norfolk Chamber Music Festival, 56-57
Orford Arts Centre for Advanced Music Studies, 133
Park City International Music Festival and Summer Institute, 121
Pianofest in the Hamptons, 101
Pierre Monteux School for Conductors and Orchestra Musicians, 75-76
Quartet Program, 114
Rossborough Festival, 77
Round Top, 119
Sarasota Music Festival, 63
Sewanee Summer Music Festival, 118
Southampton Chamber Music Festival, 101-2
Stanford Jazz Workshop, 48-49
Steans Institute for Young Artists, 70-71
SummerTrios, 114
Taos School of Music, 89
Vermont Mozart Festival, 123
Yellow Barn Music School and Festival, 124

Masterclasses

Aspen Music Festival and School, 51-52
Baroque Performance Institute, 106
Brandeis Summer Music Festival, 79-80
Bravo! Summer String Institute, 84
Brooklyn Conservatory, 90
Central City Opera, 52
Chamber Music at Mannes, 91
Close Encounters with Music, 61
Colorado College Summer Conservatory and Music Festival, 53
Conducting Masterclass, 111
Domaine Forget, 132
Eastern Music Festival, 104
Encore School for Strings, 108
Garth Newel Music Center, 125
Glickman-Popkin Bassoon Camp, 104-5
Irving S. Gilmore International Keyboard Festival, 84
Kent/Blossom Music, 109
Kerrville Songwriters School, 118-19
Kneisel Hall Chamber Music School and Festival, 75
Le Mont Wind Chamber Music Seminar, 95
Long Island Recorder Festival, 95
Magic Mountain Music Farm, 96
Manchester Music Festival, 121-22
Manhattan School of Music, 96-97
McGill Early Music Workshop, 132-33
Meadowmount School of Music, 99-100
Music and Sound at Banff, 129-30
Musicians Institute, 46
National Orchestral Institute, 76
New Arts Festival, 61
New Haven Festival Masterclasses, 55
New World Symphony, 62-63
North Carolina School of the Arts, 105-6
Northwestern University School of Music, 69-70
Orford Arts Centre for Advanced Music Studies, 133-34
Park City International Music Festival and Summer Institute, 121
Pianofest in the Hamptons, 101
Pierre Monteux School for Conductors and Orchestra Musicians, 75-76
Raphael Trio Summer Chamber Music Workshop, 122
Rossborough Festival, 77
Sarasota Music Festival, 63
Southeastern Music Center, 66
Stanford Jazz Workshop, 48-49
Steans Institute for Young Artists, 70-71
SummerTrios, 114

Handicapped Access

Academy of Gospel Music Arts, 116
American Conservatory of Music, 67-68
Appalachian State University School of Music, 103
Arkansas State University Department of Music, 41-42
Aspen Music Festival and School, 51-52
Atlantic Center for the Arts, 60-61
Audition and Performance Stress Reduction, 77-78
Baroque Performance Institute, 106
Berklee College of Music, 78
Blanche Bryden Sunflower Music Festival Institute, 73
Bloom School of Jazz, 68
Boston University School for the Arts Music Division, 79
Brandeis Summer Music Festival, 79-80
Bravo! Summer String Institute, 84
Brigham Young University Department of Music, 120-21

Broadway on Sunset, 43
Brooklyn Conservatory, 90
Brown University Department of Music, 115
Capilano College Jazz Studies Program, 130-31
Central City Opera, 52
Chamber Music at Mannes, 91
Chautauqua School of Music, 92
Chicago's New Music Festival, 68
Christian Artists' Seminar in the Rockies, 52-53
Cleveland Institute of Music, 106-7
Close Encounters with Music, 61
Colorado College Summer Conservatory and Music Festival, 53
Conducting Masterclass, 111
Cornish College of the Arts, 126
Country Music Week, 131
Crossroads Music Exposition, 116
Domaine Forget, 132
Duquesne University School of Music, 113
Eastern Music Festival, 104
Eastman School of Music, 92-93
Fairbanks Summer Arts Festival, 40
Garth Newel Music Center, 125
Georgia State University School of Music, 65
Glauser School of Music, 108
Gospel Music Week, 117
Grandin Festival, 108-9
Hartt School of Music, 54
Helene Wurlitzer Foundation, 89
Hot Springs Music Festival, 42
Indiana University School of Music, 71-72
Indiana University Summer Festival, 72
Irving S. Gilmore International Keyboard Festival, 84
JazzTimes Convention, 87
Juilliard School, 93-94
Kent/Blossom Music, 109
Kerrville Songwriters School, 118-19
Kneisel Hall Chamber Music School and Festival, 75
Le Mont Wind Chamber Music Seminar, 95
Lionel Hampton School of Music, 67
MacDowell Colony, 86-87
Manchester Music Festival, 121-22
Manhattan School of Music, 96-97
Mannes College of Music, 97-99
Mannes Jazz and Contemporary Music Program, 99
Marlboro Music, 122
Mason Gross School of the Arts, 88
McGill Early Music Workshop, 132-33
Mills College Music Department, 45
Music Academy of the West Summer School and Festival, 45-46
Music and Sound at Banff, 129-30
Musicians Institute, 46
Musicorda Summer String Program, 80
Nashville Songwriters Association Workshops, 117
National Orchestral Institute, 76
New Arts Festival, 61
New England Conservatory, 80-82
New Haven Festival Masterclasses, 55
New World Symphony, 62-63
Norfolk Chamber Music Festival, 56-57
North Carolina School of the Arts, 105-6
Northern Arizona State University School of Performing Arts, 41
Northern Illinois University School of Music, 69
Northwestern University School of Music, 69-70
Oberlin Conservatory of Music, 109-10
Ohio State University School of Music, 110
Oklahoma City University School of Music and Performing Arts, 110-11
Park City International Music Festival and Summer Institute, 121
Peabody Institute, 76-77
Pianofest in the Hamptons, 101
Pittsburg State University Department of Music, 73
Quartet Program, 114
Red Deer College, 130
Rome School of Music, 59-60
Rossborough Festival, 77
Round Top, 119
Samford University School of Music, 39
San Francisco Conservatory of Music, 46-47
San Francisco State University Department of Music, 47-48
Sarasota Music Festival, 63
Sewanee Summer Music Festival, 118
Smith Summer Workshops, 82
Songwriters Guild of America Workshops, 48

Southampton Chamber Music Festival, 101-2
Southeastern Music Center, 66
Southwest Texas State University Department of Music, 119-20
Stanford Jazz Workshop, 48-49
Steans Institute for Young Artists, 70-71
SummerTrios, 114
Symphony at Sea, 49-50
Taos School of Music, 89
UCLA Department of Music, 50
University of Alabama School of Music, 39
University of Arkansas Department of Music, 42
University of Colorado at Boulder College of Music, 53-54
University of Delaware Department of Music, 58-59
University of Hawaii at Manoa, 66
University of Louisville School of Music, 74
University of Miami School of Music, 63
University of Montana Department of Music, 85
University of Nebraska, Lincoln, School of Music, 85-86
University of Nevada, Las Vegas, 86
University of New Orleans Jazz Studies, 74
University of Oregon School of Music, 111-12
University of South Florida Department of Music, 64
University of Texas at Austin School of Music, 120
Vermont Mozart Festival, 123
West Virginia University Division of Music, 128
Winter Music Conference, 64
Winter Wonderland Workshop, 123
Yaddo, 102-3
Yale Institute of Sacred Music, 57
Yale School of Music, 57-58

Financial Aid

Alden B. Dow Creativity Center Residency Program, 82-83
American Conservatory of Music, 67-68
Appalachian State University School of Music, 103
Arkansas State University Department of Music, 41-42
Ash Lawn-Highland Apprenticeship Program, 124
Aspen Music Festival and School, 51-52
Baroque Performance Institute, 106
Berklee College of Music, 78
Blanche Bryden Sunflower Music Festival Institute, 73
Boston Conservatory, 78-79
Boston University School for the Arts Music Division, 79
Brandeis Summer Music Festival, 79-80
Bravo! Summer String Institute, 84
Brevard Music Festival, 103
Brigham Young University Department of Music, 120-21
Broadway on Sunset 43
Brooklyn Conservatory, 90
Brown University Department of Music, 115
Byrdcliffe Arts Colony, 90-91
Capilano College Jazz Studies Program, 130-31
Centrum Artist Residency Program, 126
Chamber Music at Mannes, 91
Chautauqua School of Music, 92
Cleveland Institute of Music, 106-7
Colorado College Summer Conservatory and Music Festival, 53
Cornish College of the Arts, 126
Curtis Institute of Music, 112-13
Duquesne University School of Music, 113
Eastern Music Festival, 104
Eastman School of Music, 92-93
Encore School for Strings, 108
Folk Alliance Annual Conference, 59
Garth Newel Music Center, 125
Georgia State University School of Music 65
Grandin Festival, 108-9
Hambidge Center, 65-66
Harris Institute for the Arts, 131-32
Hartt School of Music, 54
Hot Springs Music Festival, 42
Indiana University School of Music, 71-72
Juilliard School, 93-94
KentMusic, 55
Kerrville Songwriters School, 118-19
Kneisel Hall Chamber Music School and Festival, 75
Le Mont Wind Chamber Music Seminar, 95
Lionel Hampton School of Music, 67

Manchester Music Festival, 121-22
Manhattan School of Music, 96-97
Mannes College of Music, 97-99
Mannes Jazz and Contemporary Music Program, 99
Marlboro Music, 122
Mary Anderson Center for the Arts, 72-73
Mason Gross School of the Arts, 88
Meadowmount School of Music, 99-100
Mills College Music Department, 45
Music Academy of the West Summer School and Festival, 45-46
Music and Sound at Banff, 129-30
Musicians Institute, 46
Musicorda Summer String Program, 80
Musitechnic, 133
National Orchestral Institute, 76
New Arts Festival, 61
New England Conservatory, 80-82
New World Symphony, 62-63
Norfolk Chamber Music Festival, 56-57
North Carolina School of the Arts, 105-6
Northern Arizona State University School of Performing Arts, 41
Northern Illinois University School of Music, 69
Northwestern University School of Music, 69-70
Oberlin Conservatory of Music, 109-10
Ohio State University School of Music, 110
Oklahoma City University School of Music and Performing Arts, 110-11
Omega Institute for Holistic Studies, 100-101
Orford Arts Centre for Advanced Music Studies, 133-34
Park City International Music Festival and Summer Institute, 121
Peabody Institute, 76-77
Pianofest in the Hamptons, 101
Pierre Monteux School for Conductors and Orchestra Musicians, 75-76
Pittsburg State University Department of Music, 73
Ragdale Foundation Residency, 70
Rome School of Music, 59-60
Round Top, 119
Samford University School of Music. 39
San Francisco Conservatory of Music, 46-47
San Francisco State University Department of Music, 47-48
Sarasota Music Festival, 63
Sewanee Summer Music Festival, 118
Smith Summer Workshops, 82
Southampton Chamber Music Festival, 101-2
Southeastern Music Center, 66
Southwest Texas State University Department of Music, 119-20
Stanford Jazz Workshop, 48-49
Steans Institute for Young Artists, 70-71
SummerTrios, 114
UCLA Department of Music, 50
University of Alabama School of Music, 39
University of Alaska Fairbanks Music Department, 40
University of Arkansas Department of Music, 42
University of Colorado at Boulder College of Music, 53-54
University of Colorado at Denver Department of Music, 54
University of Delaware Department of Music, 58-59
University of Hawaii at Manoa, 66
University of Louisville School of Music, 74
University of Miami School of Music, 63
University of Montana Department of Music, 85
University of Nebraska, Lincoln, School of Music, 85-86
University of Nevada, Las Vegas, 86
University of New Orleans Jazz Studies, 74
University of Oregon School of Music, 111-12
University of South Florida Department of Music, 64
University of Texas at Austin School of Music, 120
Vermont Mozart Festival, 123
Villa Montalvo Artist Residency Program, 50-51
Virginia Center for the Creative Arts, 125-26
Walnut Street Theatre School, 115
West Virginia University Division of Music, 128

Westminster Choir College, 88
Yale Institute of Sacred Music, 57
Yale School of Music, 57-58
Yellow Barn Music School and Festival, 124

Web Sites

Academy of Gospel Music Arts, http://www.GOSPELMUSIC.ORG,116
Appalachian State University School of Music, http://www.acs.appstate.edu/dept/music, 103
Arkansas State University Department of Music, http://www.astate.edu, 41-42
Aspen Music Festival and School, http://www.aspenonline.com/musicfestival, 51-52
Berklee College of Music, http://www.berklee.edu, 78
Blanche Bryden Sunflower Music Festival Institute, http://www.wuacc.edu/cas/music/, 73
Boston University School for the Arts Music Division, http://web.bu.edu/SFA, 79
Brandeis Summer Music Festival, http://www.brandeis.edu/sumsch/Rabb.html, 79-80
Brevard Music Festival, http://www/lightnin.brevard.edu/bmc, 103
Brigham Young University Department of Music, http://www.byu.edu, 120-21
Broadway on Sunset, http://www.members.aol.com/bosmt, 43
Central City Opera, http://www.ossinc.net/opera, 52
Chicago's New Music Festival, http://www.indiefest.org, 68
Cleveland Institute of Music, http://www.cwru.edu/CIM/cimhome.html, 106-7
Duquesne University School of Music, http://www.duq.edu/music/music.html, 113
Eastman School of Music, http://www.Rochester.edu, 92-93
Encore School for Strings, http://www.cwru.edu/CIM/cimhome.html, 108
Folk Alliance Annual Conference, http://www.hidwater.com/folkalliance/, 59
Gospel Music Week, http://www.gospelmusic.org, 117
Harris Institute for the Arts, http://www.ampsc.com/metronome/harris/index.html, 131-32
Indiana University School of Music, http://www.music.indiana.edu, 71-72
Kerrville Songwriters School, http://www.fmp.com/~kerrfest, 119
Mannes Jazz and Contemporary Music Program, http://www.jazzcentralstation.com; http://www.NewSchool.edu., 99
Music and Sound at Banff, http://www.banffcentre.ab.ca/, 129-30
Musicians Institute, http://www.mi.edu, 46
Nashville Songwriters Association Workshops, http://songs.org/NSAI, 117
New World Symphony, http://www.nws.org, 62-63
Norfolk Chamber Music Festival, http://www.yale.edu/norfolk/, 56-57
North Carolina School of the Arts, http://www.ncarts.edu, 105-6
Northern Arizona State University School of Performing Arts, http://www.nau.edu/~spa, 41
Northern Illinois University School of Music, http://www.niu.edu/acad/music/index.html, 69
Northwestern University School of Music, http://www.nuinfo.nwu.edu/musicschool/, 69-70
Oberlin Conservatory of Music, http://www.oberlin.edu, 109-10
Ohio State University School of Music, http://www.cgrg.ohio-state.edu/other/music/, 110
Omega Institute for Holistic Studies, http://www.omega-inst.org, 100-101
Peabody Institute, http://www.peabody.jhu.edu, 76-77
Philadelphia Music Conference, http://www.gopmc.com, 113-14
Pittsburg State University Department of Music, http://www.pittstate.edu/music, 73
Rome School of Music, http://www.cua.edu/www.musu/, 59-60

Rossborough Festival, http://www.intlcomp@umdacc.umd.edu, 77
Round Top, http://www.rtis.com, 119-20
San Francisco Conservatory of Music, http://www.sfcm.edu, 46-47
San Francisco State University Department of Music, http://www.sfsu.edu/~music, 47-48
Sarasota Music Festival, http://www.sarasota-online.com/symphony/festival, 63
Smith Summer Workshops, http://www.westernwind.org, 82
Stanford Jazz Workshop, http://www.leland.stanford.edu, 48-49
University of Colorado at Denver Department of Music, http://www.cudenver.edu/public/SOA, 54
University of Louisville School of Music, http://www.louisville.edu/music, 74
University of Nebraska, Lincoln, School of Music, http://www.unl.edu/wmus/wmb/wmb.hyml, 85-86
University of Texas at Austin School of Music, http://www.utexas.edu/cofa/music, 120
Westminster Choir College, http://www.Rider.edu, 88
Winter Music Conference, http://www.members.aol.com/wmcconfac/home.html, 64
Winter Wonderland Workshop, http://www.westernwind.org, 123
Yellow Barn Music School and Festival, http://www.users.aol.com/ybarn, 124

In researching this book, we asked our featured progams to list the areas of study they offer. There was not space, as it turned out, to convey all this information in the program descriptions themselves—though we did our best. So we provide it here, in a list of programs sorted by category.

Business of Music

Academy of Gospel Music Arts, 116
American Conservatory of Music, 67
Appalachian State University School of Music, 103
Ash Lawn-Highland Apprenticeship Program, 124
Berklee College of Music, 78
Brigham Young University Department of Music, 120-21
Broadway on Sunset, 43
Brooklyn Conservatory, 90
Capilano College Jazz Studies Program, 130-31
Chicago's New Music Festival, 68
Christian Artists' Seminar in the Rockies, 52-53
Country Music Week, 131
Crossroads Music Exposition, 116
Curtis Institute of Music, 112-13
Folk Alliance Annual Conference, 59
Gospel Music Week, 117
Harris Institute for the Arts, 131-32
Hot Springs Music Festival, 42
JazzTimes Convention, 87
Juilliard School, 93-94
Kerrville Songwriters School, 118-19
Le Mont Wind Chamber Music Seminar, 95
Manhattan School of Music, 96-97
Mannes Jazz and Contemporary Music Program, 99
Mills College Music Department, 45
Music and Sound at Banff, 129-30
Musicians Institute, 46
Musitechnic, 133
New World Symphony, 62-63
North Carolina School of the Arts, 105-6
Northern Arizona State University School of Performing Arts, 41
Northern Illinois University School of Music, 69
Oberlin Conservatory of Music, 109-10
Oklahoma City University School of Music and Performing Arts, 110-11
Philadelphia Music Conference, 113-14
Red Deer College, 130
Round Top, 119
San Francisco Conservatory of Music, 46-47
San Francisco State University Department of Music, 47-48
Songwriters Guild of America Workshops, 48

Stanford Jazz Workshop, 48-49
UCLA Department of Music, 50
University of Colorado at Denver Department of Music, 54
University of Louisville School of Music, 74
University of Miami School of Music, 63
University of South Florida Department of Music, 64
West Virginia University Division of Music, 128
Westminster Choir College, 88
Winter Music Conference, 64

Chamber Music

American Conservatory of Music, 67-68
Appalachian State University School of Music, 103
Arkansas State University Department of Music, 41-42
Aspen Music Festival and School, 51-52
Audition and Performance Stress Reduction, 77-78
Baroque Performance Institute, 106
Berklee College of Music, 78
Blanche Bryden Sunflower Music Festival Institute, 73
Boston Conservatory, 78-79
Boston University School for the Arts Music Division, 79
Brandeis Summer Music Festival, 79-80
Bravo! Summer String Institute, 84
Brevard Music Festival, 103
Brigham Young University Department of Music, 120-21
Brooklyn Conservatory, 90
Brown University Department of Music, 115
Chamber Music at Mannes, 91
Chautauqua School of Music, 92
Cleveland Institute of Music, 106-7
Close Encounters with Music, 61
Colorado College Summer Conservatory and Music Festival, 53
Conducting Masterclass, 111
Cornish College of the Arts, 126
Domaine Forget, 132
Duquesne University School of Music, 113
Eastern Music Festival, 104
Eastman School of Music, 92-93
Encore School for Strings, 108
Fairbanks Summer Arts Festival, 40
Garth Newel Music Center, 125
Georgia State University School of Music, 65
Glauser School of Music, 108
Glickman-Popkin Bassoon Camp, 104-5
Grandin Festival, 108-9
Hartt School of Music, 54
Hot Springs Music Festival, 42
Indiana University School of Music, 71-72
Indiana University Summer Festival, 72
Juilliard School, 93-94
Kent/Blossom Music, 109
KentMusic, 55
Kneisel Hall Chamber Music School and Festival, 75
Le Mont Wind Chamber Music Seminar, 95
Lionel Hampton School of Music, 67
Long Island Recorder Festival, 95
Magic Mountain Music Farm, 96
Manchester Music Festival, 121-22
Manhattan School of Music, 96-97
Mannes College of Music, 97-99
Marlboro Music, 122
Mason Gross School of the Arts, 88
McGill Early Music Workshop, 132-33
Meadowmount School of Music, 99-100
Mills College Music Department, 45
Music Academy of the West Summer School and Festival, 45-46
Musicorda Summer String Program, 80
New Arts Festival, 61
New England Conservatory, 80-82
Norfolk Chamber Music Festival, 56-57
North Carolina School of the Arts, 105-6
Northern Arizona State University School of Performing Arts, 41
Northern Illinois University School of Music, 69
Northwestern University School of Music, 69-70
Oberlin Conservatory of Music, 109-10
Ohio State University School of Music, 110

Oklahoma City University School of Music and Performing Arts, 110-11
Orford Arts Centre for Advanced Music Studies, 133-34
Park City International Music Festival and Summer Institute, 121
Peabody Institute, 76-77
Pittsburg State University Department of Music, 73
Quartet Program, 114
Raphael Trio Summer Chamber Music Workshop, 122
Red Deer College, 130
Rome School of Music, 59-60
Round Top, 119
Samford University School of Music, 39
San Francisco Conservatory of Music, 46-47
San Francisco State University Department of Music, 47-48
Sarasota Music Festival, 63
Sewanee Summer Music Festival, 118
Smith Summer Workshops, 82
Southampton Chamber Music Festival, 101-2
Southeastern Music Center, 66
Southwest Texas State University Department of Music, 119-20
Steans Institute for Young Artists, 70-71
SummerTrios, 114
Symphony at Sea, 49-50
Taos School of Music, 89
UCLA Department of Music, 50
University of Alabama School of Music, 39
University of Alaska Fairbanks Music Department, 40
University of Arkansas Department of Music, 42
University of Colorado at Boulder College of Music, 53-54
University of Colorado at Denver Department of Music, 54
University of Delaware Department of Music, 58-59
University of Hawaii at Manoa, 66
University of Louisville School of Music, 74
University of Miami School of Music, 63
University of Montana Department of Music, 85
University of Nebraska, Lincoln, School of Music, 85-86
University of Nevada, Las Vegas, 86
University of New Orleans Jazz Studies, 74
University of Oregon School of Music, 111-12
University of South Florida Department of Music, 64
University of Texas at Austin School of Music, 120
Vermont Mozart Festival, 123
West Virginia University Division of Music, 128
Westminster Choir College, 88
Winter Wonderland Workshop, 123
Yale School of Music, 57-58
Yellow Barn Music School and Festival, 124

Choral Music

American Conservatory of Music, 67-68
Appalachian State University School of Music, 103
Arkansas State University Department of Music, 41-42
Aspen Music Festival and School, 51-52
Audition and Performance Stress Reduction, 77-78
Baroque Performance Institute, 106
Berklee College of Music, 78
Boston Conservatory, 78-79
Boston University School for the Arts Music Division, 79
Brevard Music Festival, 103
Brigham Young University Department of Music, 120-21
Brooklyn Conservatory, 90
Brown University Department of Music, 115
Capilano College Jazz Studies Program, 130-31
Cleveland Institute of Music, 106-7
Conducting Masterclass, 111
Cornish College of the Arts, 126
Domaine Forget, 132
Duquesne University School of Music, 113
Eastman School of Music, 92-93
Fairbanks Summer Arts Festival, 40
Georgia State University School of Music, 65
Glauser School of Music, 108
Hartt School of Music, 54
Indiana University School of Music, 71-72

Indiana University Summer Festival, 72
Juilliard School, 93-94
Lionel Hampton School of Music, 67
Long Island Recorder Festival, 95
Manhattan School of Music, 96-97
Mannes College of Music, 97-99
Mason Gross School of the Arts, 88
Mills College Music Department, 45
Music and Sound at Banff, 129-30
Musicians Institute, 46
New England Conservatory, 80
New Haven Festival Masterclasses, 55
North Carolina School of the Arts, 105-6
Northern Arizona State University School of Performing Arts, 41
Northern Illinois University School of Music, 69
Northwestern University School of Music, 69-70
Oberlin Conservatory of Music, 109-10
Ohio State University School of Music, 110
Oklahoma City University School of Music and Performing Arts, 110-11
Peabody Institute, 76-77
Pittsburg State University Department of Music, 73
Red Deer College, 130
Samford University School of Music, 39
San Francisco Conservatory of Music, 46-47
San Francisco State University Department of Music, 47-48
Smith Summer Workshops, 82
Southwest Texas State University Department of Music, 119-20
UCLA Department of Music, 50
University of Alabama School of Music, 39
University of Alaska Fairbanks Music Department, 40
University of Arkansas Department of Music, 42
University of Colorado at Boulder College of Music, 53-54
University of Colorado at Denver Department of Music, 54
University of Delaware Department of Music, 58-59
University of Hawaii at Manoa, 66
University of Louisville School of Music, 74
University of Miami School of Music, 63
University of Montana Department of Music, 85
University of Nebraska, Lincoln, School of Music, 85-86
University of Nevada, Las Vegas, 86
University of New Orleans Jazz Studies, 74
University of Oregon School of Music, 111-12
University of Texas at Austin School of Music, 120
West Virginia University Division of Music, 128
Westminster Choir College, 88
Yale Institute of Sacred Music, 57
Yale School of Music, 57-58

Composition

American Conservatory of Music, 67-68
Apostle Islands National Lakeshore Artist-in-Residence Program, 128
Appalachian State University School of Music, 103
Arkansas State University Department of Music, 41-42
Aspen Music Festival and School, 51-52
Atlantic Center for the Arts, 60-61
Audition and Performance Stress Reduction, 77-78
Berklee College of Music, 78
Boston Conservatory, 78-79
Boston University School for the Arts Music Division, 79
Brevard Music Festival, 103
Brigham Young University Department of Music, 120-21
Broadway on Sunset, 43
Brooklyn Conservatory, 90
Brown University Department of Music, 115
Byrdcliffe Arts Colony, 90-91
Capilano College Jazz Studies Program, 130-31
Centrum Artist Residency Program, 126
Christian Artists' Seminar in the Rockies, 52-53
Cleveland Institute of Music, 106-7
Cornish College of the Arts, 126
Department of Music, Southwest Texas State University, 118
Djerassi Resident Artists Program, 43-44

Domaine Forget, 132
Duquesne University School of Music, 113
Eastman School of Music, 92-93
Fairbanks Summer Arts Festival, 40
Georgia State University School of Music, 65
Glauser School of Music, 108
Hambidge Center, 65-66
Hartt School of Music, 54
Headlands Center for the Arts, 44
Helene Wurlitzer Foundation, 89
Indiana University School of Music, 71-72
Indiana University Summer Festival, 72
JazzTimes Convention, 87
Juilliard School, 93-94
Kerrville Songwriters School, 118-19
Lionel Hampton School of Music, 67
MacDowell Colony, 86-87
Manhattan School of Music, 96-97
Mannes College of Music, 97-99
Mannes Jazz and Contemporary Music Program, 99
Mary Anderson Center for the Arts, 72-73
Mason Gross School of the Arts, 88
Mills College Music Department, 45
Musicians Institute, 46
Musitechnic, 133
New England Conservatory, 80-82
Norfolk Chamber Music Festival, 56-57
North Carolina School of the Arts, 105-6
Northern Arizona State University School of Performing Arts, 41
Northern Illinois University School of Music, 69
Northwestern University School of Music, 69-70
Oberlin Conservatory of Music, 109-10
Ohio State University School of Music, 110
Oklahoma City University School of Music and Performing Arts, 110-11
Peabody Institute, 76-77
Pittsburg State University Department of Music, 73
Ragdale Foundation Residency, 70
Red Deer College, 130
Samford University School of Music, 39
San Francisco Conservatory of Music, 46-47
San Francisco State University Department of Music, 47-48
Sewanee Summer Music Festival, 118
Songwriters Guild of America Workshops, 48
UCLA Department of Music, 50
University of Alabama School of Music, 39
University of Alaska Fairbanks Music Department, 40
University of Arkansas Department of Music, 42
University of Colorado at Boulder College of Music, 53-54
University of Colorado at Denver Department of Music, 54
University of Delaware Department of Music, 58-59
University of Hawaii at Manoa, 66
University of Louisville School of Music, 74
University of Miami School of Music, 63
University of Montana Department of Music, 85
University of Nebraska, Lincoln, School of Music, 85-86
University of Nevada, Las Vegas, 86
University of New Orleans Jazz Studies, 74
University of Oregon School of Music, 111-12
University of South Florida Department of Music, 64
University of Texas at Austin School of Music, 120
Villa Montalvo Artist Residency Program, 50-51
Virginia Center for the Creative Arts, 125-26
West Virginia University Division of Music, 128
Westminster Choir College, 88
Yaddo, 102-3
Yale School of Music, 57-58
Yellow Barn Music School and Festival, 124

Folk Music

Audition and Performance Stress Reduction, 77-78
Berklee College of Music, 78
Brigham Young University Department of Music, 120-21
Chicago's New Music Festival, 68
Cornish College of the Arts, 126
Crossroads Music Exposition, 116

Folk Alliance Annual Conference, 59
Glauser School of Music, 108
Kerrville Songwriters School, 118-19
Nashville Songwriters Association Workshops, 117
Philadelphia Music Conference, 113-14
Red Deer College, 130
Songwriters Guild of America Workshops, 48
University of Colorado at Denver Department of Music, 54
University of Hawaii at Manoa, 66
University of Louisville School of Music, 74

Jazz

American Conservatory of Music, 67-68
Appalachian State University School of Music, 103
Arkansas State University Department of Music, 41-42
Aspen Music Festival and School, 51-52
Audition and Performance Stress Reduction, 77-78
Berklee College of Music, 78
Bloom School of Jazz, 68
Boston Conservatory, 78-79
Brigham Young University Department of Music, 120-21
Brooklyn Conservatory, 90
Brown University Department of Music, 115
Capilano College Jazz Studies Program, 130-31
Chicago's New Music Festival, 68
Cornish College of the Arts, 126
Djerassi Resident Artists Program, 43-44
Domaine Forget, 132
Duquesne University School of Music, 113
Eastman School of Music, 92-93
Fairbanks Summer Arts Festival, 40
Georgia State University School of Music, 65
Glauser School of Music, 108
Hartt School of Music, 54
JazzTimes Convention, 87
Juilliard School, 93-94
Lionel Hampton School of Music, 67
Long Island Recorder Festival, 95
Manhattan School of Music, 96-97
Mannes College of Music, 97-99
Mannes Jazz and Contemporary Music Program, 99
Mason Gross School of the Arts, 88
Music and Sound at Banff, 129-30
Musicians Institute, 46
New England Conservatory, 80-82
North Carolina School of the Arts, 105-6
Northern Arizona State University School of Performing Arts, 41
Northern Illinois University School of Music, 69
Northwestern University School of Music, 69-70
Oberlin Conservatory of Music, 109-10
Ohio State University School of Music, 110
Oklahoma City University School of Music and Performing Arts, 110-11
Orford Arts Centre for Advanced Music Studies, 133-34
Philadelphia Music Conference, 113-14
Pittsburg State University Department of Music, 73
Red Deer College, 130
San Francisco State University Department of Music, 47-48
Songwriters Guild of America Workshops, 48
Southwest Texas State University Department of Music, 119-20
Stanford Jazz Workshop, 48-49
University of Alabama School of Music, 39
University of Alaska Fairbanks Music Department, 40
University of Colorado at Denver Department of Music, 54
University of Delaware Department of Music, 58-59
University of Hawaii at Manoa, 66
University of Louisville School of Music, 74
University of Miami School of Music, 63
University of Montana Department of Music, 85
University of Nebraska, Lincoln, School of Music, 85-86
University of Nevada, Las Vegas, 86
University of New Orleans Jazz Studies, 74
University of Oregon School of Music, 111-12

University of South Florida Department of Music, 64
University of Texas at Austin School of Music, 120
West Virginia University Division of Music, 128

Music Education

American Conservatory of Music, 67-68
Appalachian State University School of Music, 103
Arkansas State University Department of Music, 41-42
Boston Conservatory, 78-79
Boston University School for the Arts Music Division, 79
Brigham Young University Department of Music, 120-21
Brooklyn Conservatory, 90
Duquesne University School of Music, 113
Georgia State University School of Music, 65
Glauser School of Music, 108
Hartt School of Music, 54
Lionel Hampton School of Music, 67
Mills College Music Department, 45
Music and Sound at Banff, 129-30
Northern Arizona State University School of Performing Arts, 41
Northwestern University School of Music, 69-70
Oberlin Conservatory of Music, 109-10
Ohio State University School of Music, 110
Oklahoma City University School of Music and Performing Arts, 110-11
Pittsburg State University Department of Music, 73
Rome School of Music, 59-60
Samford University School of Music, 39
Southwest Texas State University Department of Music, 119-20
UCLA Department of Music, 50
University of Alabama School of Music, 39
University of Arkansas Department of Music, 42
University of Colorado at Boulder College of Music, 53-54
University of Delaware Department of Music, 58-59
University of Hawaii at Manoa, 66
University of Louisville School of Music, 74
University of Miami School of Music, 63
University of Montana Department of Music, 85
University of Nebraska, Lincoln, School of Music, 85-86
University of Nevada, Las Vegas, 86
University of New Orleans Jazz Studies, 74
University of Oregon School of Music, 111-12
University of South Florida Department of Music, 64
West Virginia University Division of Music, 128
Westminster Choir College, 88

Musical Theater

Appalachian State University School of Music, 103
Ash Lawn-Highland Apprenticeship Program, 124
Audition and Performance Stress Reduction, 77-78
Boston Conservatory, 78-79``
Brigham Young University Department of Music, 120-21
Broadway on Sunset, 43
Chautauqua School of Music, 92
Cornish College of the Arts, 126
Domaine Forget, 132
Eastman School of Music, 92-93
Fairbanks Summer Arts Festival, 40
Glauser School of Music, 108
Indiana University School of Music, 71-72
Indiana University Summer Festival, 72
Manhattan School of Music, 96-97
Music Academy of the West Summer School and Festival, 45-46
Northern Arizona State University School of Performing Arts, 41
Northern Illinois University School of Music, 69
Northwestern University School of Music, 69-70
Ohio State University School of Music, 110

Red Deer College, 130
Rome School of Music, 59-60
San Francisco State University Department of Music, 47-48
Southwest Texas State University Department of Music, 119-20
University of Nebraska, Lincoln, School of Music, 85-86
University of New Orleans Jazz Studies, 74
Walnut Street Theatre School, 115

Opera

American Conservatory of Music, 67-68
Appalachian State University School of Music, 103
Arkansas State University Department of Music, 41-42
Ash Lawn-Highland Apprenticeship Program, 124
Aspen Music Festival and School, 51-52
Audition and Performance Stress Reduction, 77-78
Berklee College of Music, 78
Boston Conservatory, 78-79
Boston University School for the Arts Music Division, 79
Brevard Music Festival, 103
Brigham Young University Department of Music, 120-21
Brooklyn Conservatory, 90
Brown University Department of Music, 115
Central City Opera, 52
Chautauqua School of Music, 92
Cleveland Institute of Music, 106-7
Cornish College of the Arts, 126
Curtis Institute of Music, 112-13
Duquesne University School of Music, 113
Eastman School of Music, 92-93
Fairbanks Summer Arts Festival, 40
Georgia State University School of Music, 65
Glauser School of Music, 108
Hartt School of Music, 54
Indiana University School of Music, 71-72
Indiana University Summer Festival, 72
Juilliard School, 93-94
Lionel Hampton School of Music, 67
Manhattan School of Music, 96-97
Mannes College of Music, 97-99
Mason Gross School of the Arts, 88
Mills College Music Department, 45
Music Academy of the West Summer School and Festival, 45-46
Music and Sound at Banff, 129-30
New England Conservatory, 80-82
North Carolina School of the Arts, 105-6
Northern Arizona State University School of Performing Arts, 41
Northern Illinois University School of Music, 69
Northwestern University School of Music, 69-70
Oberlin Conservatory of Music, 109-10
Ohio State University School of Music, 110
Oklahoma City University School of Music and Performing Arts, 110-11
Orford Arts Centre for Advanced Music Studies, 133-34
Peabody Institute, 76-77
Pierre Monteux School for Conductors and Orchestra Musicians, 75-76
Pittsburg State University Department of Music, 73
Rome School of Music, 59-60
San Francisco Conservatory of Music, 46-47
Southwest Texas State University Department of Music, 119-20
UCLA Department of Music, 50
University of Alabama School of Music, 39
University of Arkansas Department of Music, 42
University of Colorado at Boulder College of Music, 53-54
University of Delaware Department of Music, 58-59
University of Hawaii at Manoa, 66
University of Louisville School of Music, 74
University of Miami School of Music, 63
University of Montana Department of Music 85
University of Nebraska, Lincoln, School of Music, 85-86
University of Nevada, Las Vegas, 86
University of New Orleans Jazz Studies, 74

University of Oregon School of Music, 111-12
University of South Florida Department of Music, 64
University of Texas at Austin School of Music, 120
West Virginia University Division of Music, 128
Westminster Choir College, 88
Yale School of Music, 57-58

Orchestral Music

American Conservatory of Music, 67-68
Appalachian State University School of Music, 103
Arkansas State University Department of Music, 41-42
Aspen Music Festival and School, 51-52
Audition and Performance Stress Reduction, 77-78
Baroque Performance Institute, 106
Berklee College of Music, 78
Boston Conservatory, 78-79
Boston University School for the Arts Music Division, 79
Bravo! Summer String Institute, 84
Brevard Music Festival, 103
Brigham Young University Department of Music 120
Brooklyn Conservatory, 90
Brown University Department of Music, 115
Chautauqua School of Music, 92
Cleveland Institute of Music, 106-7
Colorado College Summer Conservatory and Music Festival, 53
Conducting Masterclass, 111
Cornish College of the Arts, 126
Domaine Forget, 132
Duquesne University School of Music, 113
Eastern Music Festival, 104
Eastman School of Music, 92-93
Fairbanks Summer Arts Festival, 40
Georgia State University School of Music, 65
Glauser School of Music, 108
Glickman-Popkin Bassoon Camp, 104-5
Hartt School of Music, 54
Hot Springs Music Festival, 42
Indiana University School of Music, 71-72
Indiana University Summer Festival, 72
Juilliard School, 93-94
Kent/Blossom Music, 109
Lionel Hampton School of Music, 67
Manchester Music Festival, 121-22
Manhattan School of Music, 96-97
Mannes College of Music, 97-99
Mason Gross School of the Arts, 88
Mills College Music Department, 45
Music Academy of the West Summer School and Festival, 45-46
National Orchestral Institute, 76
New England Conservatory, 80-82
New World Symphony, 62-63
Norfolk Chamber Music Festival, 56-57
North Carolina School of the Arts, 105-6
Northern Arizona State University School of Performing Arts, 41
Northern Illinois University School of Music, 69
Northwestern University School of Music, 69-70
Oberlin Conservatory of Music, 109-10
Ohio State University School of Music, 110
Oklahoma City University School of Music and Performing Arts, 110-11
Orford Arts Centre for Advanced Music Studies, 133-34
Park City International Music Festival and Summer Institute, 121
Peabody Institute, 76-77
Pierre Monteux School for Conductors and Orchestra Musicians, 75-76
Pittsburg State University Department of Music, 73
Red Deer College, 130
Rome School of Music, 59-60
Round Top, 119
Samford University School of Music, 39

San Francisco Conservatory of Music, 46-47
San Francisco State University Department of Music, 47-48
Sarasota Music Festival, 63
Sewanee Summer Music Festival, 118
Southeastern Music Center, 66
Southwest Texas State University Department of Music, 119-20
Symphony at Sea, 49-50
UCLA Department of Music, 50
University of Alabama School of Music, 39
University of Alaska Fairbanks Music Department, 40
University of Arkansas Department of Music, 42
University of Colorado at Boulder College of Music, 53-54
University of Delaware Department of Music, 58-59
University of Hawaii at Manoa, 66
University of Louisville School of Music, 74
University of Miami School of Music, 63
University of Montana Department of Music, 85
University of Nebraska, Lincoln, School of Music, 85-86
University of Nevada, Las Vegas, 86
University of New Orleans Jazz Studies, 74
University of Oregon School of Music, 111-12
University of South Florida Department of Music, 64
University of Texas at Austin School of Music, 120
West Virginia University Division of Music, 128
Yale School of Music, 57-58

Popular Music

Academy of Gospel Music Arts, 116
Appalachian State University School of Music, 103
Arkansas State University Department of Music, 41-42
Audition and Performance Stress Reduction, 77-78
Berklee College of Music, 78
Brevard Music Festival, 103
Brigham Young University Department of Music, 120-21
Chicago's New Music Festival, 68
Cornish College of the Arts, 126
Crossroads Music Exposition, 116
Fairbanks Summer Arts Festival, 40
Gospel Music Week, 117
Kerrville Songwriters School, 118-19
Mannes Jazz and Contemporary Music Program, 99
Nashville Songwriters Association Workshops, 117
Northern Illinois University School of Music, 69
Peabody Institute, 76-77
Philadelphia Music Conference, 113-14
Red Deer College, 130
San Francisco State University Department of Music, 47-48
Smith Summer Workshops, 82
Songwriters Guild of America Workshops, 48
Southwest Texas State University Department of Music, 119-20
University of Colorado at Denver Department of Music, 54
University of Louisville School of Music, 74
University of Nevada, Las Vegas, 86
University of Texas at Austin School of Music, 120
Walnut Street Theatre School, 115
Winter Music Conference, 64

About the Author

Gwendolyn Freed is currently a Fellow at Columbia University's National Arts Journalism Program. Previously, she was editor of *Chamber Music* magazine. She writes and edits regularly for Sony Classical International. Her work has appeared in numerous publications, including *New York Newsday, The Detroit News, Stagebill, Ovation* and *Sesame Street Parents.* An oboist, Ms. Freed holds a master's degree in performance from the Juilliard School and a bachelor's degree from Oberlin Conservatory. She is a veteran of numerous music programs, including the Aspen Music Festival and School, the New York String Orchestra and the National Symphony Young Apprentice Program.

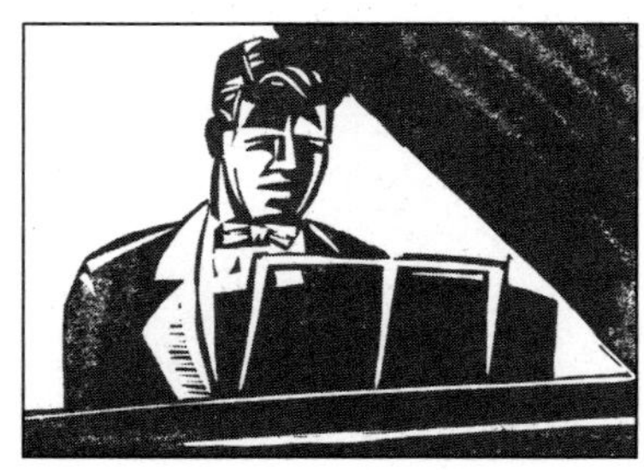

About Getting Your Act Together™

The Watson-Guptill Resource Guides to:

• Workshops • Conferences • Artists' Colonies • Academic Programs

With attendance soaring at workshops, seminars, conferences and other opportunities for continuing education, this particularly timely series presents dependable, candid resource guides tailored to meet the needs of adult artists in several specific categories.

Taking the frustration and guesswork out of the process of finding the right venue for further training, each guide offers a comprehensive and critical review of arts programs, organized alphabetically by state, covering workshops, conferences, artists' colonies and academic programs.

Each program entry provides such key information as contact name and address (plus phone and fax numbers, e-mail and Web site addresses), application requirements, financial aid opportunities and size of program. The books also cover general information on relevant associations, organizations and unions, as well as the business side of each discipline.